Last Mission for a Reluctant Patriot

Paul A. Baffico
with Ann McNamara

ISBN: 0615952089
ISBN 13: 9780615952086
Library of Congress Control Number: 2014930771
Approaching the Spot Publishing, Lake Forest, IL

Kathryn –
Thank you for
listening.
Best Always.
Paul

For The Beadle and Ken and Mike

"If you can keep your head when all about you
are losing theirs and blaming it on you,
If you can trust yourself when all men doubt you,
but make allowances for their doubting too,
If you can meet with Triumph and Disaster
and treat those twin imposters just the same,
Yours is the earth and everything that is in it,
and which is more—you'll be a man, my son"

Rudyard Kipling

And so, my fellow Americans, ask not
what your country can do for you;
ask what you can do for your country."

John F. Kennedy

The following is a true story. It is based on personal memories and is as accurate as those memories can be in my mind after many years of being obscured. The history has been thoroughly researched, but human error is bound to be extant.

Some names have been changed to preserve the anonymity of an individual.

LAST MISSION FOR A RELUCTANT PATRIOT

Prologue		xiii
Chapter 1	Wounds Re-Opened	1
Chapter 2	Growing up	8
Chapter 3	An Unlikely Memorial	19
Chapter 4	Post World War II America	23
Chapter 5	High School Goes Global	29
Chapter 6	Wall Magic	45
Chapter 7	On to College 1965	52
Chapter 8	My Buddy Jack	57
Chapter 9	Oooorah 1966 Student life	68
Chapter 10	An American Genius	73
Chapter 11	This is the End of the Innocence 1967	78

Chapter 12	The Volunteers	91
Chapter 13	The Class of 1968	99
Chapter 14	How It Works	106
Chapter 15	The Journey Begins	113
Chapter 16	Combat Orders	120
Chapter 17	To War Alone	124
Chapter 18	Close Calls	132
Chapter 19	My Rendezvous with Destiny	138
Chapter 20	Myth vs. Fact	149
Chapter 21	Taking Over	161
Chapter 22	Joining the Band of Brothers	173
Chapter 23	This is the Job	184
Chapter 24	Their War--Our Agony	205
Chapter 25	Never Forgotten	212
Chapter 26	Coming Home, Bittersweet	219
Chapter 27	"The World"	229
Chapter 28	Lifeless Integration	240

Chapter 29	Unexploded Ordinance	249
Chapter 30	Closing the Gap	259
Chapter 31	Alcohol	271
Chapter 32	The Wall That Heals	282
Chapter 33	A Safe Place for Healing	289
Acknowledgements		298
About Ann McNamara		300
References		301

PROLOGUE

I'm not a bumper-sticker kind of guy. I never have been. I don't wear my thoughts or patriotism on chrome. My car fenders and windows are pristinely blank; no knick-knacks hang from my rearview mirror; no bobble heads or hats in the rear window. I look disdainfully on my neighbor for hanging signs on her house decorated with ducks, squirrels, owls and sailboats which declare it is Summer, Valentines, Christmas, Easter....you name it. I confess I did buckle to pressure and put the necessary village stickers on some of my cars so I wouldn't be ticketed when parking at the market. I keep one loose sticker handy when needed in my convertible so I can keep my profile low and the car showroom clean.

I have always tried to keep my thoughts and feelings very close so I could fit in and not be the target of attention or derision. *Inclusion* to me is located on the outer edge of the inner circle. I enjoy the feeling of freedom too much to succumb to lemming behavior. So, it is safe to say I prefer being under the radar on a different vector.

Although I have lived a life larger than many, oddly enough, I have spent most of it under the guise of commonality with the average working person. Comfortable being a strong but silent force, I took my father's mantra to heart when he would repeatedly say, "Action speaks louder than words", thus my bumper sticker and decal phobia.

In recent years, I have had the luxury of time for reflection and contemplation. I am told this is a common behavior at this stage of one's life. In the process, I have been able to identify and understand specific pivotal events which were seminal in forming who I am. However, when I was living through them, I could not comprehend either the enormity of their importance nor their connectedness to each other. Life was life. Who was taking time to think much about it?

Most of my life seemed like a blur, as if it was flying by at supersonic speed. I occasionally wondered, 'Why am I the way I am?' I am driven. There are things to do; places to go; objects to acquire; accomplishments to collect; and competition to crush. Until now, my agenda has always been about *doing* not about *being*. At the same time, I was haunted by the insidious thought I was going to miss something if I slowed down or stopped.

Many of us assume we can understand and separate the good news from the bad news. I know I certainly did. But in my younger life, I was too caught up to do that. The ever increasing speed of modern communications and the ubiquitous presence of various information formats have created a habit in us of looking at life hastily, and seeing it in black and white terms. I fell into that trap. We've also developed an ever-growing desire for instant answers and gratifications. We tend to live in the future and not the present. It's as if we are trying to make sure our lives go according to our self-crafted plans and individual will, regardless of how outside forces might actually affect the outcomes. I fell into that trap too.

It's only recently I've come to the realization I really can't distinguish the good from the bad news. Time, perspective, context, and unplanned events affected outcomes more than I ever comprehended. When looking back through a longer lens, I can see that more clearly now.

My blistering agenda was defined early on and firmly imprinted during one critical year of my younger adult life. Now I feel like I've put the year into a better perspective. I see and realize the impact it had on me and how my life was shaped by it. It was a year I thought I would never survive. But survive it I did. What followed has been a remarkable life.

This is the story of how it happened and how the events leading to and following the year shaped me into the person I am, the non-bumper sticker kind of guy, the action-speaks-louder-than-words believer, and the admirer of the common man.

I am delighted I have somehow been accorded enough chances at The Good Life to have gained this perspective and to have been given opportunities to make a difference.

WOUNDS RE-OPENED

> If you are able, save for them a place inside of you and save one backward glance when you are leaving for the places they can no longer go. Be not ashamed to say you loved them, though you may or may not have always. Take what they have taught you with their dying and keep it with your own. And in that time when men decide and feel safe to call the war insane, take one moment to embrace those gentle heroes you left behind.
>
> *Major Michael Davis O'Donnell, 1 January 1970, Dak To, Vietnam*
> *Listed as KIA February 7, 1978*

It was a cold Saturday in Washington DC, March 4, 2006. Under the gray sky in the parks and monuments, life was hibernating. Nothing looked alive except the homeless. They were huddled on top of the exhaust grates of the State Department building on 21st Street that were belching enough steam to keep four of them from freezing.

At my request I was dropped off at the corner of Henry Bacon and Constitution Avenue to make my way alone to my destination. But at first, I didn't move.

I couldn't seem to get my legs to start towards it. I stood nervously in the cold shifting from foot to foot with hands in my pockets. I kept looking around apprehensively until I felt foolish. My chest felt tight. I told myself to get moving and to keep moving. Motion was always soothing for me.

By this time I had been home for more than 35 years and had not been able to unravel what Vietnam had embedded inside me, a convoluted network of courage, shame, anger, honor, obligation and betrayal, all in one emotional deluge. The Wall makes all of those feelings re-surface. It's uncontrollable. It takes one to another place.

I stood there alone full of sharp emotions, and I had no idea how to process them. I felt inadequate…weak. I had been there only two times before, and both times were painful. I couldn't imagine why I was doing it again…it was just too hard…and for what? As I recalled, it hurt more than it helped. I had never talked to anyone about it. I didn't want to. There was no one who could understand my feelings. When I came home from Vietnam, I took off my uniform as fast as I could and put the memories away as permanently as I could. I didn't want anyone to get at them.

But my wife Max had asked me to go. She said, "I think you should go talk to your guys at The Vietnam Memorial Wall. I think it would be good for you." In deference to her, I said I would, but only if I could do it alone. No one could be with me.

As I walked towards an information kiosk, my mind started to flood with the memories I hadn't had for years. There were just bits and pieces of floating thoughts and emotions which seemed familiar but disquieting. Embarrassed by my lack of recall, I wouldn't dare ask for help. I didn't want to talk to anyone. I'd figure out what I would do. 'I will find them myself.'

I saw a directory pedestal and began to flip through the pages…I looked slowly and carefully. I felt myself shrinking into a past which made my heart start to race. There's one, Bohrman, Sgt. Michael Dennis Bohrman, panel 10W, line 133…Delafield, Wisconsin. There's the other,

Luttel. Got him. SPC 4 Kenneth Bernard Luttel, panel 9W, line 2... Greensburg, Indiana. Wow. Both of their hometowns are within a few hours' drive from Chicago. What a coincidence. I wrote down the panel and line numbers, started walking towards them and began to recall the day: June 1, 1970.

I could see their 21 year old faces clearly. They were seared into my memory forever; full of anticipation and excitement because they were going out to the action. The loss of them and my guilt about it brought tears. It always happened the few times I let the memory take control of my consciousness. That's why I didn't want them to enter my mind if I could help it. Just keep them buried. Don't think about them...move on. As we said in Vietnam, "It don't mean nothin." But these two young men have been somewhere within me since the day of their deaths.

The other two times I had come to the Wall I had the same feelings of self-pity, remorse, guilt, regret, and shame. I was a platoon leader—responsible for my troops, and trained to take care of them. What I didn't get trained for was how to lead them in the gray area between black and white; orders and common sense; courage and stupidity; and life or death. That's the area most difficult to navigate. It is in the gray where it is most dangerous and it demands the best leadership. The quality of leadership required there comes only through hard fought lessons, mistakes and luck. It can't be taught.

When I first touched their names before, I felt the flashback. I was instantly transported back to the day: the wretched smells of rotting food and flesh, the burning shit, the smell of fear and panic; the feel of primitive living and killing; the stinking heat and humidity. I could recall the conversations I had with both men before sending them out....as though it had just happened. The Wall does that too. It is a silent and permanent representation of the vivid memory of the loss of life. Only the vet who was there when it happened has this special bond with the memory and the names on The Wall. And it is a sacred bond.

The West Wall

I walked slowly down the West Wall looking for their panels. As I approached the spot, a man with some kind of uniform came towards me and asked if I needed help. I curtly responded I didn't, as if to say, 'don't ask me to speak…this is my private moment of grief. You couldn't possibly understand.' He took my cue and backed away carefully.

I stared at Luttel and Bohrman's names, 'they shouldn't be dead…I didn't try hard enough to get out of the mission...I should be dead...I should have been with them...am I a coward for not being with them? Why did I come here again? This is pointless.'

After some minutes with my head down and deep in thought, the uniformed man approached me again and asked if I wanted a rubbing. I said no, I already had them. I just wanted to tell him to go away when I noticed his uniform said Billy O'Brien, Park Service *Volunteer*. For some reason it struck me as odd because I thought park *rangers* manned the National Parks. He also had a 1st Cavalry Division patch on his shoulder which really caught my attention. But I didn't want to ask.

With no preamble, he asked, "Are you from San Francisco? I see you belong to the Olympic Club," pointing to the logo on my sweater.

"Ah, yeah, originally from San Francisco, but I live in Chicago now. I had a career with Sears and got moved around a lot."

"When were you there?" he continued.

I was a bit taken back but reflexively replied, "70 to 71. Were you there?" He was and we had been there the same time.

I asked if he was with The Cav (as it was called) in Vietnam and he said he had been. I said, "Then you went into Cambodia in May?" Right again.

"What was your MOS?"

"I was an Infantry platoon leader," Billy replied gently with his smooth Georgia inflection. The deep southern drawl made me think he must be one of those rebel patriot military types.

I noticed he was wearing the Combat Infantryman Badge, Ranger, Airborne and Pathfinder pins on his hat. I had not seen these badges of courage and heroism since I was on active duty. Very impressive, and I thought he must have had a long Army career. Those were the symbols and decorations of a serious life-time warrior. "Lifers" we called them. For us non-lifer ROTC officers, we received the basic training prescribed for non-career types, did our jobs and then, hopefully, went home unharmed. It was the standard formula most of us signed up for then.

Billy clearly wanted to talk and I felt surprisingly okay with him, so I asked, "So, were you career Army?"

With a slight chuckle, he replied, "No. I was an ROTC graduate from the class of '68. When I finally got through all the training schools, I got shipped directly to Vietnam. When I came home from Vietnam, I was done with my obligation and I went directly to Grad School."

I said I had done exactly the same thing, only minus the formal Ranger, Airborne, Pathfinder route. Shockingly, I had been involuntarily qualified as an Air Assault officer when I got to the 101st Airborne in Vietnam. My job as a communications platoon leader was to fly daily combat assaults with the Infantry throughout their area of operations. It was not at all what I had envisioned when I signed the ROTC paperwork in college.

The similarity of our lives was eerie. Our time in combat the same, both platoon leaders with elite units, our ages the same, education equal, heavy combat time followed by rear area decompression, number of men killed identical. Finally, he had spent a good deal of his life after Vietnam living in San Francisco. We triangulated neighborhoods and hot spots in The City and we started to bond.

It felt good to be talking with him…remembering some things I hadn't thought about for years. For the first time I could recall, I felt as though I was talking with someone to whom I could reveal a dark part of my life without suffering any severe emotional consequences. It was like being with a friend in my attic looking at my old uniform and decorations.

So I asked him why he volunteered. I imagined the work was painful and difficult. It was for me just to be a visitor. Without hesitation he replied, "Standing here in front of the names of my men as a volunteer is the best I have felt in the 35 years since I've been home. It is safe for me to be here with them and safe for me to talk here."

Suddenly, I felt a gentle gravitational pull towards The Wall. Physically, I touched the names of Luttel and Bohrman again. It was what I had never allowed myself to feel: connection. I understood what Billy meant immediately. I thought of my men, their youth and enthusiasm. I needed to face the hard fact that I had never really wanted to forget their sacrifices. Disremembering was simply the easiest way to deal with the pain of their deaths.

Then something came to mind, 'Here at The Wall, it is safe and honorable to be a part of Vietnam history. There is no shame here. This is why you were given the chances at life you've had. To serve again, and this is a form of service to others, like Luttel, Bohrman and all of your men,' I realized. Billy saw my face relax with my grasp of his reply. He reflexively suggested I become a volunteer. He said I would get more than I would give. I told him I couldn't possibly do it because I live in Chicago. He said some volunteers live as far away as LA and Alaska and came when they could. He suggested I apply, gave me his contact information and said he would be happy to help me get started. Hesitatingly, I gave him my card and politely said I would consider his suggestion.

Almost an hour had passed by the time I glanced up along the West Wall path and saw Max and her son patiently waiting for me in the piercing cold. I thanked Billy for his time and courtesy, and I hurriedly walked up the path to join them.

As soon as I greeted Max she said, "Boy. That was quite some conversation you had with him. We've been up here for about 30 minutes waiting for you and didn't want to disturb you. You know, we have been talking, and I think you should consider becoming a volunteer here. We have the resources. Why not? I think it might be good for you..."

Astounded by the synchronicity of their thoughts, I pointed to Billy and said in bewilderment, "That's what he just said!"

Without a moment's hesitation Max replied, "Well, are you listening?"

GROWING UP

> If you want to give me a present, give me a good life. That's something I can value.
> *East of Eden - 1955*

Born in San Francisco in 1946 to a set of first generation Italian-American blue collar parents, I was the youngest of three and a classic first year Baby Boomer. My older brother and sister have had much different lives than I. They were caught in the first half of the tumultuous 40s decade when the culture of the nation was still reeling from the Depression, fighting a World War, rationing food, recycling rags, no new cars, women in the workforce, and no gasoline.

By the time I was born, rationing was over, unemployment was 1.2%, and television, frozen food, and credit cards were the hot new items of life.

Being a few years older, my brother and sister did not get the same intense sampling of the new life and world that characterized the Post War culture. They had strong recollections of much tougher times in their early years. I didn't. My world from day 1 was filled with new, happy, and amazing things.

The Family

My family worked as hard as any other at pursuing their post war dreams. Bathed in fantasy TV shows, we lived with the ideals born from the Allied victory... new urban living standards, and the promise of free-market capitalism delivering happiness and wealth to the multitudes. The "status race" was on in America, and my family tried to participate as best we could on limited income.

Success for us was defined as achieving an education and a material life beyond that of our parents. We were taught to be grateful for opportunities to improve ourselves through education, competition and ambition. As long as we could assure ourselves we always applied our best effort, we would achieve our dreams. It seemed a reasonable formula to my young mind.

My parents provided a sense of family, security and comfort which allowed us to grow and mature. It was quite an accomplishment in the liberal context of San Francisco and the free spirit of classic California culture. We were constantly reminded the axis of the universe may be centered in New York City, but there was *no place* which could match the caliber and quality of life in San Francisco or California. Mom was a housewife/department store clerk, and Dad a truck driver. They both worked for Sears.

Mom: The Energizer Bunny

Mom was the energy force in our family. Her positive attitude and spirit were boundless. All risk assessment, growth and improvement for the family were inspired by her. She controlled the calendar, and she made absolutely certain "family" was the top priority entry on each page. Family social events were scheduled and approved by Mom.

Her dedication to family was rooted in her major childhood trauma. In 1918 at 6 years old, the Spanish flu epidemic in San Francisco claimed her mother, father and two sisters in a matter of two weeks. Consequently, Mom, the two remaining sisters and their baby brother were scheduled to be assigned orphan status by the City Health Department. They were rescued within days by their uncles and each child was assigned to their cousin's families to be cared for and raised. This terrifying childhood episode steeled my mother for life, but also gave her a sense of gratitude few of us ever feel. She was forever faithful and grateful to family for rescuing her and her siblings from the grim life of being an orphan.

Mom was sent to her Uncle Leo whom she called Dad for the rest of her life, the wealthiest of the 6 uncles and the Capo of the Sicilian fisherman community of The Wharf. Along with Mary, his devoted and talented wife, both were brilliant substitutes as mother and father to their niece.

Formal education did not excite Mom. She left high school before graduating to work in Leo's successful fish business as the bookkeeper while her two spoiled brothers (cousins) played at their imitation of Gatsby lifestyles. Mom was exceptionally social and very intuitive. Learning by witnessing and understanding was actually more satisfying to her than was formal education. She learned by observation and was able to put her learning to good use in the most creative and productive ways.

Her Depression life was markedly different from most because it was more privileged than impoverished. She could devote time to the things she enjoyed, especially when it involved food. A lifetime gourmet cook, she never stopped learning how to create new tastes and presentations. Obviously, food and family were the most common sources of conversation for Mom.

My grandfather's company logo

She was a great story teller. She had a natural ability to tell tales of family, friends and her work life while doing great mimicking of her subjects. We listened intently and always laughed so hard that tears would inevitably squirt from the corners of our eyes. It was great fun to be in her spell while eating her delicious food. It was what our home was always about. The most talked about moment in her cooking life morphed into Baffico Family Folklore and it is still the most famous eating story.

My brother Jim played professional football for the Buffalo Bills. When the team came out to play the hated Oakland Raiders, Mom asked Jim if he wanted to have a few of "the boys" over for some raviolis after the game (that was Mom's code language for an eating marathon). Why not? Everyone was always welcome. I thought there would be no takers after playing such a big rivalry game. But, sure enough, Jim brought four teammates to the house after calling in and saying she had better prepare a large meal. Amongst the guests were Billy Shaw, All-Pro Guard and now an NFL Hall of Famer and Joe O'Donnell, a Michigan All-American lineman. Both could pass for a couple of Hoss Cartwright inflatables.

Mom was in heaven. It was Showtime! She made her usual salads, home-made antipasto, loaves of garlic bread, a baked ham, 4 vegetables, and enough home-made ravioli to feed 20 people so there would be enough for the family during the week. All of this was followed by cake, cannoli, and after dinner drinks. They ate everything, plus 10 quarts of milk.

After dessert, when Mom kiddingly asked Billy Shaw if there was anything else she could get him, he replied in the gentlest Southern drawl, "Yes, Ma'am. If you have any more of those raviolis, I'd really appreciate it." She and my sister skittered into the kitchen and made the last four batches as fast as they could. The men finished them off in complete ecstasy...theirs and Mom's. History had been made.

Dad: The Brains

Dad was the antithesis of Mom. He was a classic Depression child. Risk made him uncomfortable. Security was paramount to him. Parsimoniousness bordering on miserly was Dad's way of dealing with his insecurities. As he made his way through life, he made a point of keeping a low profile, being steady, patient, and thoughtful while cultivating his other attributes of being cerebral and artistic. To Dad, life's adventures lay in the pages of the books he always had handy and the work he could do with his hands. An inveterate reader, he read 2 books a week until he died.

In his mind, education and information were the twin pillars of The Good Life. He firmly believed formal education would provide one the answers to everything you would ever need in life. He graduated from high school against the wishes of his vegetable farmer father. As a bright inquisitive young man, he was constantly chided to work full time on the family ranch with the other "men". Although he desperately wanted to continue his education, circumstances and economics prevailed. Consequently, he became adamant his children would not suffer the same fate.

At 18 years old, he joined the Coast Artillery of the California National Guard to earn some Depression money and to avoid the full time hard scrabble life of the farming business. His father did not approve. It was considered a waste of time and costly labor to the Old World Genovese mountain farmer. But with his mother's approval to earn more money during his National Guard service and to stay clear of the farm, Dad and his younger brother George found additional work as furniture assembly and delivery men for the huge new store in town: Sears, Roebuck and Co. The year was 1930. Uncle George went on to become a college teacher. Dad stayed with Sears for the rest of his life.

Dad's truck and his brother George

Facts, current events, science, literature, music, the classics, and new frontiers were the common sources of Dad's conversation with anyone, but particularly his family. Conversation was mandatory for everyone at our dinner table. He cultivated competition during the nightly ritual, and he made it clear to each of us that good was never good enough. We learned values, facts, etiquette, protocol, and manners from the exchanges, and we learned we were always expected to be the best we could be. Nothing less would be accepted.

Dad continually dreamed of being what he never was: an explorer. But his anxieties were too great to make it happen. So he lived his life through his books and his children. Fortunately, he had the wisdom to realize his maturation model would not work for his 3 talented children. So when it came time to letting them explore the world unencumbered and independently, he had the courage to let us go.

The Twin Stars + One

My brother Jim was the early star of the family: great athlete, musically inclined, high-grade student and talented at almost everything he chose to take up. He was particularly gifted when it came to sports, the measuring stick of male success in our larger family during our growing up years. A genuine star in baseball, football and golf, Jim could intimidate anyone with his skills and size. Every accomplishment on the field was a source of great pride to Mom and Dad. He was the idol of the Baffico-La Rocca clan. He was cool and accomplished, and everybody around him knew it.

Sister Christine was also of enormous talent. A straight A student with looks and personality, she was a talented singer who showed tremendous potential in various school musicals as well as a local TV talent show. She had the makings of a child star. But the bright, well-read young girl was never really attracted to the glamorous life which was offered to her. Cool doesn't necessarily describe Chris, but she was definitely an important player in the In Crowd. Like Jim, she too was often the topic of conversation in family circles.

I was always referred to as "the baby" and repeatedly told I was coddled and spoiled. I didn't feel that way, but I didn't fight it very hard. I just always believed that as my parents became more practiced and confident in their parenting skills, the job came easier to them and I was the beneficiary of their progress. I think my siblings still don't buy this view. At any rate, the outcome is that I have been accorded a poster-like life in many ways, and the envy of much of my generation as well as that of my brother and sister. But it started out slowly and differently than most.

I was the perfect average of the lowest combined talents of my brother and sister. I was a good athlete; a better than average student; good curiosity, but not particularly ambitious; fairly artistic, but didn't have any patience; physically average; not supremely cool; and sometimes clumsy in my attempts to imitate my brother and sister. I always seemed to be in need of special attention.

I didn't speak until I was almost 3 years old. I didn't have to. My sister did all the talking for me. When I finally did try, it was obvious I had a speech impediment which needed attention. Through speech therapy I was pronounced good to go by the time Kindergarten started. But my troubles didn't end there. From severe hemorrhaging after a simple tonsillectomy, to my accidentally cutting my face when playing with my father's razor, and my obsession with food not being mixed on my plate, I was going to find trouble if it was lurking close by. I was regularly in need of something beyond that of a normal kid, whether it be emotional strength or just plain medical attention.

I did have a natural mechanical intuition most of my family thought of as cute but not particularly impressive. At 3 years old I could take complicated things apart and effortlessly put them back together with no help. My father would give me something like a flashlight to keep me entertained. I would take it completely apart, lay out all the pieces and then put it all back together again…hour after hour. Working with my hands, staying quiet and understanding how things work was the best way for me to sooth myself and to stay out of trouble. With the speech problems I had, I think some people thought I was some kind of a savant mute. I still work well with my hands in building and repairing things as a method of relaxation. But now I talk too much.

I started to show leadership talent by the time of grammar school after I learned how to speak correctly: class officer, team captain positions, honor student, etc. In relative short order, however, I realized I couldn't measure up to my sibling's gold standards of talent and attention, no matter how hard I tried. So, I looked for other dreams to inspire me.

I think I was one of the early versions of a propeller head—now called a nerd or geek. I always had a strong interest in science and the scientific events of my childhood. Our country was just starting to fire off rockets and satellites in competition with the Soviets as The Cold War steadily took on larger proportions. *Watch Mr. Wizard* was my favorite Saturday morning TV program. I couldn't wait to hear Jimmy say, "Gosharoonie, Mr. Wizard!" *Science In Action* was a local TV show I watched religiously with Dad every Monday night. Playing with radios, chemicals, electricity, and making smelly gases really caught my attention. I was hooked.

Mr. Wizard and Jimmy

This led me to thinking in a completely different way than my brother and sister. I was not going to be a professional star or talent of some sort. I was not going to live a privileged existence of celebrity like they would. I needed to find my own dream. Perhaps I would invent some breakthrough product like plastic glass or stainless steel light bulbs. In the pre-adolescent years, the world of science and mechanics seemed like a decent fit for me, and I thought it was fun.

My inimitable ambition was quite anomalous to my larger family of first generation Italian men and women who measured success through physical attributes, muscular calibrations and the amount of food one could consume. It was hard for me to show off my home-made crystal set when my brother was a colossus and breaking records, my sister was knocking down straight A's and on TV, and my mother was putting on weekend gourmet meals. My uncles and aunts didn't know what to do or say to me. To them, I was in a different zip code.

The exception was my father. He was my staunch supporter and worked tirelessly to help me further my unique interests. He would encourage me to explore and expand my science talent. Every Saturday morning he'd take me on field trips he had planned: the planetarium; a downtown tour of historical sites; the old Coast Artillery gun emplacements he used to man as a teenager; the Main San Francisco Library, his Sistine Chapel. All were intended to help me see a larger world filled with unlimited potential than I was experiencing as his youngest. I now believe he was vicariously living some of his boyhood dreams through me.

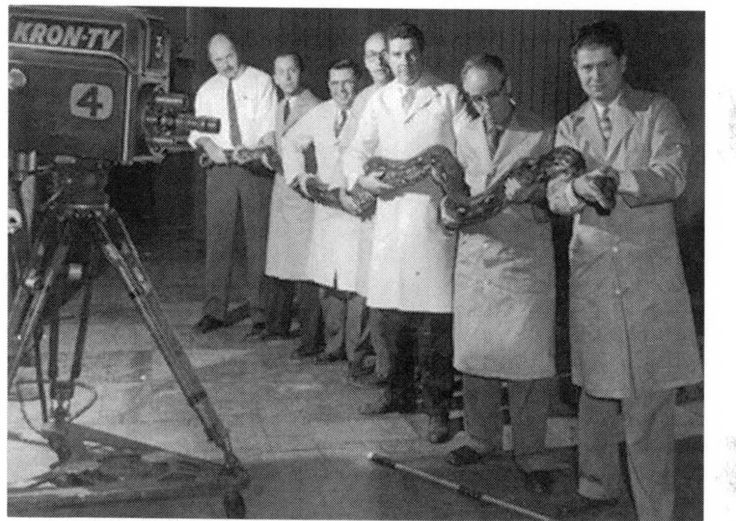

Science in Action with Dr. Earl S. Harold

I loved electronics. I'll never forget the Saturday he took me to the Allied Radio store downtown, and we bought the parts to build a small radio from a schematic drawn out on a piece of note paper by the clerk. I was so excited I couldn't wait to get home and get started. Dad helped, and we had it working that night. Magic! Dad got to play like the kid he never had the chance to be, and I got to feel like I could do something really special and different from everybody else.

I was comfortable with the sense of individuality it gave me. I remember thinking, 'I might be different,' but I was different in a special way and that was okay. I didn't have to apologize for not being out on the playing field rough-housing with the neighborhood kids like Jim. I could do that, but I actually preferred using my hands in a constructive way. I also liked the fact I was a little more under the radar than my brother and sister. It gave me a greater sense of freedom I cherished.

I liked the feeling very much.

AN UNLIKELY MEMORIAL

> The surprise was not that we got it built. The big surprise was that it did not become a fraternal monument, like many military monuments where the only people interested in them are the actual participants. This has transcended just participants in the Vietnam War. You see them there, but by and large, most visitors are not Vietnam veterans.
>
> *Jan Scruggs*

Jan Scruggs, 1982

Soldiers die in war: 116,516 Americans in The Great War; 405,399 in WWII; 36,574 in Korea; 5281 in The War on Terror, and 614,500 in our Civil War. By comparison, our Vietnam losses were modest for the 20 years we fought: 58,300.

Our culture has a habit of burnishing the history of our wars by glorifying the nobleness of the cause or exalting the victory, or both. It is a way of avoiding and neutralizing the obvious fact that war is savagery.

Vietnam was the first war for which we couldn't glorify the cause *or* the victory. The lives of men and women had been sacrificed. Yet even today it puzzles us as to what happened and why. So, erecting monuments and statues to the greater glory of this war was an embarrassing enigma for our country. When we had finally extricated our troops from Vietnam, collectively, we were at a loss about what to do other than forget it--until one man developed an idea.

Jan C. Scruggs, a wounded and decorated infantryman from Bowie, Maryland, wanted Vietnam Veterans to have a tangible symbol of recognition from the American people. He felt strongly a memorial and national reconciliation was needed. He contributed the first $2,200 of his own money to start the Vietnam Veterans Memorial Fund, Inc., a nonprofit, charitable organization which was subsequently incorporated by a group of Vietnam Veterans whom Scruggs knew.

He established The Fund in order to raise money for the construction of the Memorial to those who sacrificed their lives in Vietnam. By separating the issue of the service of the individuals from the issues of policy and tactics, Scruggs hoped to begin a process of national reconciliation.

Initial public support came from U.S. Senators Charles Mathias, Jr. and John W. Warner. On Nov. 8, 1979, Sen. Mathias introduced legislation to authorize a site of national park land for the Memorial. The first significant financial contributions to launch the national fundraising campaign were raised by Sen. Warner.

More than $8,000,000 was raised, all of which came from private sources. Corporations, foundations, unions, Veterans groups and civic organizations contributed, but most importantly, more than 275,000 individual Americans donated the majority of the money needed to build the Memorial.

On July 1, 1980, Congress authorized a site of three acres in Constitution Gardens near the Lincoln Memorial. In October of that year, VVMF announced that a national design competition for the Memorial was open to any U.S. citizen over 18 years of age. By Dec. 29, 1980, there were 2,573 registrants, and the competition became the largest of its kind ever held in the United States.

On the deadline date of March 31, 1981, 1,421 design entries had been submitted. All were judged in a blind competition anonymously by a jury of eight internationally recognized artists and designers who had been selected by VVMF and none of whom were Vietnam Veterans. The jury presented its unanimous selection for first prize on May 1, 1981. The selection was accepted and adopted enthusiastically by VVMF.

And the Winner Is...

The winning design was submitted by a 21 year old senior architect student from Yale University. Controversy over it was immediate, explosive and voluminous. The design was called The Black Gash of Shame by dissenters. They said it was wrong. The shape, the concept, the materials, the designer, the symbolism and positioning were all deemed unacceptable by a highly critical public. Moreover, the Memorial was not a statue nor had statuary as a part of it. The debate over the design was fanatical and vitriolic. It subsided only when a compromise about statuary was finally reached almost a year after the original competition was concluded.

In January 1982, a decision was made to add a flagstaff and sculpture on the Memorial site in order to provide a realistic depiction of three Vietnam servicemen and a symbol of their courage and devotion to their country. VVMF selected Washington, D.C. sculptor Frederick Hart to design a sculpture of the servicemen to be placed at the site. Once Hart's design was approved, work was allowed to proceed on the construction of The Wall.

On March 11, 1982, the Wall design and plans received final federal approval, and work at the site was begun. Ground was formally broken on Friday, March 26, 1982. Construction was completed only 6 months later in late October 1982, and the Memorial was dedicated on Nov. 13, 1982.

The Three Servicemen statue was eventually added in 1984, two years after the dedication. That same year, the Memorial was given as a "gift" to the American people in a ceremony presided over by President Ronald Reagan.

During the competition, design and construction phases the Wall made sensational news. Many Veterans paid little if any attention to the news or the design controversy of the Memorial. Personally, it made me angry any energy was spent on something that would symbolize and memorialize a war that was not a war; a war that shamed and shunned the soldiers who fought it; and a war that was singled out as the "only war the United States ever lost".

Vietnam already stood out as a despicable international embarrassment, so it was difficult to understand why anyone wanted to build a memorial--a memorial *to* what and *for* what? The bitterness in the country was so pronounced that other Veterans from other wars steered clear of Vietnam Veterans. Most of us who served there spent a lot of energy silencing our memories and trying to be invisible. Suddenly, with the controversy over The Wall, the country's dysfunctionality and its divisive streak was again highlighted and on display. The Memorial was having the opposite intended effect.

I wanted nothing to do with any of it. I was done. I had served my time as prescribed, did the best I could, and wanted nothing more than to keep my memories compartmentalized and hidden from public scrutiny. I didn't need a monument in our nation's capital to remember the loss of my men. I carried their memory inside me remorsefully and privately. And I wanted it kept out of view from everyone. Others could flail and debate and scorn all they wanted. My anger about Vietnam was so sharp and held so fiercely, I felt I would explode if I participated in any dialog. As I saw it, I was on borrowed time and wanted to make the best of it I possibly could. To remember an agonizing part of my life was not my idea of a good use of the time.

Post World War II America

> We witness today in the power of nuclear weapons a new and deadly dimension to the ancient horror of war. Humanity has now achieved, for the first time in its history, the power to end its history. This truth must guide our every deed. It makes world disarmament a necessity of world life. For I repeat again this simple declaration: the only way to win World War III is to prevent it.
>
> *Dwight D. Eisenhower, 1955*

The Cold War and The Eisenhower Presidency

Like all Baby Boomers, my early childhood was inexorably tied to the gravitational forces exerted on global peace by the Cold War. The navigation and leadership through these problematic force fields rightly fell to the job of the President of the United States as a result of our role in WWII and the fact we had dropped the first atomic bomb. Dwight D. Eisenhower was the leader of the free world. As the planet transitioned into a messy and difficult Post WWII rebuilding phase charged with high drama about new conflict, Eisenhower projected a proper confidence.

Quietly and powerfully he held a steady hand on global and domestic issues in his first term while restoring the confidence of voters and allies after President Truman's tumultuous ride out of the White House. Ike was the ideal U.S. president for the Cold War environment. He won his first term in a landslide and was a popular president who ended the Korean War and kept the U.S. out of the possibilities of other wars. The only true emergency of his first term was the heart attack he suffered in September 1955. And as soon as his doctor pronounced him fully recovered in February 1956, Eisenhower announced his decision to run for re-election.

The Democrats set up a replay of the 1952 contest by nominating Adlai Stevenson. But two world crises helped cement Eisenhower's lead in the final days of his second campaign. The Soviet Union invaded Hungary, and Britain, France, and Israel attacked Egypt in an effort to take over the Suez Canal. Eisenhower kept the United States out of both conflicts.

The result was an even more spectacular Republican landslide as Americans registered their anxiety over entering another war. Ike was their man. The world felt safe and secure with this iconic warrior leading us through the treacherous new waters of the Cold War. It was the critical issue to all constituencies both domestic and foreign, and Eisenhower had a commanding grasp of the situation.

As were most young children of the times, I was completely oblivious to the international tensions and their importance to our electoral process or my well-being. With Ike as the ultimate father figure and heroic warrior, we were insulated from the Cold War tensions and were confident it was safe for us to go out and play. Eisenhower's gentle demeanor and public unflappability masked his commitment to a nuclear strategy of massive retaliation should there ever be an attempted attack on U.S. soil. But the confidence and security Ike carefully provided the country through his unwavering dedication to the strategy wore thin during my later childhood as the Cold War drama intensified with unremitting Soviet nuclear rhetoric. Evacuation drills went from occasional in grammar school to regularly scheduled events in junior high. At the time, they seemed like small annoyances in my educational advancement.

Text from Eisenhower 1955 Electronic Media Re-Election Campaign

"Four years ago it was a different story. Many of our young men were on Heartbreak Ridge in Korea. And that was no game: A vicious, grinding war that went on and on, as if forever.

Of course, today it's all over and the young men are trying to forget. But for one day this year, they'll remember. And that one day is Election Day, November 6th, when not only these young men, but Americans of all ages will be thinking long and hard about how to vote for the surest road to peace during the next four years. What are some of their thoughts?

COLLEGE STUDENT: I'm engaged this time, and I'm planning to get married, and I don't want to look forward to military service in war. I want my children to grow up in a country that's in peace. I think that Ike is the man who can do this for us.

MOTHER: I will vote for President Eisenhower because I am a mother of three children. And I feel, with President Eisenhower in command of our country, I can raise my children with great security.

FATHER: I'm going to vote for Ike because of his outstanding record in the past four years, and because I believe, through a Republican administration, we will have peace and prosperity for my children to grow up in for at least the next 20 years."

Junior High School

As I progressed though grammar and junior high schools, my bias for the sciences continued to grow. The Space Race was a subset of the Cold War, and I wanted to understand it and be a part of it. I performed well enough to begin to consider expanding my education in the sciences. I was chosen for some special programs and won a few awards which made me feel I was on track. I participated in an advanced placement for a high school electronics class, and I won a Ford Foundation competition for a mechanical drawing design I submitted. Dad was impressed. Cool stuff for me.

Simultaneously my body temporarily took on new features and my athletic skills began to be less and less competitive. Others passed me by. Even though I had been a decent baseball, football, and soccer player during my Junior High School years, puberty didn't do the right things in the right places. That was a big blow to my confidence and self-esteem.

But I remained hopeful I would head to the same elite private high school my all-star cousins and brother had attended to be a student and a star. Saint Ignatius College Prep was a family tradition, and I looked forward to getting my share of treasured memories from this venerated institution. I knew I would have the family athletic reputation to uphold and enhance, and I was concerned about living up to the standard set. There was a lot to worry about following in big footsteps. But I soon realized sports stardom was only one small worry.

Saint Ignatius was a private Catholic Jesuit all male school in the heart of the City bordered by the Haight-Ashbury district. It was also part of the campus of The University of San Francisco. Most of the cream of the City had gone to S.I. and then on to U.S.F. They were the sons of San Francisco's politicians, lawyers, doctors and industry moguls. They were sent there to prepare for the Good Life of fame and fortune. It boasted alums like Gerry Brown, three time governor of California, Gordon Getty of oil fame, Richard Egan, famous actor, Dan Fouts, Hall of Fame footballer, and many more. It was an esteemed institution then and it continues to have a proven formula for success today after 149 years. I had to get in.

In order to be accepted into S.I., you had to pass a rigorous entrance exam. It was designed to be difficult enough to keep the bar and breed of student high. Besides the math, science, writing and literature sections, there was also a test of your religious knowledge.

Religion was actually not a big concern for most. Even if you were going to make the shift from the public school system to this private

Catholic institution as much of my family did, the religion portion was not a significant hurdle for most applicants. It was designed to simply verify you were a practicing confirmed Catholic--no problem. This was true for others, but not for me. I failed the religion part of the exam. I couldn't do it. Four correct out of 100 questions. I think I broke the record for the worst score for someone claiming to be Catholic. I probably would have been better off if I had declared I was Jewish. They always let a few smart Jewish kids get in to keep the competition intense. I didn't get in. I was wait-listed.

My brother and sister did not have the religion problem I had. That's because they attended the mandatory Sunday school Catechism classes, did the work, and made real Confirmations (early post-war discipline displayed at its best!). I, on the other hand, had cut all my Catechism classes and was confirmed just so the nuns could get me off their roster. So there I was again, an anomaly. I was ashamed. I felt like I had besmirched the family name.

Was this the price I had to pay for my truancy? The possibility of my getting into S.I. looked slim. My penalty for failure was to sweat out the summer waiting. Worse yet, I had thumbed my nose at all my public school friends and classmates because for years I bragged I was going to this exclusive school everybody hated. Suddenly and unexpectedly, I was looking at the possibility of eating a super-sized serving of humble pie.

Fortunately, Dad came to the rescue. He wrote a drippy, teary letter to the Principal pleading for me to be given the same opportunity for this education his other son had earned. Coddled again. Special attention again. Dad had to grovel for *me!* And it worked. They let me in.

I was embarrassed, but determined to prove I was not the spoiled, geeky wimp I appeared to be. I resolved to excel at everything I did and be the best of the best. I felt that as long as I had gotten my foot inside the door, I could get on an even playing field with the future superstars. I got ready to meet cool people and learn how to integrate into the cool circles of San Francisco social and then professional life. I committed myself to make the best of it.

It was an exciting proposition and I was beyond thrilled. Saint Ignatius was and is a machine for producing winners. It was a place to learn how to be a Renaissance Man in the classic Jesuit definition and the envious place to attend high school in the San Francisco Bay Area. Losers there were sorted out efficiently, expelled, and never let back inside. I finally felt like I was included with the winners. I was on my way.

High School Goes Global

> We stand today on the edge of a new frontier -- the frontier of the 1960s, a frontier of unknown opportunities and perils, a frontier of unfulfilled hopes and threats. The new frontier of which I speak is not a set of promises -- it is a set of challenges.
>
> *John F. Kennedy*
>
> *January 20, 1961 Inaugural Address*

A Heady Beginning

The John F. Kennedy Inauguration 1961
The Times They Were a Changin'

The year was 1961, and it was my high school freshman year. I was ready to begin my journey from pre-adolescent to responsible young adult.

That same year John F. Kennedy assumed the reigns of the world's most powerful nation. As a country we were beginning to transition from the old WWII Eisenhower democracy model to the New Frontier with a bright new leader who was eager to guide us through the next phase of our country's maturing process. Ike was gone. The memories of World War II faded a little faster. There was fresh, young and glamorous leadership on Pennsylvania Ave.

Politically, no greater symbol of the nation's imperial character could be found than in the newly elected leader. Young yet rational, stylish yet cautious, Kennedy behaved the way the leader of a great nation was expected to behave. In the air and on the streets there was a true sense of excitement. More than a symbol of the nation's brash self-confident mood, JFK epitomized an American ideology which began to emerge in the mid-50s, reached a climax in 1960, and continued until about 1965, all during my high school years.

Kennedy's ideology was built on six basic assumptions. 1. American capitalism works, creates abundance, and it has the potential to solve social problems. 2. Growth is the key to the potential thereby eliminating anticipated conflict for resources. 3. Abundant resources can solve global social problems. 4. Middle Class expansion eliminates inequality (workers become members of the middle class). 5. Democratic capitalism works for us; therefore, export it. *It is our destiny to bring it to the world.* 6. Contain communism. The obvious threat to this ideology is from communism.

Over the course of my high school years, the Kennedy ideology would be intentionally woven into the curriculum in various classes either as a topic for current debate or through recitations on political rhetoric. There was no question that the Jesuits felt duty-bound to create good Democrats for the world.

Intrusive Global Politics

With the anticipated modernization of archaic Roman Catholic dogma via Vatican II, the revitalized Church appeared to blend perfectly with the freshness of Kennedy's view of our country's profile in the geopolitical landscape. His Catholicism which had been a mild campaign negative turned out to be of little concern. It actually provided a timely relevancy which could add value to his presidency. And it created an atmosphere of great and genuine hope in the world on his Inauguration Day.

However, post-WWII U.S. foreign policy and diplomatic ideology had instituted the U.S. primary pillars of the Containment policy against Communism of *superior power and portable force.* Both were direct threats to the Soviets, and Khrushchev was determined to challenge the U.S and Kennedy cunningly and aggressively. Ike had remained very cool yet firm with Khrushchev's theatrics. When Kennedy took office he was immediately challenged. Soviet sabre rattling and hyperbolic proclamations about nuclear conflagration collaterally touched everyone on the planet. Arms superiority became the macabre objective of the Cold War. Fear and frustration mounted speedily and unexpectedly inside the U.S. and from Allies who had hoped for peaceful coexistence.

"We will beat the United States with small wars of liberation or popular uprisings...of colonial peoples against their oppressors across the developing world."
Nikita Khrushchev, January 1961

Kennedy's Presidency was tested mercilessly within the first 12 months by Soviet leader Khrushchev and the dream of the New Frontier stalled. The last two points of the ideology became the initial sources of serious and irreparable tears in the fabric of America which would become unremitting far beyond Kennedy's brief term in office. The dynamics and weight of the Cold War became centric to the Kennedy Administration very quickly. World reaction was confused and unpredictable around a plethora of mismanaged titanic issues which grabbed all the lustrous hope Kennedy represented.

Five days after his Inauguration, two USAF crewmen were released by Khrushchev after their Stratojet was shot down. Kennedy ignored the opportunity to discuss the Cold War implications. Khrushchev was furious. Soviet aggression was promulgated in every bed of colonial unrest. The Bay of Pigs was a humiliating failed Castro assassination attempt by Kennedy's Whiz Kids in the first 3 months. The Berlin Wall built in August represented a microcosm of the ideological battle with no U.S. comment or action. U.S. and Russian tanks squared off at Checkpoint Charlie in Berlin in October. The world gasped. Intense nuclear proliferation went unchecked. The nuclear arms race produced scorekeeping headlines. Revolutions boiled simultaneously in Latin and Central Americas, The Congo, Hungary, Nigeria, Algeria, et al. Military actions percolated in Laos, Thailand, Burma, and Vietnam. Who would we support, and why?

In his second year, the Cuban Missile Crisis produced a nerve jangling button-pushing high drama threat of world war. Simultaneously, the Green Berets were developed as the U.S. guerilla anti-insurgent force and utilized Vietnam for proof of concept. Meanwhile, missile-equipped U.S. Nuclear subs sat silently off the Russian shorelines waiting to strike a moment's notice.

The enormity of nuclear war was so overwhelming and such a new phenomenon to the world it was difficult to comprehend for all humanity. One fact outweighed others. The conflict would be final for all living beings regardless of geography or ideology. Eisenhower had made that clear in the 50's. Hiroshima was a distant event, but it had left a lasting impression on the world. It presented every person on earth with the same question. How could we survive the struggle for world power which had become more complex and incendiary every day? War which would be like no other the U.S. or the world had ever seen. It would involve our land, homes and infrastructure. Older generation's wars had no relevancy to this new form of hostility. Only two equally matched superpowers were playing a global game of "Who Will Blink First?", but it affected every living thing.

For the Boomer Generation, our high school agendas became naturally oriented to the mega-power struggle. The news stories were so sensational and of such magnitude they could not be ignored. Announcement of Russia's 100 megaton bomb by Khrushchev; the tense daily confrontations at the Berlin Wall and Kennedy's acceptance of them; Russia's first human orbit of Earth; and the failed Vienna conference of Kennedy and Khrushchev kept the drama high and lethally serious.

To exacerbate matters, Kennedy's staff of "The Best and Brightest" was totally unprepared to be confronted with events of this magnitude so early in his Presidency. They had great difficulty interacting with a world which did not respect or worship their academic achievements or their pedigree. Simply stated, they were long on brainpower but woefully short on pragmatism and practical wisdom. As a country, we were accustomed to Eisenhower's paternal administrative profile which had subtlety but powerfully manipulated the balance of power in our favor. Now the Soviet Union wanted to take advantage of the odd naivety and arrogance of the Kennedy Administration. As Kennedy's Whiz Kids faced mounting affronts, the best performance they could muster was to insure the Kennedy Camelot story was attended to for public consumption in every dimension.

Inside San Francisco City Hall House Protest, May 1961

Furthermore, unruly internal protestations against facets of the Kennedy ideology kicked off during his first year. In May, the House Un-American Committee riots in San Francisco sent a clear message that the McCarthy witch hunt tactics of the Fifties were a violation of individual rights and not a matter of autonomous patriotism. Going forward, the government would be confronted in this regard. This particular gauntlet was being thrown in the face of the new Attorney General and former McCarthy aide, Robert Kennedy.

I remember watching young people *inside* San Francisco City Hall being washed down the front stairs of the regal building with fire hoses on full power like leaves in a gutter, because they were demonstrating for the rights of individuals. Rights that I thought were clearly spelled out in The Constitution. It had to be explained to me that rights were not written in The Constitution as clearly as a set of assembly instructions for an Erector Set. But the bigger question I had was, 'Are those people right or are they wrong? Whose side would I be on if I had to make a choice?'

> **"The layman's constitutional view is that which he likes is constitutional, and that which he doesn't like is unconstitutional."**
> ***Justice Hugo Black, New York Times, 26 February 1971***

Increasingly, seeds of backlash were sown in the young minds of the post-war generation. Revolution within our own borders was fomenting. An endless information feeding frenzy became a new part of the culture with the phenomenon of videotaped world news availability. Instant, repetitive news was anywhere in the world there was a television. Intense media competition formed and shaped opinions by means of sensational sound bite editing as each network did its best to surpass the other in the powerful Nielsen ratings. Concurrently, world leaders' reactions to the events became quicker than ever, particularly with Kennedy and Khrushchev at the controls. Both were masters at using the media for parrying.

Kennedy was the adored fresh leader of the Free World. But constant Soviet histrionics and the early diplomatic blunders of his Administration eventually forced him to take a stand against the communist aggression. He had to act. However, Berlin was too high profile and directly confrontational with Russia. The Soviets had crushed Eastern European freedom movements. Africa was not strategically and economically valuable to the U.S. at the time. Kennedy had lost Cuba by an embarrassing comprehensive military blunder which eventually led to major problems.

Although he inherited trouble in Laos, Vietnam was where Kennedy eventually chose to take his stand under the advice and guidance of retired

General Maxwell Taylor who had been brought into the White House by Kennedy to investigate the Bay of Pigs catastrophe. Taylor took the opportunity to plan and implement a new, greater role for the Army (who had lost resources and prestige to the Air Force in the Cold War environment) by instituting a policy of "flexible response for small brush-fire" conflicts to justify an Army role in U.S. diplomacy. Vietnam presented Taylor and, albeit, JFK with ideal ground for testing the concept, and it conveniently tied to the U.S. policy of Containment of communism. Taylor was the leading proponent of the Kennedy inner circle to promote action in Vietnam despite significant opposition.

> **"Now we have a problem in making our power credible, and Vietnam is the place"**
> ***John F. Kennedy, 1961***

At the time, the black and white analytics of U.S. Cold War policy did not differentiate versions or degrees of communism. If a small country was tied in any way to communist doctrine, it carried enemy status equal to that of a major power. China and Russia's historic limited interest in Vietnam was enough for the U.S. to justify Vietnam as a threat which had to be met. And the Domino Theory held that if one fell all nearby would fall. The theory had been naively developed without a rigorous assessment of its assumptions during the Truman/Eisenhower Presidencies as the justification for Containment.

Kennedy adopted the Taylor strategy as a way for the U.S. to engage Third World anti-colonial conflicts. Vietnam superficially appeared to be a suitable location for Kennedy's ideology and to sample Taylor's theory of fighting "brush-fire" type conflicts with new specially trained small fighting units called Special Forces. However, the designated role of the Green Berets as "advisers" whose mission was to "win hearts and minds" in a conflict unlike any we had ever encountered was misplaced. Vietnam was a multi-dimensional guerilla civil war. The enemy <u>*and*</u> the friendlies were impossible to separate. The counter-insurgent tactics of the elite, highly trained and motivated Berets fell short of the mark while the Viet Cong systematically choked the life out of village after village with invisible but deadly force.

As unimpeded Viet Cong aggression escalated and was openly denied by the US military, the self-immolation of Buddhist monks protesting the Diem government on the streets of Hue and Saigon horrified the civilized world. Kennedy was pressed for a U.S. strategy for Vietnam. To the media, he glibly positioned the war as "their fight" and suggested we were just helping. Privately he had serious doubts and had to deal with heated staff disagreements. With the failed Special Forces experiment, Taylor and the Joint Chiefs of Staff then pressed for the use of old style WWII force and fighting via ground troop deployments and intense aerial bombing, the same essential tactics that had failed for the French.

Arrogance among staff, fostered by National Security Advisor McGeorge Bundy that U.S. superiority would prevail over the perceived weaker, poorly equipped, and ignorant enemy was persuasive. However, a minority expressed serious doubt we understood the dynamics of the Vietnamese culture to be dedicating resources to it. The French, who had lost at Dien Bien Phu in 1954, strongly advised against U.S. aggression. But the elite Kennedy inner power circle had a difficult time comprehending traditional U.S. military advantages were woefully misplaced in a political conflict like Vietnam.

> "I don't think that unless a greater effort is made by the (South Vietnamese) Government to win popular support that the war can be won out there. In the final analysis, it is their war. They are the ones who have to win it or lose it. We can help them, we can give them equipment, we can send our men out there as advisers, but they have to win it—the people of Viet-Nam—against the Communists. We are prepared to continue to assist them, but I don't think that the war can be won unless the people support the effort, and, in my opinion, in the last 2 months the Government has gotten out of touch with the people."
>
> *John F. Kennedy, Cronkite CBS Interview, September 2, 1963*

Confusion and misinformation about the situation intensified in the White House. South Vietnam was politically leaderless. It was not within our diplomatic or political competence to fill that void. Kennedy was humiliated by the confusing direction and obfuscation of the American-initiated Diem coup. He agonized over what to do next, but held firm against military advice and refused bombing or the commitment of ground troops. Independent of the conflicting reports and outright lies of some of his staff, he realized a ground war would be a fatal path that held no hope for a reasonable outcome. By October of 1963, Kennedy decided privately he wanted out of Vietnam after the 1964 elections.

Customized Curriculum

Throughout these high-drama years, the Jesuits struggled with adapting their Classics curriculum into the hostile context of the Cold War while simultaneously attempting to align with the Kennedy ideology. In my sophomore year, as Laos and Vietnam heated up on the world stage, not so coincidentally, the 1958 best-selling book (and 1963 Marlon Brando movie), *The Ugly American,* became required reading for my World History class. It was a thinly veiled phantom novel of the misguided politics, diplomacy, and arrogance of American presence in Southeast Asia. It correctly portrayed the unwelcomed application of inappropriate American behaviors and policies in a culture that wanted few of our ideologies. The authors declared in their introduction, "Our aim is not to embarrass individuals, but to stimulate thought — and, we hope, action." The book presented an eerily accurate vision of what was to come in South Vietnam in a few years.

But the new geopolitical order was more than theory or intellectual gaming; it was a whole new troubling reality. The Eisenhower insulation had been stripped away by The New Frontier. Suddenly, the traditional Jesuit concept of being a Renaissance Man became vague and less relevant in the new threatening world. It was harder to buy into the concept that as long as you were smart and could speak Latin and recite Shakespeare; you were going to do just fine in life. The curriculum modified around the current events of enormous proportions spoke volumes about the state of the world.

Busy becoming a newly minted Ignatian, I didn't devote much time to the mounting global tensions—I did only as instructed. Frankly, the excitement of being a part of an exclusive academic fraternity was enough to keep me on task. I had little choice but to be a good student. The rigors of study kept my mind occupied trying to prove I deserved to be a part of the community. There was no time in my world for the contemplation of the consequences of global disorder.

I started out as a great student my freshman year getting a 4.0 average. In my second year, the honors class competition became significantly tougher. A measurably more difficult curriculum and my sophomoric overconfidence combined with continuing physical changes made for a shaky year. I struggled mightily.

Along the way, my fear of being an athletic outcast in the hotbed of talent proved to be well founded. I didn't make the cut for football or baseball in my first 2 years, so the anticipated damage to our family sports "brand" became a reality. Junior year, the growth hormones kicked in and I grew 6 inches. As soon as the coach saw me, I was instantly put on the varsity football team (a huge honor since the team went on to win 22 straight games and was named the #1 high school football team in the nation). Unfortunately, before playing one minute of real game time, I was injured permanently in a practice and my sports career was over. Did it again!

In the third year, I got very serious about many things and recovered nicely academically. I did manage to improve a little in coolness too. I became a peripheral participant with the shakers and movers in the class. I was the editor of the school paper, a fairly accomplished guitar player and singer (Hootenanny was in full swing), an A.P. pre-med course participant, a member of various committees and societies, and consistently a class officer.

As my self-confidence grew, more sharply defined facets of my personality began to emerge. Challenging the status quo became comfortable to me (must have been the influence of the times and environment), and I was less fearful of being contrary to the thinking of the masses. I liked thinking independently. I was not a robotic follower. I got comfortable against the flow.

By senior year I managed a solid GPA and was accepted to a four year university for pre-medical undergraduate study. Disturbing global events had built up rather than abated throughout my high school years and the questions the events highlighted were fully integrated into the school curriculum. The world was transitioning again to a more violent and dangerous place and we all imagined what it might imply for the future of our generation.

As we tackled various global issues, the cloud over all humankind darkened more and took on menacing proportions. As outlandish as it might have seemed, the possibility of world destruction had to be considered. It was unnerving to reconcile this real possibility against the idyllic post-WWII dream that had been so hard-earned. It required planning and reflection. People were encouraged to build and provision home bomb shelters. More importantly, there was a complete disconnect from the context of the present day to a clear and reasonable vision of the future. It was a reality gap.

Ideals and principles closely held and protected by one generation did not reconcile at all with the uncertain and cloudy future the younger generation was facing.

Just when humankind thought peace had been achieved, a new Age of Fear, Revolution and War dawned. No one imagined the power of its grip on our everyday lives going forward. Worse yet, the younger generation realized how completely unprepared we were to deal with this forbidding unknown. Disillusionment came rapidly.

Coincidentally, immense issues within our borders caused our foundation to suffer seismic damage. We lost our way as a country and world leader, and we agonized over the unheard-of and uncontrollable embarrassments in our own yard. Race riots in the largest cities swept across the country. Desegregation and the ugliness of unvarnished bigotry received high-level exposure. American historian Richard J. Hofstadter wrote a seminal essay in *Harper's* about "movements of suspicious discontent" that ignited political paranoia. Political conspiracy discussions led by Arizona Senator Barry Goldwater conservatives began taking control of the Republican Party based on a platform of anger and discontent.

November 22, 1963, the day the world changed.

Then on Friday, November 22, 1963, the assassination of JFK took away our breath and hope simultaneously, regardless of where in the world you were. In one hour of one afternoon, The End felt frighteningly close. Like everyone who lived through that moment, I will never forget every detail.

I was in the process of delivering the first ever full-color school magazine I had designed, printed and edited. It was supposed to be a momentous day in S.I. history. But the distribution of the first edition was interrupted by the somber announcement over the intercom that President Kennedy had been shot in Dallas and was not expected to live. Forty-five minutes later he was dead. Words cannot describe the emotional flood we collectively felt. For the next four days the funeral services and the live murder of Lee Harvey Oswald were televised on every TV in America. It was a national and personal agony for each individual who gorged on the coverage. One of the most important pieces in all of American history laced with horror, grief, honor, majesty, power, violence, murder, and more unfolded in real time in our homes.

Kennedy parade Dallas, Nov. 22, 1963

Chicago West Side rioting, 1963

Six months earlier Pope John XXIII had died suddenly and the Catholic world lost its rudder. Then Kennedy was gone. Three weeks later on the first night of Christmas break of 1963, I watched my classmate Dennis Carter die of a burst aneurism in a routine basketball game as he scored with 3 seconds left in the half. He was the first person I ever saw die. His became the third major funeral Mass in our cathedral in 5 months.

At this point in our history, never did the world seem so lost and out of control. It was frightening high drama in real time. Chaos was at the front door of my generation and it had grown more intense each year. Festering paranoia replaced the peace and serenity of childhood. The year 1963 ended solemnly. Fear and anxiety had anesthetized the world psyche.

Post-Assassination Presidency and the Fall Elections

LBJ's sudden ascension to the Presidency appropriately focused his immediate attention on the transition of power after the trauma of the assassination. Associated issues to the transition that occupied most of the public's attention were the retention of key Kennedy cabinet members, global relations, Cuba, Berlin, the stalled Civil Rights Bill and budgets. In Vietnam the U.S. continued to communicate confusing signals about supporting a weak government. The confusion was the result of Kennedy's unspoken strategy of pulling out after the fall '64 U.S. elections. Consequently, the strongest argument mumbled about supporting South Vietnam was the Domino Theory, and Johnson did not seem particularly convinced by either side. Therefore, six weeks into the Johnson Presidency, it was back page news.

> We are not about to send American boys nine or ten thousand miles away from home to do what Asian boys ought to be doing for themselves.
> *Lyndon B. Johnson, April 1964*

In June, however, the impending presidential election of 1964 ignited serious debate about the precarious and unwinnable U.S. position in Vietnam. The Republican Party, with a Goldwater presidential primary win in California, developed a "he's weak on Communism" strategy similar to what had defeated Truman after the losses of China and North Korea. Then Hofstadter's "movements of suspicious discontent" began to surface. Johnson needed to demonstrate command of the situation or risk his first election. He decided to solidify his re-election hopes by using his old Senate powers to trump the argument while he simultaneously clarified his position on Vietnam.

On August 2nd and then again on the 4th, three months before the elections, Vietnam suddenly moved to front page copy when the USS Maddox, while "patrolling international waters" near North Vietnam, was allegedly attacked by the North Vietnamese. The Johnson Congressional machinery was poised and ready for action. Within 5 days, the Gulf of Tonkin

Resolution was passed (Senate 88-2; House 416-0) and signed into law on August 10th. The Resolution gave Johnson virtually unrestricted discretionary authority to use *conventional* military force in Southeast Asia to wage war on North Vietnam. It had been primed by Johnson *before* the alleged attack at the most desirable time for the fall elections.

The Resolution instantly guaranteed the sitting President the election. Johnson back room politics took precedence over moral examination, intellectual rigor, constitutional process, diplomacy and sound military strategy. It gave him the opportunity to enforce the policy of Containment against communism—a powerful theme for Johnson and a cooperative Congress. The U.S. prepared for war with North Vietnam but would not admit it. Military hubris had convinced almost all politicians it would only take a few weeks to beat some sense into the "little yellow men".

> **Tell the Vietnamese they've got to draw in their horns or we're going to bomb them back into the Stone Age.**
> *Gen. Curtis Le May, May 1964*

For me and my classmates, high school ended in May 1964. We had no idea how much the next four years would permanently scar our souls. We graduated, enjoyed a brief summer break and then things got serious. We were draft eligible and had to register. I never considered it would mean anything or that I would ever serve. Besides, everyone knew only suckers got drafted or volunteered. The few friends who decided to serve were going to be put in harm's way. In light of the Tonkin Resolution I thought they were fools who had taken the wrong path. I was certain my pre-med route would keep me from the grips of service and my path would be problem-free.

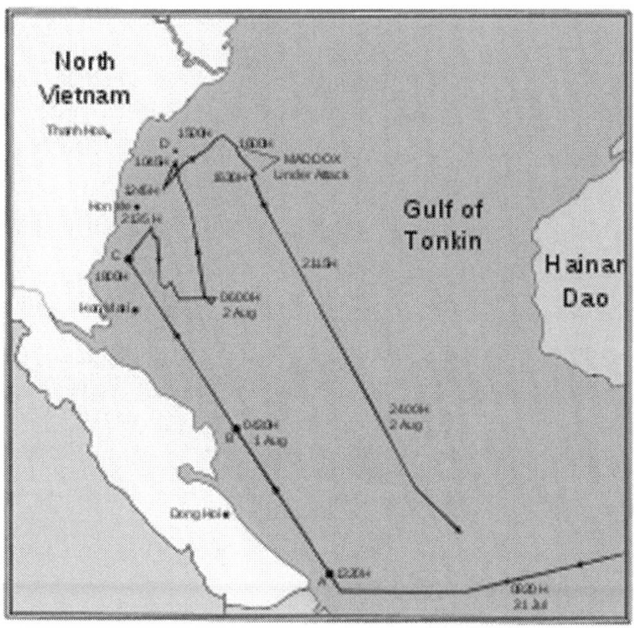

The route of the Maddox through Tonkin Gulf

WALL MAGIC

> Above all, Vietnam was a war that asked everything of a few and nothing of most in America.
> *Myra MacPherson, 1984*

The Trial Run

With the encouragement of Billy and my wife Max, I applied to become a volunteer at The Wall and was accepted. I thought I would give it a try for at least one weekend to see what it felt like. A part of me was understandably reticent. A part of me was excited, too. There was much unknown territory in my head I hadn't dare traverse in all those years.

The first opportunity to volunteer was the Memorial Day weekend of 2006. The crowd was expected to be 350,000 to 400,000 over the 3 days, including the annual ceremony. I was a bit nervous about what to expect and about making mistakes, so hypervigilence was on full power and I calmed myself with the thought of escaping if I had to.

I dutifully adorned my volunteer shirt and hat with a patch or a pin of the 101st Airborne Division and some of my miniature medals because I was told that wearing your decorations made you more approachable to visitors or Veterans. I had not worn the patch of the 101st since I came home on January 28th, 1971, and had never worn any of the medals. But for this occasion, I wanted to be as professional and proper as I could be. I put them on and felt a fleeting flash of pride I had experienced the day I came home 35 years before.

I was ready to be initiated. The day was bright and sunny and the crowd was very large. I took up a position away from most of the other volunteers in front of panels W5 through W12, the panels that represent the time I was in Vietnam. I was adjacent to Billy who stood in front of his men's names. My position made it convenient for me to ask him questions. And I had a lot of questions. I had studied hard, but I still needed plenty of help.

Surprisingly, I immediately felt I was a part of the Memorial and the activity it ignited for Memorial Day, almost naturally. Nervousness dissipated effortlessly the more I talked with people. I was at ease meeting the public here as I was for years working on the sales floor in a Sears store. As the time passed that first day, I came to understand what Billy had told me the day we met. The Wall made him feel the best he had felt since he came home. It did for me also, proud not ashamed. I had put my life on the line for my country when others didn't. At The Wall I didn't have to apologize, defend or explain to anyone why I had done it. I could see there were memories I needed to process and not avoid. Losses I needed to grieve and honor about people, places and events.

A Memorial Day Crowd

It was fitting for me to stand in front of my men's names and the others who I knew. I allowed myself to feel a personal connection to them. In the past, The Wall hurt when I didn't understand its relevance to my memories, but this day it called to me. I realized a part of me was inscribed on it, and I felt an instinctual bond. A bond I could finally accept. I stood tall.

One man came up to me who recognized my 101st Airborne patch and asked if I had been with them in Vietnam. I said I had been and he asked me when. I told him and then we exchanged a few more points of coincidence about our service time. He paused for a moment and looked at my name badge questioningly and said, "Wait, are you the Paul Baffico who went to the University of San Francisco?"

I hesitated and slowly took off my dark glasses to get a better look and thought, 'It couldn't be.' I asked him if he was the Major Gerry Landry that had taught ROTC at The University of San Francisco when I was a sophomore in 1966, exactly 40 years before. It was him! I couldn't believe it. We shook hands and embraced then started to trade 101st war stories.

We did some catching up on people and exchanged contact information before Landry took off. I was so pleased about this blast from the past I ran over to Billy to tell him.

Major Gerry Landry, 1967

"Yeah," he said. "Some people call that Wall Magic, and it happens all the time." I asked if he had ever had it happen and he said he had many times: men from his platoon, his company commander, and others. The possibility of meeting more people from my past made volunteering even more special for me. I wanted to experience more.

Time passed quickly that first day. To hear the personal stories unfold throughout the day was moving—as was helping those Veterans who had come for their first time to find the names of those they had known or been with when they died. I felt close to them and their heart-wrenching memories. I had them too. And to help or even observe the relief of a significant other who had also suffered was equally poignant. The years of suffering were over for both.

There were also the family members of the names carved in the black granite—their loss still so unforgettable after all the years, and their vivid recall of the day they were notified—the sickening news they prayed they'd never hear. I was moved by the vigil that continues to follow the number of people missing in action and the memories of them—bracelets, memorabilia, letters, searches, friends and relatives that will not forget them.

More than half the visitors were there for the first time, tourists from other countries, student tours, some locals, and lots of families touring DC for the Memorial Day weekend. No matter where they came from or what their background, the sheer number of names and the peaceful presentation of them struck most visitors silent and somber. The finality of losses and their permanent compounding effect is never felt more than at The Wall.

There was so much for me to absorb the first day I couldn't take it all in in one weekend. I had to do it again. I felt compelled to return. The consistency of the questions was fascinating. How are the names arranged? How many names? Why does it say 1959? When did the war start? Did you go?

The last question was a surprise because no one had ever asked me in 35 years of being home. It was never a relevant question in the context of my everyday life after my service. At The Wall, it was a new phenomenon because the question was based on a sincere interest about me and my history, not based on animosity or my political beliefs about the war. Each and every time I answered in the affirmative, the response was invariably, "Thank you." Wow. That was amazing. I had never been thanked before. It felt special. It made me realize I had lived for years with an unconscious and unfulfilled need to be acknowledged for my service and the sacrifices all of us made in going to war. And on my first day of being a volunteer at The Wall the need was fulfilled for the first time since I had come home.

Safe Memories

The day was absolutely packed with new and unique encounters. The meeting of Gerry Landry after 40 years was a highlight. It made me think of other people I would want to know about. The first name that came to mind was my best friend from my time in Vietnam: Jack Hopke, a Dartmouth Distinguished Military Graduate of 1968, Ranger, Airborne, and Pathfinder.

Jack had greeted me warmly the first day I reported to the 101st and we fast became close buddies—I from California and he from New Jersey. The most striking characteristic was Jack's great sense of humor and wit that played well in the absurd world of combat. It came naturally to him, and it helped me carry a sensible perspective about the incongruous dynamics of combat. He always gave me sane advice and guidance. He carried his calm and confidence off with equal parts of intelligence and mischief. He was smart, tough, and well respected by everyone.

I never really got to say a proper thanks or goodbye to him. Just before he rotated home in October of '70 he gave me some of his personal belongings to use (fan, small cooler, and other comfort items for our Spartan living conditions) and asked me to sell them for whatever I could get when I rotated back. I did a few months later when I came home in January of '71, but we never connected again. 'He shouldn't be that hard to find,' I thought.

When I got back to my hotel room that night, I went to work on the internet to try to resurrect some of my 101st history as a starting point in my new search for Jack. When he had left us, Jack went to the 2/506th Infantry Battalion that was fighting a fierce battle on a mountaintop called Firebase Ripcord. The 2/506th was the same unit that had taken Hamburger Hill just 10 months before, and their history went all the way back to *The Band of Brothers*. So I searched for whatever I could find about it.

As I read details about Ripcord, memories were triggered I had long put out of my mind. Completely surrounded by nine NVA battalions against the 2/506th, Ripcord was almost impossible to land on because it took so much fire or was shrouded in fog day in and day out. My men, Eason and Biason, were two great kids who stayed on the firebase until the last minutes of its existence before being completely overrun. Hopke sent them back to me alive on one of the last choppers. He did it for me. It was a traumatic day for all involved. There were four killed in the evacuation to add to the many killed and wounded throughout the 3 month battle.

Hopke on left and LTC Lucas, middle, killed on Ripcord

After some quick skimming of research data I found on the internet in my hotel room, I became obsessed with finding Jack. I was charged and motivated to have the memories come back after so many years. It was hard to imagine, but my enthusiasm got me started that night. I soon realized I needed quiet time to do the search justice. It meant continuing in the privacy of my home. But the magic had done its work. I was hooked.

On to College
1965

"Stay in college, get the knowledge. And stay there until you're through. If they can make penicillin out of moldy bread, they can sure make something out of you!
Muhammad Ali

As was to be expected, my college choices were relatively limited by comparison to my brother and sister.

Jim had won a full ride scholarship to any of 46 colleges who were pursuing him for football. He chose Nebraska, and, of course, went on to a fabulous collegiate career. Mom and Dad were more than thrilled for him to get a "free education" while playing football for a national power. Dad's buttons popped every time he told anyone who would listen to him that his son was on TV playing football for Nebraska.

Chris was a National Merit Scholarship finalist. She could have had a full academic scholarship to almost any school in the country, but instead chose San Francisco State College as an impermanent alternative because she really wanted to enter the convent with six of her best friends from high school. Dad insisted she try at least one year of secular school before making such a big decision. S.F. State was her choice. It turned out to be the right one because she went on to study in Italy and Germany, eventually finding the man of her dreams whom she married after finishing her degree. It was a fairy tale story partially engineered by Mom and Dad. They could not have been more proud.

My Son's going to be a Doctor

I chose to go to The University of San Francisco, like 72 others of my high school graduating class. It was a safe choice for a number of reasons. USF was a de-facto extension of the high school, so there was no cultural adjusting with which to be concerned. It was local so I could work part-time to help pay tuition since Mom and Dad were partially paying (they didn't have to pay a nickel for Jim or Chris). It had a great reputation in the Bay Area, so future career opportunities could theoretically be enhanced. And I didn't have to leave the safety and security of home. As the youngest, I felt I was somewhat obligated to be the stay-at-home child. Best of all, USF was co-ed for the first time in its 110 year history. Girls!

I entered as a pre-med major, full of surreal visualizations of being a great doctor. The pre-med program was small but highly regarded. For most candidates accepted into the program, laboring through the rigors of the curriculum would almost guarantee success in getting into a good medical school. I had passed the entrance requirements so I thought its degree of difficulty would be well within my capabilities. For the first time in my life, my family was genuinely impressed with me. The thought of one of the clan becoming a great doctor really stirred the pride in many.

I began full of energy to make the dream come true for myself and for my family. My best friend from high school, Mike Girolami and I went into the program together so we could support each other. He was a serious student and was supposed to set a great pace and example for me. He did. However, it did not take long for me to admit to the disappointing fact that I just couldn't be like Mike. I simply didn't have the commitment to sacrifice everything it takes to become a doctor. Zoology and German were the first 2 speed bumps I hit hard, and they aren't even difficult courses. Romance was the second big disruption. When I fell in love the first semester, I just couldn't seem to concentrate.

Her name was Mary, and she captured me the first day I sat behind her in orientation classes. She seemed perfect. She was smart, beautiful, vivacious, and very composed. She was a pioneer too. She was one of the first 14 on-campus coeds of the class. I was completely smitten when she agreed to go on a date with me on my first try. We hit it off well and continued to date seriously for the balance of our first year. My vision of being a cool college guy was coming true. But my pre-med passion and energy dissipated progressively as the majority of my waking concentration easily shifted to Mary.

Along with this romantic distraction was a part-time job. I got one at the Sears store on Geary Street around the block from the campus to help pay bills. The work provided a little tuition, books, gas, and dating money. I worked about 20 hours a week at nights and on Saturdays with other young college students. It was an enjoyable respite from the classroom, but it caused more distraction from academics. Unfortunately, it also drained me of all incentive to do well in the pre-med program while funding my love life. I couldn't study, work and be in love simultaneously. I could feel the jaws of the pedagogic vise squeezing the life out of my dream of doctoring.

Vietnam an Instant American War

In the second semester of my first year, March of 1965, a world-changing event took place in Vietnam that was hardly noticed. The 3rd Marine Division landed on the beaches of Danang, walking though the waves with great drama as though returning to the Philippines. No one paid much attention to the theatrics. In fact, few people realized the significance of it in the context of the military activity in Vietnam. I know I didn't. For more than 8 months the Johnson administration had proceeded with the bombing of North Vietnam as a way to get Ho to yield to U.S. wishes. It didn't work. Consequently, outdated U.S. WWII tactics and the conventional wisdom of the times dictated that if limited bombing didn't work, increased bombing would achieve the desired results. We tried that and it also didn't work. It caused more trouble.

The North Vietnamese retaliated by mercilessly attacking the U.S. airbase in Danang from which most of the 2500 sorties per day originated. The vicious attacks on the base to slow down the bombing were constant and effective. Complicating the condition was the fact that the U.S. could not count on South Vietnamese forces to protect American men and assets there. President Johnson as the Commander in Chief, then, acting against the advice of many and using his Gulf of Tonkin Resolution powers, decided the U.S. Marines would take on a new and aggressive mission. It was to protect Danang Air Base as well as to fight offensive missions called "search and destroy". Johnson's decision authorized the first U.S. ground forces to directly engage the enemy. Suddenly, on March 8, 1965, we were no longer advisers. The ground war was on. Vietnam was instantly an American war to win or lose.

Many saw the precipitous introduction of U.S. ground troops as madness from its inception. It was based on an erroneous assumption that force, firepower and technology would easily snuff out the insurgent opposition, and it underscored a U.S. admission that the South Vietnamese could not fight their own war. Regardless of whether we were wanted there (unlike the French) or not, we made a conscious decision to fight for South Vietnam for unclear reasons. Portentously, the engagement became more dangerous for U.S. troops fighting conventionally against the highly invisible insurgents.

The introduction of U.S. ground warfare was the incendiary ingredient that generated the rapid escalation of the war. In any kind of warfare, an undefined goal is inconceivable. In insurgent warfare it is fatal. 'How many ground troops would ever be enough?' was the unanswered question in Washington on the day of the landing. That single question went on to become the subject of heated and emotional debate, headlines, embarrassment, and eventual tragedy while the U.S. groped for a logical answer. Today, it is a question that is still not posed without emotional debate.

Finally, for those paying attention, the Danang landing triggered a plethora of pointed and logical queries for which there were no lucid official responses. Overnight, moral questions began to unfold. Is it a just or unjust war? Why? What is the goal? Who is the enemy and why? Why is American blood being spilled? What is the relevancy of a country with a corrupt government so far from our shores to U.S. interests? If the use of force is necessary, why are we providing it in the absence of a credible government? What do we know about The Domino Theory?

When all the political rhetoric was stripped away, the Johnson White House could not rationally explain its actions to the global community through the questioning media. It was not a war, it was a policing action. We needed to stand by our friends. We couldn't let Vietnam be the first domino. We were fighting communism with/for the South Vietnamese; all communism is the same and must be stopped anywhere in the world; etc., etc.

Like most Americans of my generation, I didn't consider the just or unjust morality of our military actions. I was conditioned to think that we, the good guys, didn't make those kinds of ominous decisions unless they were honorable. Besides, I was as convinced and lazy-thinking as everyone else that it would be over quickly. Our superior power would prevail easily and we'd sort out the morality later. Moreover, no one had any idea what our leadership was doing or going with the war.

Thoughtlessly, I felt I was safe from the perils of the action. I had a student deferment to keep me out of the service for the 4 years I was to be in college, so I was free of anxiety. My first year ended. I was in love. I had to worry about changing majors. I had to make more money to support my love life. I had lots to think about before my second year started. My selfishness told me the war would be over by the end of summer vacation anyway.

My Buddy Jack

> Thus nature has no love for solitude, and always leans, as it were, on some support; and the sweetest support is found in the most intimate friendship.
> *Cicero*

1LT Hopke and 1LT Baffico at Camp Eagle

I had to find Jack Hopke. I couldn't be sure this time would be any different from the other times I had tried in the last 15 years. But I had new tools and fresh leads visitors and Vets had given me during my first day volunteering at The Wall. I went to work on the search giving it my full attention.

Some 101st visitors I met told me a couple of ways to track him down. There was the 101st Airborne Association I had heard about, and there was a Ripcord Association about which I knew nothing. They told me there was a book written called *Ripcord, Screamin' Eagles Under Siege* and an Oliver North TV special about the Ripcord battle as a result of it being declassified after 25 years. I was dumbfounded. I knew it was a horrific battle, but had no idea it had such a high profile. It was the last major confrontation between United States ground forces and North Vietnam in the war, so the action was classified at the time to keep public protest at a minimum. The new information I picked up gave me great motivation to push through the available resources to see if I could possibly find my buddy.

After being a commo platoon leader for the 501st Signal Battalion where we had become good friends, Jack had been sent to a combat line job with the 2/506th Curahees, the "Band of Brothers" unit, on Fire Support Base Ripcord to run the communications for the battalion. Jack's predecessor with the 2/506th, John Darling, was shot down and killed days before, so he had to report in the middle of heavy activity.

Ripcord was under constant mortar and rocket attack by the NVA who had it surrounded. That made it the most difficult firebase for my platoon to support on a day to day basis. The only way to get in or out of the treacherous mountain top terrain was by helicopter and it was always a perilous mission. The constant shelling, the fog, or the 30-70 knot winds at the top of the mountain always made Ripcord a scary place to land. I had to have my best men, Eason and Biason there. They were extra reliable and had to be almost self-sufficient because it was such a hot firebase. On the days when we could get in, I flew some of my most harrowing missions. From April to July, 118 choppers sustained various degrees of damage and 17 were shot down by enemy fire.

On July 1, 1970, after weeks of reconnaissance, the North Vietnamese Army launched a surprise attack. During the next 22 days, 75 US were killed in action and 444 wounded, including the Battalion Commander Lt. Colonel Andre Lucas, Medal of Honor recipient, and 1st Lt. Bob Kalsu, the only active pro athlete to be killed during the war. By the 22nd of July, after the relentless siege, a decision was made to evacuate FSB Ripcord on the 23rd and then bomb it and the NVA out of existence. The night before, evacuation planning for Ripcord became my highest priority. We had to keep the communications working until the very last minute, and then get Eason and

Biason off the hill safely. I prepared a two man crew to help, got a chopper ready to go in under fire and took off at day break for Ripcord.

But under intense enemy fire when the NVA began to overrun the perimeter during the extraction, word came to me that Jack waved off my chopper. He said he would get my men off the hill, so I had to wait at Camp Evans for them. While I listened to the radio traffic, I kept looking up at the mountain only to see flashes and smoke while evac choppers labored in and out one at a time. Eason and Biason finally got off the hill on one of the last runs. Hopke volunteered to stay behind as a ranking officer to help final evacuees. At the time I didn't know it, so I kept waiting for the next run to drop him safely. It was an agonizing morning.

At around noon, when one of the last choppers whopped its way down to a soft landing in front of me, off jumped Hopke smiling and running. Tucked into his flak jacket peeking out at his neck was Rip, the battalion puppy Jack just had to save before getting off the overrun firebase. Typical cool Hopke, a big grin on his face and his little pal safe. He was awarded a Bronze Star for valor for exposing himself repeatedly to direct and indirect enemy fire while keeping wire and radio communications going during the final three days of siege at Ripcord. Years later I still felt I had to say a better thanks to him for what he had done for me and my men.

Hopke (first on left) being promoted to Captain while on Ripcord

FSB Ripcord Official After-Action Report

EXTRACTION FROM FSB RIPCORD: At 230545 July 70, the 3d Brigade began operations for the extraction of the 2-506 Infantry from FSB RIPCORD and field locations south of the firebase. During the nights of 22-23 July, massive artillery and air fires were employed throughout the area against known and suspected enemy locations. More than 2232 mixed caliber artillery rounds were fired in support of the extraction. The US Air Force, Marines and Navy flew 35 preplanned and immediate air strikes, for a total of 74 sorties. Fourteen CH47 aircraft were employed commencing at 0545 hours to extract 22 sorties, which included 1 155mm howitzer battery (6 tubes), 2 M-405 dozers, communications equipment, 1 M55 multiple machinegun (Quad-50), and 1 damaged 105mm howitzer. The CH47 extraction operations proceeded smoothly until 0740 hours when 1 CH47 was shot down on the firebase by enemy 12.7mm machinegun fire. The aircraft was forced to land amidst the 105mm howitzers which had been destroyed on 18 July and thus prevented the landing of additional aircraft to extract the remaining artillery pieces and two 106mm recoilless rifles. The CH47 received a direct hit by an unknown type enemy mortar round, causing the aircraft to burn and explode. The aircraft was destroyed. Eight additional CH47 aircraft received hits during the extractions; 4 are non-flyable. B/2-506 Infantry began extracting at 0745 hours by UH1H aircraft but was delayed until 0935 hours by heavy enemy 60mm and 82mm mortar fires. The extraction was conducted by infiltrating one UH1H aircraft at a time into the firebase. The extraction from FSB RIPCORD was complete at 1214 hours. Companies A and D/5-506 Infantry extracted from a pickup zone 1 1/2 kilometers south of FSB RIPCORD commencing at 1301 hours. Sporadic small arms fire was received during the extraction. There were no casualties or damage. The extraction of 2-506 Infantry units from the RIPCORD area was complete at 1407 hours. During the extraction, FSB RIPCORD was under constant fire from numerous enemy mortars of 60mm and 82mm caliber. Several hundred rounds impacted throughout the firebase during the operation. Heavy 12.7mm anti-aircraft fire was directed against the aircraft flying into the firebase. Air, artillery, and ARA destroyed several enemy mortars and 12.7mm machineguns. In addition, numerous enemies driven into the open by CS were killed by air, artillery, and ARA.

> ...the decision to extract from RIPCORD was made, and operations into the AIRBORNE-BRADLEY areas will be undertaken as a part of operations CHICAGO PEAK. Additional factors of critical importance in the decision to close FSB RIPCORD were the domestic and foreign political implications of another US firebase undergoing a KHE SANH or DIEN BIEN PHU siege. RIPCORD, if given an inordinate amount of adverse publicity, might well have jeopardized the program of Vietnamization. RIPCORD operations caused heavy NVA casualties and drew the enemy from his cache sites causing him to mass and thus to present numerous targets vulnerable to heavy air attack and artillery fire.

My search started with the 101st Airborne Association. It was a dark emotional cave littered with old unit numbers, acronyms, and places I had long forgotten. When I separated from the Army in 1971 I was automatically enrolled in the 101st Association but I never participated in any activities or communications because I wanted no contact with that part of my life. Eventually they just gave up on me. Now I scoured their website looking for clues about Jack.

There was no listing for him, but I found out he had participated in a Ripcord Association reunion a few years before in Louisiana. That led me to find some information on a Hopke who lived in New Orleans. I couldn't imagine my Dartmouth/New Jersey friend living in the South because he was such a New Yorker. At the time, it was only 9 months after Katrina had wiped out over 1800 lives and scattered about a third of the population. Not very good odds, I thought, but I pushed on.

Next I discovered that the Hopke in New Orleans had participated in a few 10K runs around the area, and my level of hope increased. Jack was a distance runner in high school and college. The running discovery led me to a connection with WWNO, the NPR station in New Orleans where the runner was employed. Could it be? A few things seemed to fit, so it was worth a try.

Fire Support Base Ripcord during the 23 day battle

Ripcord, July 23rd 1970 in the afternoon after B52s bombed it out of existence

I looked up the station phone number and dialed it. A woman answered, and with significant hesitation I asked if there was a Jack Hopke that worked there. She replied, "Yes. He's on the air right now. Do you want to talk to him?" I couldn't believe it, but said I would really appreciate it if it was possible. She nonchalantly gave me the okay and the phone clicked.

A moment later I heard his unmistakable voice say, "Jack Hopke." I was momentarily taken back, but composed myself and asked, "Is this the Jack Hopke that was the Distinguished Military Graduate of the Dartmouth Class of 1968, and the Airborne Ranger Jack Hopke of the 101st Airborne?

"Yeeeesssss," he said quizzically, "Who is this?"

I was thrilled. Connected, but unsure if he wanted any contact, I identified myself. "My name is Paul Baffico, and I have been wondering about you for many years."

"I remember you! How did you find me? Do you know who stole my Ranger watch? I know it's not you, but I'm trying to remember that ring knocker from West Point who was relieved. He was the guy. Do you remember him? Oh my God!

What are you doing and where are you?" His excitement was absolutely infectious as it always was.

"Well, I live in Chicago now. I had a career with Sears after I came home. I'm retired now and have a little time on my hands in between my part-time consulting jobs. I've been looking for you for a long time, and I am so relieved to finally find you so I can settle a debt," I intoned.

"A debt? What debt?" He sounded a little frantic.

"Do you remember when you left Eagle to go out to Ripcord you left me with some of your personal stuff? Remember a fan, some old speakers, and other pickings for a comfortable bunker? I was supposed to sell all of it when I left and send you the money. Well, I could never find you based on the simple address you gave me of Teaneck, New Jersey. So I've been holding your money for 35 years."

"I don't remember this at all. The only thing I remember is that I am still really pissed about my Ranger watch."

"I don't have your damn watch, but I have a check here for $3,202.97 made out to you if you want it." Dead silence. Deafening silence. "Hello, are you still there?"

"Yeah, I'm here, but I have to go back on the air in a minute. Can I call you back on the next break? What's your number?"

I gave him my mobile number and said goodbye, not sure if he would really call me back. His silence was troubling, and I was hopeful I had not touched an old nerve of some kind.

About 5 minutes later my phone rang with a New Orleans area code. It was Jack.

"Can you really talk while you're on the air?"

"Yeah, it's no problem with the long sets I have pre-recorded. Now what's this about a check? I don't remember a thing."

"Trust me, Jack. It happened just as I described, and it has been on my mind since I got home in one piece that I owe you the money. Since I had a career in retailing, you can guess I got top dollar for your stuff: $300! Being a Dartmouth graduate, I would assume you would have invested the $300 wisely and made decent interest on it for 35 years. So my calculation says it has grown to $3,202.97. I have this check in my hand I wrote while waiting for you to call back. You called back. It's yours."

"I don't know what to say. I am ashamed to admit it, but I could really use it. I got wiped out in Katrina and had to temporarily evacuate. I just got back into my neighborhood, and I am struggling to clean up and dry out my apartment. I've been in Atlanta as a refugee broadcasting from the NPR station there back to New Orleans. I can't believe this. Are you really serious?"

The rest of our conversation was giddy. We exchanged addresses, phone numbers, histories, and much more. There was more to say than one conversation could satisfy either one of us. We were friends again in 20 minutes of talk after 35 years of separation. It was absolutely a special moment in both of our lives.

I couldn't help being struck by the richness of a friendship that had lived on quietly and had almost eluded both of us. I felt as close to Jack from a distance as the day he and Rip jumped off the chopper with my men back on July 23rd 1970. My chance to say thanks had arrived.

I sent the check off and followed it up with a phone call a few days later. It took five or six days for the check to get to him because FedEx was hampered finding addresses and access to the more severely affected areas of the city. Jack lived about a half a mile from Bourbon Street where things were still pretty bad.

We were both excited to continue re-connecting and to catch up more about each other than ever before. I arranged a weekend trip in August to make it happen. I was a bit cautious about how it might go, so I arranged to stay in a hotel and not impose my presence in case it was too uncomfortable for either of us. I needn't have worried.

101st Area of Operation, the A Shau Valley decimated by Agent Orange
The most fought over terrain in South Vietnam

When I found his apartment and he opened the door with his charismatic grin, we comfortably hugged each other and began a 2 day stream of steady conversation that was marvelously therapeutic. He talked about his life after the Army that took him through many record industry jobs and 2 wives, and I talked about my corporate career and my life after Sears. Consistent throughout the conversation was the enormous respect for each other that had been there when we first met, and was reinforced by the story telling of the ups and downs of our lives after Vietnam.

On the second day we broached the subject of Vietnam and compared our recollections of people, places and battles. Yes, he had gone to the Ripcord reunion and had taken his then current girlfriend Angie as his guest. He needed the moral support of a close friend. Angie was perfect because she was too young to know anything about the war, so she had no baggage. He did report she was struck by the closeness of the group even after all the years.

Initially hesitant to talk about it, we eventually segued to the details of our shared conflict and confusion about what we had seen and done in the war and the collateral damage that took years to identify. The emotional and mental wreckage of combat that could no longer be compartmentalized was closer to the surface than ever before for both of us. I found, once again, Jack's intellect and thoughtfulness to be of great comfort because we were again dealing with the same fears and pain he had helped me with when I first met him 35 years before. I also felt I could be of help to him as he put his life back together. The timing and fit seemed perfect.

Over the course of the next few years Jack and I exchanged phone calls, emails and holiday visits. We both helped each other work through the physical and mental scars of our service. Jack's set of concerns were particularly difficult because he had few resources.

His broken marriages had cost him dearly, and his career in the record industry ended when he decided he hated the seediness and tawdriness of the business. Now he is doing what he had always wanted to do of being an on-air host for the NPR station in New Orleans. The problem is it pays so poorly. But he is dedicated to his craft and is very good at it.

I was able to encourage him to navigate through the labyrinth of public health and VA services he needed. He was helpful in showing me how to face my problems with PTSD and Agent Orange. For whatever the reasons, I feel okay about my problems knowing Jack is there for me if I need him. It is a carryover of the bond forged many years ago in the ambiguous environment of combat. When facing death, it is somehow comforting to know the other guy is there.

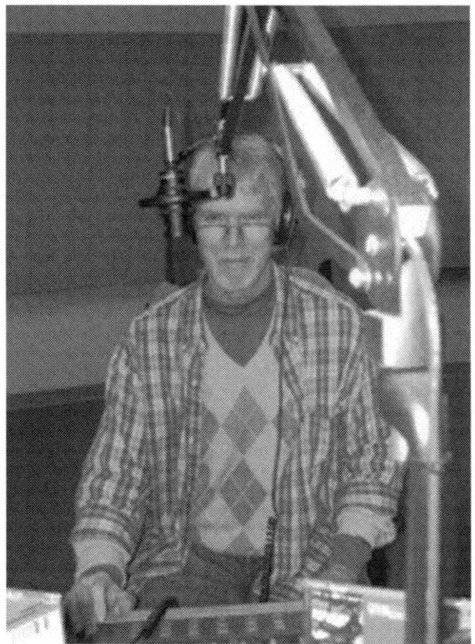

Jack Hopke on the air

Since our first visit in New Orleans our renewed friendship has blossomed into an unofficial brother relationship for both of us. I have taken Jack to The Wall so we could experience it together. It was a moving time for both of us. We have spent Thanksgivings, the 4th of July, and other occasions together at my home and I was honored to be Jack's best man at his wedding to Barbara, a wonderful woman he met in New Orleans and with whom he fell madly in love. She gives him the life he has been pursuing for decades, and it is satisfying for me to know I may have had some influence in his getting it.

Every day I am grateful to Max who encouraged me to heed Billy's suggestion that I volunteer at The Wall. The gifts I have received as a result of volunteering there have been plentiful and meaningful...and one of the best is that I found my friend Jack.

OOOORAH
1966 STUDENT LIFE

This is not a jungle war, but a struggle for freedom
on every front of human activity.
Lyndon B. Johnson

Full Division Air Assault

Life is What Happens When You're Making Other Plans

By mid-semester of sophomore year, I had to change my major to Clinical Psychology. Continuing in medicine would have been futile since I couldn't get into a medical school with my middling grades.

Clinical Psychology was a choice of convenience rather than a vocational calling. My credits easily transferred to the new major; it was cheaper than taking more required courses for a different major; and I got to stay in school for 2½ more years as a full time student. That became more important as each semester passed. But the transition to the new major was not smooth.

One of the problems was facing the disappointment of my family for giving up so easily on the dream of being a doctor. That was hard for them to understand. Mom and Dad did their best to accept it as a good choice on my part rather than a broken commitment, but they couldn't effectively hide their disillusionment. I felt guilty.

The other problem with the change was the draft. In quick order, the system was overstressed with a larger demand for ground troops to deploy into the expanded war and the manpower requirement was more than the normal draft formula could produce. Volunteers were fewer and fewer so things became much more intense at the draft board. Reserve and National Guard units were immediately filled by draft eligible men because they were excluded from Vietnam deployment per Presidential direction so Johnson could pretend it was not a war. This coupled with too many deferments or physically unqualified people and there simply weren't enough bodies in San Francisco to fill the board's growing quota.

The unfolding situation demanded more draftees from college campuses. In 1966, the count of U.S. troops deployed in Vietnam went from 184,300 to 385,300, a 110% increase in a year. The draft became significantly more important in the lives of millions of young college men who thought their student deferments were good until they graduated. Initially, a student deferment had worked if you were in school full time ....barely. But then Grade Point Average became a criterion for draft eligibility, and the heat on male students increased exponentially with each uptick in the war.

Consequently, military obligation became a more personal and frightening issue. Some classmates started to get drafted directly out of class because of poor grades. Others dropped out of school and into the draft just to get it over. Some overdosed on drugs. Some declared they were gay. Some got married and pregnant. One took a hammer to his knee to permanently damage it, and some just disappeared. Almost everyone was desperately looking for a way out, me included. I couldn't find a legitimate way to fulfill my service obligation and stay at home safely.

All Reserve and National Guard units quickly had waiting lists and you had to know someone to get in the back door. The Coast Guard needed no one. I couldn't stand the thought of taking some exempt job like being a Merchant Marine deckhand and living an isolated and difficult existence, all the while hiding from an obvious obligation. The Peace Corps was full up. All I knew was I didn't want to be drafted.

I was struggling with my integrity. I had changed majors because I couldn't master the rigors of the pre-med program. I didn't really like the new major either. Yet I needed to get better grades to avoid the draft. I worked part time at Sears and was a full time student. So as a laborer and commuter I didn't feel connected to campus activities. The carefree innocence and idealism of freshman year were distant memories while heavy debilitating thoughts collected in my mind.

I was completely confused about a career path. My grades did not reflect my capabilities, only my meager efforts. Mary and I were seriously dating and the relationship was causing me to grow more distant from the close group of friends with whom I had hung out in high school and college. Mine was becoming a lonely existence.

On campus, fiery emotional skirmishes between hawks and doves over the draft and Vietnam became everyday occurrences. All of us had draft cards, and each of us knew a day of reckoning regarding obligation was fast approaching. At some point, it seemed, you were going to have to make a critical decision.

At the same time, San Francisco came into its own as the Cultural Revolution capital of the world right in our campus front yard. The influence of the neighboring Haight-Asbury scene was noxious and deleterious.

Student union debates inevitably revolved around one of two key issues: fear of the draft and war or your acceptance or revulsion of the illicit activities of our neighboring generational cohorts. Opining was not fun because many times the debates got very personal and heated.

Moreover, our natural academic instinct to make sense out of the rightness or wrongness of Vietnam was pure madness. We were totally ill-equipped and ill-informed to be able to discern the morality of the war given our idealized "classics education". Add to that the media manipulation by the White House, and it simply amplified the futility of trying to find the truth, e.g. Johnson's transparent paranoia was exacerbated every day as the press exposed the inconsistencies of his Vietnam and Great Society proclamations. Suspicion regarding the launch of the war based on a lie by Johnson and McNamara through the Tonkin Resolution surfaced but was carefully suppressed. The suspicion was eventually confirmed and admitted by McNamara 35 years later in his book, *In Retrospect*.

By end of my second year, I was at a personal crossroads. Life had changed radically for me. School was a minor issue. I had more serious obligations. I either had to sign an ROTC contract that included 2 years of active duty and a possible all-expenses paid trip to Vietnam, or take my chances with the unpredictable draft and the voracious appetite for manpower Vietnam demanded of it. Mary and I wanted to get married after we graduated. It seemed like the logical next step in our relationship. These obligations, together with the promise to finish college in 4 years were more critical decision making than I had the maturity to handle. I felt absolutely claustrophobic about my future, but was determined to press on.

March 8, 1966: The U.S. today announced it will substantially increase the number of its troops in Vietnam.
The Washington Post

March 26, 1966: Demonstrations are held across the United States against the Vietnam War.
The New York Times.

Decision Time

At the eleventh hour, I reluctantly concluded I had to be ready to put my life on the line or have the courage to stand up as an objector and pay the consequences. The latter was neither a desire nor a viable option. I had no heart, conviction or rationale that could support such a noble decision. I was humiliated to be trapped in my own conflicted thinking, and I could not bear the thought of being embarrassed by the internal conflict.

Agonizing to admit it, I could feel a decision being forced by fear and cowardice. I wanted to avoid dishonor or being rejected by my family or The Establishment or both. That ignominy was more powerful than volunteering to be an officer and going to war. There was no loyalty or patriotism involved in the decision-making process. I had no idea what it meant to be patriotic at that point in my life. So I chose ROTC. I signed on to become an officer of the United States Army at graduation. And my heart and head were not in it. The decision was based purely on pragmatism not patriotism, nothing more.

At the time, everyone in my world was avoiding the obligation and saying service to country was wrong and/or immoral. I couldn't de-code the morality of my reluctance to participate in the Army. I was simply scared. I knew I wanted to be safe in my service, and I naively wanted to feel good about it. But I couldn't. There was a chronic tightness in my chest about my decision, and for not taking a principled stand on clear and present danger. Others officially judged me as a "hawk" but I didn't believe it. I secretly hoped the war would be over before I was needed and I would never serve. Pitiful mixed up emotional conflict was constantly swirling in my mind.

Friends went in different directions. They peeled away rapidly. I did too. I didn't want anyone second-guessing me or my decision.

An American Genius

> I deliberately did not read anything about the Vietnam War because I felt the politics of the war eclipsed what happened to the veterans. The politics were irrelevant to what this memorial was.
>
> *Maya Lin*

Maya Lin

Maya Lin was born on October 5, 1959 in Athens, Ohio. The daughter of intellectuals who had fled China in 1948, Athens is also the home of Ohio University, where Lin's mother, Julia Chang Lin, was a literature professor. Her late father, Henry Huan Lin, was a ceramicist. The couple immigrated to America from China in the 1940s, leaving behind family that included a well-known lawyer and an architect. Lin's family in America includes her mother and an older brother.

During her childhood, Maya Lin found it easy to keep herself entertained, either by reading or by building miniature play towns. She loved to hike and bird watch as a child and also enjoyed reading and working in her father's ceramics studio. From an early age she excelled in mathematics, which led her toward a career in architecture. While in high school Lin took college level courses and worked at McDonalds. She considered herself a typical mid-westerner, in that she grew up with little sense of ethnic identity. She admits, however, to having been somewhat "nerdy," since she never dated nor wore make-up and found it enjoyable to be constantly thinking and solving problems.

She received her bachelor's degree in 1981 from Yale University in New Haven, Conn., where she studied architecture and sculpture. During her senior year she entered the nationwide competition sponsored by the Vietnam Veterans Memorial Fund to create a design for a monument honoring those who had served and died in that war.

The design for the Memorial was her term project. She got a B+. The brilliance of her design was not rewarded with the highest mark by her professor, but by a unanimous vote of a panel of eight prestigious judges over 1420 competitors in the first round of voting of the competition. From the moment the entry was chosen, a storm of controversy over the simplicity and uniqueness of her concept became a national headline issue. The cultural battle was played out in the Legislature as well as the press. It reflected the lack of resolution over the national struggle with the war as well as the lack of consensus over what constituted an appropriate memorial to those who had served and sacrificed their lives. Additionally, the controversy was not limited to the Memorial or its design, but also centered on Lin because she was too young, a woman, and an Asian-American.

Lin's design consisted of a polished black granite V-shaped wall inscribed with the names of the men and women who were killed or missing in action. The minimal plan was in sharp contrast to the traditional format for a memorial, which usually included some interpretation of figurative, heroic sculpture. The controversy of Lin's design was the absence of statuary. Congress resolutely insisted on its inclusion. Lin argued its irrelevancy to the purpose and the design requirements of The Wall which were to be reflective and contemplative; harmonize with its surroundings; contain the names of those who died or were missing; and make no political statement.

Eventually, a compromise was reached with the commissioning of a traditional statue depicting three servicemen with a flag to stand at the entrance to the Memorial. After The Wall was dedicated on Veterans Day in 1982 on the Mall in Washington, D.C., it became a popular and affecting tourist attraction. In 2005 the American Institute of Architects conferred upon the monument its 25-Year Award, given to a structure that has proved its worth over time.

After the controversy was settled, Lin sought anonymity by returning to academia. She began graduate studies in architecture at Harvard University in Cambridge, Mass. In early 1983 she left Harvard to work for a Boston architect, and in 1986 she completed a master's degree in architecture at Yale.

Today Maya Lin is one of the most prominent architectural designers of the 21st century. Her vision and focus have always been on how space needs to be in the future and what it means to the people. Her focus is less on how politics influence design and more on what emotions the space creates and what the design of the space symbolizes to the user. Amid all of Lin's brilliant works, the Vietnam Memorial captures this vision the best.

Statement by Maya Ying Lin, March, 1981

"Walking through this park-like area, the memorial appears as a rift in the earth, a long, polished, black stone wall, emerging from and receding into the earth. Approaching the memorial, the ground slopes gently downward and the low walls emerging on either side, growing out of the earth, extend and converge at a point below and ahead. Walking into this grassy site contained by the walls of the memorial we can barely make out the carved names upon the memorial's walls. These names, seemingly infinite in number, convey the sense of overwhelming numbers, while unifying these individuals into a whole.

"The memorial is composed not as an unchanging monument, but as a moving composition to be understood as we move into and out of it. The passage itself is gradual; the descent to the origin slow, but it is at the origin that the memorial is to be fully understood. At the intersection of these walls, on the right side, is carved the date of the first death. It is followed

by the names of those who died in the war, in chronological order. These names continue on this wall appearing to recede into the earth at the wall's end. The names resume on the left wall as the wall emerges from the earth, continuing back to the origin where the date of the last death is carved at the bottom of this wall. Thus the war's beginning and end meet; the war is 'complete,' coming full-circle, yet broken by the earth that bounds the angle's open side, and continued within the earth itself. As we turn to leave, we see these walls stretching into the distance, directing us to the Washington Monument, to the left, and the Lincoln Memorial, to the right, thus bringing the Vietnam Memorial into an historical context. We the living, are brought to a concrete realization of these deaths.

"Brought to a sharp awareness of such a loss, it is up to each individual to resolve or come to terms with this loss. For death, is in the end a personal and private matter, and the area contained with this memorial is a quiet place, meant for personal reflection and private reckoning. The black granite walls, each two hundred feet long, and ten feet below ground at their lowest point (gradually ascending toward ground level) effectively act as a sound barrier, yet are of such a height and length so as not to appear threatening or enclosing. The actual area is wide and shallow, allowing for a sense of privacy, and the sunlight from the memorial's southern exposure along with the grassy park surrounding and within its walls, contribute to the serenity of the area. Thus this memorial is for those who have died, and for us to remember them.

"The memorial's origin is located approximately at the center of the site; its legs each extending two hundred feet towards the Washington Monument and the Lincoln Memorial. The walls, contained on one side by the earth, are ten feet below ground at their point of origin, gradually lessening in height, until they finally recede totally into the earth, at their ends. The walls are to be made of hard, polished black granite, with the names to be carved in a simple Trojan letter. The memorial's construction involves re-contouring the area within the wall's boundaries, so as to provide for an easily accessible descent, but as much of the site as possible should be left untouched. The area should remain as a park, for all to enjoy."

> "It terrified me to have an idea that was solely mine to be no longer a part of my mind, but totally public."
> *Maya Lin*

This is the End of the Innocence 1967

Oh beautiful, for spacious skies,
Now those skies are threatening.
They're beating plowshares into swords,
For this old man we elected king.
Armchair warriors often fail,
Poisoned by their fairytales
Lawyers clean up all details…
This is the end of the innocence.

The End of the Innocence
Livingston Taylor

A 101st patrol

My third year of college was culturally, socially and emotionally difficult.

Mary had transferred to an all-women's suburban Catholic college. She needed the distance from me in order to concentrate on being a better student. Since I couldn't see her every day, I was determined to work harder for her love. Consequently, more of my time would be devoted to commuting 30 miles to see her. Therefore, there would be less time for others in my life. That was okay, because she supported me emotionally while my other friends found reasons to avoid me. The differences in the beliefs of my friends and me had taken on a sharp edged definition.

And the same was true on a national scale. Divisiveness between friends and families had progressed deeper and wider by 1967. It spread across the country like a brush fire that started from the Atlantic and Pacific coasts and moved with gathering momentum until it exploded uncontrollably in the middle: Illinois, Ohio, Missouri, Kansas, Oklahoma, and Texas. No geography real or imaginary went untouched by the combustible emotions of the war in Vietnam.

War at the Door

As my time to serve drew closer, I couldn't conceive of being a combat soldier. The amount of courage it would take was beyond my ability to visualize. Nor did I ever pretend I could find the vision some place in my being. In fact, I was convinced I never could. As a child, I had actually prayed I would never have to face the possibility or that I would have to be trained to be a killer or suffer a violent death.

But my military obligation was official and irremediable. I had signed the papers and was committed to 2 years. Since there was no possibility of revocation, I continually replayed the reasoning I used when I signed up: avoid being drafted; the promise to complete college in 4 years; embrace the practicality of being a married officer; the obligation of service had to be fulfilled. Furthermore, I had been challenged years before by JFK's daring charge, "Ask not what your country can do for you; ask what you can do for your country."

All those rationalizations made sense. I just never believed it would really come down to my going to a war which I didn't understand or clearly support. What would I be fighting for? How did Vietnam help my country? Why over there? But it was going to be my reality if the war didn't end before I graduated. The thought of real combat was simply inconceivable, and yet it seemed closer than ever. And the closer it became, the more questions, fears, and apprehensions I had.

Family Dilemma

We had never been overly patriotic in our family (no flags, banners or bumper stickers, remember?), but we were conditioned to have an enormous respect for Veterans and the authority of government. There were models of military service both good and bad. Dad, Uncles George, Guido and Babe served proudly while Uncles Shoulders (Al) and Pat never did and never talked about it. Actually, war was rarely discussed in our family.

It was, however, fiercely studied. In fact, as a child, I eagerly watched Victory at Sea with Dad and my brother every week while my mother and sister excused themselves. It was a thrill to be included with "the men". I was mesmerized by the drama created by the blending of music and action with the real-life footage of warfare that was unlike anything else on television. I was simultaneously captivated and terrorized by what I saw men do, the putting of their lives on the line and the willful killing of others. When I watched it on TV as a young boy, it was difficult to imagine it was real. It was the romance, heroism and excitement of victory I saw. All of those feelings dissipated as the requirements for manpower continued to increase in Vietnam. They faded from view when I put myself in the picture.

While the daily news from Vietnam occupied much of my student life, it simultaneously created frustration and contradiction for me in my family. Talk about Vietnam politics did not creep into the dinner table conversations at home. It was as though Vietnam didn't affect us and didn't exist topically in our family. So we didn't deal with it. Mom avoided the subject and Dad was just as bewildered as most Americans because he could not find the facts which would help him understand it. Of course, that was true for most of my family. But for me, it was no imaginary intellectual exercise. I was right in the sweet spot for recruiting and the draft---a primary target for serving and very much alone with my anxiety.

My brother was called for the draft in 1965, but he flunked the physical because he was overweight and had torn cartilage in his knees. He was a professional football player for the Buffalo Bills at the time, and it does seem ridiculous a professional football player would be unfit for military duty. But in the mid-sixties, a lot of things seemed ridiculous. And they were. The next year, 1966, Jim was called again and he flunked the physical for the same reasons. And by 1968, he was married and a father, so his chances of being drafted all but disappeared.

My brother-in-law, Hans, was a new immigrant from Germany. He had been in the U.S. for less than a year. He was married with no children, so he was a prime candidate for the draft. He was willing to serve if he had to in exchange for U.S. citizenship, but at 25 years old and newly married, military service was not in his plans. Nevertheless, he was drafted for active duty. The day before he was to report to Oakland Army Terminal to be processed, he received a student deferment in the mail. To this day he has no idea how it happened or why.

I still have trouble with the vast difference in the standards of both sides of the Vietnam service argument and the willingness to serve or run from war. But it is fair and accurate to say that logical, linear thinking was completely useless in 1967. The depth of the differences between those who served and those who fled are as wide today as they ever were. Only today, the Vietnam Veteran has hallowed status.

Campus Friends

On campus, contemporaries mocked me each week on drill day. Every Thursday we were supposed to be in Army Class A's, the classic green dress uniform all day for drill. Nobody was. In order to minimize the amount of abuse from students and others we changed from street clothes to uniforms and then changed back to civvies as fast as we could. And for us commuters, since there were no facilities on campus to change and store our clothes, we did it in our cars on the streets of the surrounding neighborhood. Not a very proud way to wear the uniform.

Besides the weekly skirmishes on campus, I found I was consistently running directly into the headwinds of the anti-war, anti-draft, anti-government movements and the endless dissent which captured ours and eventually every other campus in America. All causes and splinter groups were suddenly legitimized as the Boomer Generation desperately sought comfort and security in their own tailor-made play groups.

Simultaneously, more and more classmates who didn't get drafted disappeared into the neighboring psychedelic world of the Haight-Ashbury scene to find escape. There was a festering anger and frustration that was visibly rising in the streets, campuses, and neighborhoods. Ours was no different. It was easily felt. Detroit, DC, Buffalo, Newark and Minneapolis were making the news with race riots which had surfaced again and were becoming all too common.

The media images of conflict in the streets at home combined with the nasty war in the fetid jungles of Vietnam were disturbing. The relentless sound bites, whether from Detroit or Pleiku were powerful, graphic, unrehearsed images of violence never before seen by so many in their living rooms, in their kitchens, or in their bedrooms. It was difficult to comprehend these confrontations were happening every day. By comparison, the victorious struggle that *Victory at Sea* had so dramatically depicted a decade before looked like a synthetic docudrama made for TV, as out of date as the family sitcom, *Father Knows Best.*

If You're Going to San Francisco...be sure to wear...

From within the bowels of the San Francisco revolutionary scene and my parochial perspective, I struggled to understand my evolving environment.

The Haight in 1967

The gap between *what was* and *what was supposed to be* grew ever wider with each shocking event. The gap was filled by radical ideas and the idealism of an immature generation. My old value system was useless in the new reality. The orderly road to adulthood was hijacked, perverted and sidetracked by new social primacies. A perfect ideological rupture formed and spread wider than just between the generations in my world. Progressively, it appeared to affect the entire country and continued to gather momentum in the Western World.

Boomers contested existing morals and the authority which defended those morals. The modest entitlements with which we had grown up became expressed as extreme rights, demands and ultimately outright revolt. The founding of The Weather Underground, SDS, The Free Speech Movement, NOW, SNCC, Black Panthers, Black Power, CORE, and others were promoted in this time of discontent and cultural meltdown. California was the proud birthplace of many of them and the San Francisco Bay Area was the epicenter.

There, an arrogant army of youth wrestled control, voice, and power from the disdainful reigning structure and produced a complete and categorical breakdown of order on Bay Area campuses. Anti-draft, anti-war demands were augmented with demands for ethnic studies, ending state education, and any number of student activism issues. The strength in numbers and energy of the young was powerful and irresistible. The logic of their ideas was essentially unopposed by a flummoxed and confused older generation who easily relinquished their authority and responsibility.

Youth took control precipitously. We assumed a right and mandate to change the world we felt we had been preordained to do since the start of the Cold War. Self-actualization flourished and was the bonding agent for the narcissistic orientation of the generation. To many, the time had "arrived" for revolution. Not all of us, however, bought it.

In the midst of the disorder, with my dream of being a doctor a faded memory, my obligation to finish college in 4 years became more intense. I had given my word on it and wouldn't renege. I was hopeful the war would end in another year, but the chances of it happening continued to decrease. The Army would wait for me. Time could not be wasted or misused. I had to stay in school with a good GPA. I had to do whatever it took to earn a commission and avoid the draft. My energies, therefore, were focused on meeting those obligations. Mary was the support I needed. Her faith and confidence reassured me. Junior year ended. It was time to prepare for future military duty.

The Summer of Love

The summer of '67 was not much of a Summer of Love for me. I went off to Fort Lewis, Washington for 6 grueling weeks_of boot camp as an ROTC cadet....the lowest rank in the Army. When I reported, I didn't know it was not any ordinary ROTC boot camp. The rapaciousness of Vietnam action put a special spin on 1967 Summer Camp. It was akin to a Special Forces hazing process for future officers headed to war.

> Duty, Honor, Country
> Those three hallowed words reverently dictate what you ought to be, what you can be, what you will be. They are your rallying point to build courage when courage seems to fail, to regain faith when there seems to be little cause for faith, to create hope when hope becomes forlorn.
>
> *General Douglas MacArthur*
> *Thayer Award Speech -(1962)*

The Army needed to weed out those weak of heart or unqualified for leadership given the increasingly precarious and protracted status of the war in 1967. By then, the U.S. troop count had risen to well over 400,000 and there was no appreciable evidence the U.S. had made progress against the VC or NVA. Therefore, all training exercises were designed as realistic and graphic simulations of live actions that had taken place "across The Pond". And just in case we forgot where we were headed, not a sentence from an instructor went by without "NAAAMMM" being inserted, even if it didn't belong. The instructors made sure of it and made sure we knew they were seasoned pros.

Being an ROTC summer camp instructor required some special qualifications. All were battle-hardened enlisted men or officers who had proven themselves under fire. By the summer of '67, every one of them had had at least one and possibly two tours behind them. The knowledge and perspective from their time in combat was incredibly respected.

They were professional survivors. I couldn't help but have a deep respect for them. They were not sophisticated, but they had sincerity and credibility. They were stand-up people. What they said and taught simply made common sense. Their unfettered patriotism was not something about which they were ashamed. Their word was their bond. That was oh-so different from the campus atmosphere from which most of us had come. Academics are book smart by design with little pragmatism, and there is much to be said for the contributions of great academics throughout history. But boot camp was my first glimpse at how much practical experience can be more valued than being book smart.

Even though I harbored a faint hope that somehow Vietnam was not going to happen to me, I paid attention to the threats and teachings of the instructors. I actually had some fun during camp--getting the most fit I had been since my would-be football days in high school; meeting others with similar fears and concerns from colleges of the Western U.S.; and, getting a greater sense of confidence about developing some leadership abilities.

I was by no means a star cadet. A little better than mediocre might be the right note. But the training was vital for me to learn important things about myself I would have otherwise never have known. I wasn't a wimp. I could take a fair amount of pain and abuse. I needed to be mindful of my mouthing off, and I needed to learn how to be a good leader. I found out that honoring diversity and having genuine respect for each individual are critical ingredients in good leadership, and especially for leading men into battle. I began to experience how a team is made up of multiple levels of individual contributors of different talents who learn to function together as a team with the right leadership. I also learned a leader's primary job is to be accountable *to* the team and *for* the team, not himself. And the greatest reward for the leader is when he says, "Follow me," and his team does it willingly to the very best of their capabilities. It was a breakthrough for me.

ROTC Boot Camp, June, 1967

When I completed summer training, I went back to part-time work at Sears before the final year of college. The months ahead would be a stress test of what boot camp had taught me. I had a new sense of confidence and purpose. I had passed a small milestone of personal importance. The lessons learned in boot camp would serve me well in life.

While gone, the Boomer Generation's fissiparous activities proceeded unimpeded. The steady dissonance continued to be fueled by conflict and confrontation. Obscene choices, weird and straight, multiplied in the culture.

- Hip vs. Straight; Hawk vs. Dove; Commie Pinko vs. Patriot; Revolutionary vs. Lemming.
- Sex, drugs and Rock and Roll were status symbols. They were openly flaunted and sometimes violently protected.
- Authority and tenets were flouted at every opportunity and in every venue.
- Questioning status quo was the order of the day. If it feels good, do it. If it doesn't, stop it. The Anti-draft, Hell No, We won't go. Burn your draft card! Anti-War, No More War! Free Speech on campus.

We are not part of the military industrial complex! Free sex! Love Ins, Be-Ins and Flower People were the chants of the times.

Simultaneously, two important rights movements continued to run on parallel tracks: Civil Rights and Women's Liberation.

As the predominately white and increasingly female college population got distracted by women's rights, free love, speech, and drugs, the non-violent Civil Rights Movement of Martin Luther King became somewhat marginalized. The Black Power Movement had formed and it demanded more and faster action than the non-violent approach could deliver. This coupled with the outrageous volume and ascendancy of the Boomers did not bode well for the movement. The drowning out of the voices of Civil Rights set the stage for a future violent outcry.

The Women's Liberation Movement, meanwhile, got started in 1967. As was the case with the Civil Rights Movement initially, the focus was more about rights. But that eventually changed and evolved into a focus on gender equality. The Women's Movement's careful coordination of their tactical plans proved to be a positive influence for their survival during the disorderly Cultural Revolution of the 60's.

As this tumultuous year of rhetoric and revolution came to a close, _Time_ Magazine named the Twenty-five and Under the Man of the Year for 1967. I remember looking at the cover reading the article and thinking the WWII Generation (The Greatest Generation) had made a formal generational capitulation, "It's all yours. We can't do any more".

1967 Time Magazine Man of the Year
Twenty-five and Under

> I see light at the end of the tunnel (in Vietnam).
> --*Walt W. Rostow,*
> *National Security Adviser, Dec. 1967*

How could that possibly be? The country was in a massive crisis. The war had heated up feverishly. The Revolution was in full swing. Young men and women tuned in, turned on and dropped out. University campuses were no longer institutes of higher education but had become ideological battlefields strewn with violence and anger. Disorder and confusion seemed to reign supreme. Youth had taken control. The generational gap widened to maximum distance. Its repair was abandoned to the dysfunctional Boomer Generation to fix it or close the gap.

Being thoroughly muddled by living in the epicenter of chaos, and not being the daring sort, I continued to hang on fiercely to the principles and beliefs with which I had been raised. I had no desire to experiment with revolution, drugs, or dropping in or out. I was determined to follow the conservative behavioral model that felt comfortable to me: traditions and rituals. After 3 serious years of dating Mary, we were formally engaged.

I was determined to control my own destiny in the face of all the pandemonium around me.

THE VOLUNTEERS

All the wrong people remember Vietnam. I think all
the people who remember it should forget it, and all
the people who forgot it should remember it.
Michael Herr, 1989

Come shine. . .

...or Rain

So Billy was right. Volunteers do come from all around the country and there is such a thing as Wall Magic. If you get to appreciate the spirit of service at The Wall you can easily get habituated. I did because to participate as a volunteer is an honor. Volunteers come when they can make the trip or they make it on special days like Memorial Day, Veterans Day, In-Memory Day, or special occasions. They show up from Chicago, Los Angeles, Alaska, Boston, New Jersey, Philadelphia, Pittsburgh, Indianapolis, and more.

Almost all are Veterans of Vietnam or are strongly connected to a Veteran of the war. They are some of the most delightful people I have ever met in my life. They give of themselves in any weather and at any time, asking nothing in return but to serve in the memory of those who didn't make it home. The Wall gives them the opportunity to tell a living history of our country's most misunderstood and mysterious war. It is a story rarely told except at The Wall.

If you were to ask a volunteer why they come to The Wall, you would surely get a different answer from each one of them. But there are a few consistent themes that run through everyone's response which are at the heart of their generosity.

First, is to recognize and honor the loss of life in any war that is so very clearly presented by The Wall. The overwhelming number of names permanently carved in stone demonstrates how serious war is, and that no matter the cause or the politics, loss of life is the ultimate price paid.

Second, The Wall is an opportunity to teach and inform others about a part of United States history which is fraught with folklore, misinformation, controversy, and shame. It is not an easy period in history for our current population to understand with clarity or without the archaic presumptions and bias that still prevails. As younger generations come to visit the memorial, they are hungry for basic information about who, what, when, where and why. Wall docents are dedicated teachers of the history. Facts are well researched, vetted, and presented in an informative but serious way so the listener gets a full briefing for as much time as they are willing to spend. Many times a simple question leads to a long informative conversation.

Third, volunteers are indefatigable in their efforts to help the Vietnam Veterans. For many Veterans, it is a crucial moment in their lives. We are there to help them work through the recall and the grief the experience provokes. That is why we wear our unit identifications on our uniforms. They function as ice breakers for the reticent Veteran. The familiarity of a unit patch allows one to approach a Vet who is having trouble and needs to talk to someone.

Frequently, family members are inexplicably aware their loved one needs some kind of support and they respectfully stay in the background as they watch years of repressed memories be released to a docent. They are glad the journey and the suffering are over. The process is a form of healing that is long overdue, and no matter what side of the catharsis you are on, it is rewarding to witness.

The majority of the volunteers are local and there is usually at least one at The Wall every day. Some dutifully wash it at 6 am every Saturday morning. Others help the Park Rangers with cleaning and picking up the things left at The Wall to be cataloged and stored. Some work at the Information kiosk or do the countless rubbings of names requested every week by those who cannot make it to Washington. Each volunteer has their own special talents, devotions and contributions.

Wall washing on Saturdays

Allen McCabe, a rich baritone voiced non-Veteran is a regular weekly speaker and is known for his flawless facts and gripping 30 minute talks about the history of The Wall. He started volunteering when the date he had arranged to meet at The Wall never showed up. He looked around at what was happening while he waited and liked it so much he became a volunteer.

Annmarie Emmet is 80+ years old and has volunteered all her life in various locations throughout DC. Her two current favorites are The White House and The Wall. She is at both every week, and has been for over 25 years. In addition to a fabulous career in the financial world with which she spent 3 years in China, she later became a Peace Corps volunteer at the age of 70 and took off for Africa. There is nothing she hasn't seen as a volunteer. She is an icon.

Dan Kirby has been a volunteer since he retired a few years back. A native of Alexandria, Virginia and a Purple Heart recipient, he was opposed to the war as a college student like many. But he was drafted and became a fast track Infantry NCO and then sent to Vietnam. While leading a patrol he hit a booby trap which severely wounded his leg and took him out of action. He went back out when he healed, and eventually made it home. He is fully committed to his volunteering at The Wall every week for those who were not as fortunate as he was.

Betty Henry is another local volunteer with Vietnam service and a family who served. We call her Kissin' Betty. She left her native Pittsburgh when she was 18 years old to work for the Navy in Washington, D.C. Then at the age of 25 she volunteered to be a civilian administrator for the Navy in Vietnam. It was 1967. She spent 2 years of her young life in Saigon during the Tet Offensive when most of the U.S. population was doing anything and everything it could to stay away. While in Vietnam, two of her brothers were sent, one a Marine and the other with the Air Force. They both made it back as did Betty. She married a Marine who was part of the Presidential Honor Guard. Marines old and young are Kissin' Betty's very favorites. She is there every week to thank them for serving, and to give them a kiss, a rubbing of a name, a hug or a pep talk.

Michael McMahon is a retired Merrill Executive Vice President and a decorated combat vet from New Jersey as is Mike Coale, a retired Fire Captain. Both were infantry men. McMahon served with the 9th Infantry Division and Coale with the 25th Infantry. They drive down from New Jersey every 4-6 weeks to spend a weekend at The Wall. Whether it is rain, heat, sleet, snow or humidity, they will stand and serve for hours each day. It is therapy for them as it is for many of us.

John Berry and his wife Angela are both local Veterans. John is a decorated Vietnam Marine and Angela a recently retired Navy Chief. He joined the Marines and volunteered for combat because it's what you did in his family for generations. John is still the model Marine he was when he was an 18 year old rifleman. He caught the tail end of the time Marine ground forces were still deployed in the northern most sector of South Vietnam and was badly wounded a number of times. The Berry's show up as a team, and their humor and sense of life is a delight to be around.

And there is soft-spoken Jim Debenport from San Angelo, Texas. He served as radio technician aboard *The America* with the Navy during Vietnam. Jim works in the DC area even though he makes his home in San Angelo, Texas. There is no other volunteer who delights visitors more than Jim educating the public at The Wall. His sweet Texas drawl captivates his audiences as he helps young and old appreciate his respect for this history

Billy was one of the best. He was a special friend for a number of reasons. He recruited me; our similar chronologies and time in Vietnam; our age was identical; our interests and humor; and he had lived in San Francisco for a number of years. It is where he met his wife Mollie, who is also a close friend. Like good combat buddies, we could anticipate the thoughts and feelings of each other without ever saying a word.

Every month he would be there when I arrived and we would work the visitors side by side like a well-rehearsed two man show, attending to Veterans, teaching students, sharing stories if appropriate: always humble, never overdone, just factual. It was the most important thing Billy taught me, be right with what you say. There has been so much bad information communicated about Vietnam; The Wall is the place where people should be able to get it right and straight from the people who lived it.

Often, Billy and I didn't get to talk much during the day because we were so focused on visitor needs. So we would leave and grab a break or a meal together. That's when we would share some of our most private thoughts and memories, slowly building trust in each other. Being an Infantry platoon leader, Billy's war stories were more gruesome than mine, but he was comfortable sharing them with me. I felt privileged because I understood how difficult those memories could be. Survivor's guilt for both of us was chronic. He would never admit he felt it, but I knew he did. I never found it necessary to say any more. Leading and directing your men to execute your orders is something for which you are trained and prepared. When they are killed doing it, there is nothing which cushions the guilt and finality of the loss that haunts you forever.

Second guessing is an instinctive reaction for most people. In the heat of combat and engagement, you have no time to second guess. It is only in the solitude of your mind after time has given you room to think when you re-assess the facts you can recall, no matter how ineffectual an exercise it is.

And in order to get some relief from the guilt, you have to talk with someone who has gone through the same kind of loss. We did that. It helped both of us a lot.

Billy won the Silver Star saving one of his men who jumped on a grenade to save him. They both lived to tell about it, but serious damage had been done to both. The man he saved won The Congressional Medal of Honor and is totally disabled. Billy lived with shrapnel painfully imbedded in his spine and the horrific memories of his combat time.

We became good friends and socialized as couples on the occasions when Max came to town with me. We needed each other's support, but I didn't realize how serious Billy's hurt was for years. Then he started complaining about his back, his level of energy, his attitude, other volunteers and the darkness of his existence, but only to me I suspect.

He started to carry pictures from Vietnam he wanted me to see. Most were pictures of his men but some were of the people they had killed. Alarms went off in my head. Not only were the photos contraband, they signaled a much more serious issue with Billy's emotional state. I encouraged him to get some help with his pain, both physical and mental. Like most of us, he denied it. He said he was fine.

During my June trip in 2008, we met at The Wall as usual and I could tell his physical pain and depression were significantly worse. We talked more over that particular weekend than ever before. My July plans had already been made, so I told him I would plan my August trip for weekdays so we could spend quality time together. He seemed pleased.

But on July 11th all Wall volunteers received an email from the Vietnam Veterans Memorial Fund informing us Billy O'Brien had passed away suddenly that morning. I thought it was a mistake, so I called Allen McCabe to ask what had happened. Apparently the shrapnel in Billy's back shifted suddenly and severed his spinal cord. He died within minutes from asphyxiation. Once again, I felt I had seen death coming and could not do anything to stop another life from being taken by the hideous grip of Vietnam.

Billy O'Brien's burial at Arlington Cemetery

On September 30, 2008, Billy O'Brien was buried with full military honors and a 21 gun salute at Arlington Cemetery. He was finally at peace. His silent solitary suffering was over. Almost every volunteer was at his Mass and at Arlington to say their farewells: Annmarie, Betty, Allen, Kirby, Jim, the Michaels from Jersey, the Berrys, Max and I and more.

We all had to say goodbye. We needed to pause and reflect on the pain of the loss the likes of which we wouldn't have dared to consider when we were in combat. I am still grieving about Billy as are all of us who volunteered with him. But rather than be compelled to compartmentalize and expel his death from our conscience as we did in Vietnam, we are able to support each other with fond memories of his time with us. We don't have to block Billy out of our heads. It is okay to remember a fallen comrade, because, "It *does* mean somthin".

THE CLASS OF 1968

> "By and large, the past two generations have made such a colossal mess of the world that they have to step down and let us take over."
>
> *Pete Townshend*

1968 Democratic Convention in Chicago

The Pivotal Year of the 20th Century

The most formidable and profound year for the Boomer Generation had to be 1968. Whether we wanted it to be or not, the time to step up to a responsible leadership role was at hand. But we were completely unqualified to bring order and reason to the world. The structural deterioration resulting from events of the 12 months metastasized beyond our imagination and shocked every living being. At home, every headline felt personally painful for almost every American citizen. The daily news exacerbated a sense of despondency which bordered on hopelessness. For many, the year 1968 could possibly be considered the worst year of the 20th Century.

The significance and rhythm of disasters, month by month, was extraordinary: January: the USS Pueblo is the first U.S. warship ever captured. Tet Offensive is the worst day of US casualties in Vietnam, 246 Americans killed. February: the Battle of Khe Sanh begins….U.S. Marines under siege for months. Cronkite declares the war unwinnable. March: the My Lai massacre kills 350-400 villagers. Johnson announces he will not run for re-election. April: Martin Luther King delivers his mountain top speech and is assassinated and 114 cities in America riot and burn: New York, Chicago, Detroit, Philadelphia, L.A., San Francisco, DC, Baltimore; 46 dead. May: the Paris Peace Talks are agreed to. Five thousand students riot at the Sorbonne for Free Speech. June: Robert F. Kennedy is assassinated in Los Angeles after his California victory speech. July: Abbie Hoffman, Jerry Rubin and Paul Krassner, disrupt the trading floor of the New York Stock Exchange and destroy the Clocks at Grand Central Terminal. August: Republicans nominate Richard M. Nixon in Miami. "The Yippies go to Chicago": The Democratic National Convention sparks riots in Chicago. Mayor Daly states, "The policeman isn't there to create disorder; the policeman is there to preserve disorder." Democrats nominate Hubert Humphrey. They are completely embarrassed. Johnson doesn't even attend. September: the Miss America Beauty Contest is protested and Women's Liberation garners media attention. October: black athletes Tommie Smith and John Carlos protest in the medal ceremony at the Mexico Olympics. November: Nixon is elected. National Turn in Your Draft

Card day is observed across U.S. campuses. December: astronauts Borman, Lovell and Anders are first humans to see the far side of the Moon and planet Earth as a whole making the Apollo 8 mission successful.

Of note, buried in these headlines, was The Tet Offensive launched in late January. It was the pivotal point of the Vietnam War and in U.S. presidential politics. The all-out attacks by North Vietnam overshadowed the capture of the *Pueblo* only 3 weeks before. They took place in every major city in South Vietnam and throughout the countryside. It was a well-timed offensive against high profile targets. Enemy sacrifices were suicidal with no regard for their own massive loss of life. Regardless, the United States military was embarrassed in front of the entire world. Tet was a complete surprise and easily declared a major public relations victory for Ho and the NVA. Anti-war and anti-U.S. sentiments moved to a more vociferous plateau at home. U.S. World leadership was badly and permanently damaged.

Accentuating the embarrassment for the U.S. was the fact that the McNamara strategy had failed so publicly and conclusively. Even though the NVA lost 45,000 KIA and had 6,991 captured versus U.S. casualties of 543 killed and 2547 wounded, the world was convinced the U.S. had lost the battle and was well on its way to losing the war. Facts had no bearing in the court of world-wide public opinion because perception prevailed. Simply stated, the North Vietnamese were more than willing to sacrifice enormous numbers of lives for their cause. We weren't and couldn't justify it. No other evidence could demonstrate more clearly that a U.S. victory by attrition of the enemy was a cataclysmically flawed strategy.

> You can kill 10 of my men for every 1 I kill of yours, but
> even at those odds, you will lose and I will win.
> *Ho Chi Minh to the French*

Johnson and McNamara publicly staggered in the days following Tet. The Administration's already marginal credibility was completely destroyed as was Johnson's political career. All semblance of a unified White House evaporated in a matter of days because of the misaligned mendacious statements made to the media and to the American public. Johnson confirmed his failure to lead a few months later in March with the surprise announcement to not seek re-election. In less than 5 years, the U.S. had unexpectedly lost two presidents to equally demoralizing but completely different tragedies: assassination and megalomania.

Personal Loss

Such was the world in 1968. Tucked into these events of global magnitude was a tragic personal event for me. It was the first combat death in Vietnam of a classmate and friend, Art Timboe on February 1, 1968 during Tet Offensive.

Art was an ROTC graduate of U.S.F. and S.I. He was 2 years ahead of me in school for 8 of my formative years, and was the first person I actually knew who was killed in the war. He was not a gung-ho ROTC student or crazed combatant. He was a modest, unimposing, smart and well-liked young man fulfilling his obligation, like many.

After his college graduation, marriage, commissioning and stateside training, he was subsequently sent to Vietnam to be an Infantry platoon leader. Just months after reporting, he died in a vicious firefight trying to save a wounded man. Art's death hit close to home for me. I imagined it could be me in a matter of months. The thought of that fate made me withdraw into my own fears. My nightmare of an early violent death like Art's became more real with his striking so close.

Graduation was in May for my class, and it marked the final point of estrangement from friends and classmates. Overnight, our life paths moved miles apart and became more indelibly defined. Most commonality had evaporated when I had taken a stand about going into the Army 2 years before, but graduation made it official and unalterable. It felt as though the weekend of graduation and commissioning marked the end of one life for me, and the following Monday I was very much in another...the silence was deafening...there wasn't even an echo of the last 8 years. Life felt so different.

I was 21 years old. Officially, I was a legal adult, an officer and a gentleman by an act of Congress, and obligated to develop a well-defined course for my life. In my passage towards adulthood, I had tried the best proven behaviors of the previous generations, but the formula didn't seem to give me any buoyancy or peace of mind. My head was crammed with a list of very serious "to-dos". I had to marry my college sweetheart in October, find work to support us, find a place to live, and my military obligation was getting closer. I was completely uncertain of where my life would go if I were to make it through the Army commitment unharmed. That was a central concern, and I only hoped I could figure it out if and when the time came. The weight of the obligations was overbearing.

I couldn't get comfortable enough to order my priorities logically. Fear of war and the fate of Art Timboe clouded my decision making. I became depressed and a major crisis of confidence took control of me. To relieve some tension, fill in time, and make some money, I took a most unglamorous job with Sears as a trainee before I had to report for active duty. No one else would hire me except Sears with my military departure imminent. Even though I detested the work, I reasoned I would abandon Sears after the Army and start a real career in some other field. Still nothing seemed right in any part of my life. 'It isn't *supposed* to be this way,' I kept telling myself.

It felt like I was losing control of my life at breakneck speed and that the obligations were strangling me. Marriage had become just another compulsory check-off on my to-do list rather than a joy to embrace. I couldn't handle the thought of making a lifetime commitment in my state of depression. I doubted I loved her at that point. So six weeks before the wedding while sitting on the floor of the empty apartment we had just rented, I told Mary I couldn't go through with the marriage. I was embarrassed and ashamed beyond explanation. In my rush to find relief from my anxiety, I handled it poorly. As expected, she was crushed. We were finished.

My lack of maturity overwhelmed me. I was not prepared to face life-sized decisions in the real world. Unfortunately, I had a naïve notion that adulthood would be triggered at the magical age of 21 and I would be blessed with the wisdom and expansiveness to handle a full, challenging and rich life. That didn't happen. The concept of gradual maturation through trial and error was unknown to me. In short, I suddenly realized I was facing adult-sized accountabilities with severely limited tools. I had tried to make intelligent, informed decisions, but instead of feeling strong and independent, I felt woefully inadequate. My few coping skills evaporated as I struggled mightily to deal with life on life's terms.

I had reluctantly chosen ROTC with my fiancée's encouragement. At the time I thought it was an honorable way to stand up for something in which I could say I believed. Now it was different. Mary was supposed to be my partner in my passage through these dangerous and uncharted waters of life. But she was gone. I was hopeful the Peace Talks would end the war before I got there, but that hope was snuffed out by the crush of the Tet Offensive. The war was worse and I knew I was going. I was on my own, afraid and had to wrestle with the cross currents of life which were about to knock me harder. I wanted to call a time out. I wanted someone to pity me and tell me it was all going to go away. I felt ineffectual under the weight of my obligations. I wanted to run. I wanted a place to hide but could find none.

HOW IT WORKS

> They carried the soldier's greatest fear, which was the fear of blushing. Men killed, and died, because they were embarrassed not to. It was what had brought them to the war in the first place, nothing positive, no dreams of glory or honor, just to avoid the blush of dishonor. They died so as not to die of embarrassment.
>
> *The Things They Carried*
>
> *Tim O'Brien*

There are no politics at The Wall; no right or wrong; no policy or diplomacy debating; and no glamour of battle and victory. Just names of those who died or are missing, 58,300 of them over a twenty year period. It is intended to be contemplative space for both visitor and Veteran.

Confronted with the commanding presentation of combat casualties, one can physically feel the horror and the sacrifice of youth in war...regardless of time, place or cause. The names of the dead and missing etched in polished black granite present a staggering contrast to the reflected images of the living through the names. The names speak to you as you walk by, some simple names like Billy B. Bull and others more intricate, like Faleagafula Ilaoa or Frank W. Jealous-of-Him. They each have a story which now must be told by another.

As one tries to understand the order in which they are inscribed on the Wall, the names engage you. The most common question a visitor asks is how the names are arranged. That is intentional.

The names are arranged in chronological order by date of casualty, and they are alphabetical within each day so there is a way to separate days and to see how many were lost on a given day. They represent a permanent and powerful recitation of the loss of life in Vietnam. If they were arranged in alphabetical order the story wouldn't be as potent because there are 667 Smiths; 526 Johnsons; 406 Williams; 383 Browns; and 350 Joneses.

The Memorial starts with July 8, 1959 on panel 1E and ends on panel 1W with May 15, 1975. It starts in the center and finishes in the center. The first and last casualties lay side by side in the apex to symbolize the war is over. In effect, The Wall is a circular timeline. It is 246 feet, 9 inches long in both east and west directions and 10 feet, 6 inches tall at apex.

The shape of The Wall is as subtle as it is severe. It is a polished black granite gash in the ground to symbolize the wound in the heart of America which the war caused. The grass on the north and south sides of The Wall are a gentle symbol of the wound growing back together and healing. Black represents death, granite a permanent separation of the living and the dead, and polished granite reflects the images of the living in the chronology of those who died. The Memorial is about healing the wounds the war caused by honoring those who gave their lives. It is a living Memorial so the healing is self-sustaining. It was designed as such.

Almost all visitors to The Wall ask how many names are on it. When answering their question, we always explain that the number changes every year. To a person, they are surprised to learn that new names and symbols are carved into the black granite in early May.

For those who have died as a result of their wounds, their name is inscribed as close to the day they received the mortal wound as space is available. The status symbols which accompany names are also changed at the same time names are added. A diamond with the name represents a confirmed dead. A cross represents a Missing in Action. A cross with a diamond superimposed on it represents a Missing in Action who has been found. In 2014 there were 13 names added and 3 MIA's changed from missing to found.

A ceremony is held on Memorial Day at The Wall for the families of those whose names have been added or their status has been changed so proper honors and respect can be paid for the sacrifice. It is a fitting way to complete the story of the service and sacrifice for many.

The Wall was conceived, and designed in a cauldron of controversy just 5 years after the official collapse of South Vietnam under siege from the North. The design of the Memorial was initially heavily criticized and demeaned by many, both military and civilian. Emotions and allegiances were still intense and deeply imbedded in the country in the few years after the war ended.

At the time of its dedication, who was right and who was wrong about Vietnam was still a part of the American narrative. Some Veterans were puzzled and frustrated with the controversy over The Wall. When we came home, we had been shamed, shunned, vilified and excluded. We were told we were losers; the war was not only wrong, but it was a waste; that most of us were psychopathic murderers; that if we had just said no to going, the country would have been better off. Most of us worked hard to be invisible about our service and our tour of duty. To many, the Memorial was an irrelevant monument in the context of the lives we were then trying to live. We just wanted to forget. So why would anyone want to build a Memorial?

The answer was simple and transcendent. It was to remember the people who sacrificed their lives in the prosecution of the war, right or wrong. Their sacrifice earned them an honorable place in the history of our country. Those of us who made it back safely attest to that silently every day.

When considering the depth of the emotions and the bitter aftertaste that was inescapably tied to Vietnam, The Wall represents incredible insight on the part of its founder, Jan Scruggs. Healing was absolutely necessary for all who lived through the tragedy of the war and its time in our country's history. It was also an astonishing accomplishment that would be difficult to duplicate in today's governmental environment. The fact it was completed in less than 3 years from concept to dedication, and it was built entirely with private funds amidst continuing rancor, criticism and polarity borders on the miraculous. It is an achievement which will never be repeated.

The Things We Carried

There is a special grieving ritual which started at The Wall before it was completed and it continues today. The leaving of common or uncommon personal items has become a way to remain connected to those who sacrificed. It started unexpectedly during construction when a Veteran passing by the site asked if he could leave his Purple Heart in the concrete which was being poured for the pilings. The foreman said he had no objection, so the man dropped his medal into the fresh concrete of the support pilings where it remains today.

The gift left behind is a private act made for all the public to see in monumental space. This special ritual has come to define The Wall itself as well as to become a solemn act of grieving which has been re-created throughout the world. Things left vary from the deceptively ordinary to the incredibly symbolic or personal: flowers, cigarettes, drugs, C-Rations, weapons, ammo, old uniform pieces and patches to pictures, love letters, undergarments, diamond rings, stuffed animals, an old baseball glove, signed high school yearbooks, keys to cars, and even a brand new hand-made Harley Davidson. Each piece has a story and a relationship which it memorializes.

Many items are left by families, loved ones and relatives. But there are just as many left by Veterans who made it home and were a buddy or a witness to the death inscribed on the panel which the precious remembrance is laid in front of. In some cases, the item left was of critical importance to an individual when he was there. Often we carried some peculiar thing because it was familiar, or for superstition or emotional security. Many were connected with some meaningful act or event—the particular item may have soothed our fears or given us courage and inspiration to press on at a critical time. Mine was my P-38 C Ration can opener on my dog tag chain. It was the opener I used my first day in Vietnam after I had survived being booby trapped and heavily mortared…it was my good luck charm which I still carry today.

Legend has it the first object left was a Purple Heart. Many more have been left since.

The panties were left with no explanation

Memorial Day and the hand-made Harley Davidson

My P38

Every night the items are picked up by the Park Service and catalogued then stored in a national warehouse. Some items have been on display at 'The Price of Freedom' in the Smithsonian's National Museum of American

History. There are over 150,000 items preserved. Eventually, all of them will be put into a permanent rotating presentation along with a picture of every person inscribed on The Wall in the Vietnam Veterans Learning Center across the street from The Wall when the center is completed.

The Gathering and the Grieving

There is no better place which unfalteringly communicates the sacrifice and loss of life in war than the Vietnam Memorial. To look at the number of names and realize each name represents a real life and a hope snuffed out, evokes an unexpected flood of anguish about the insanity of war.

Even though American losses in World War II were seven times greater in three and a half years of fighting than the 20 years in Vietnam, The Wall stands as a brilliant work of art and a Memorial which tells a difficult story in every dimension of its design. It is a work in which you become immersed and captivated as you walk it. No other memorial has this power.

After 32 years, The Wall is the most visited memorial in the world. Almost 5 million people per year come from all over to see it, feel it, and relate to it both physically and emotionally. Some come many times. Others can only do it once. It is an opportunity for a visitor to learn something about a war which gripped the attention of the world every day for 10 solid years, and yet its history has barely been taught. It is also an opportunity for each individual to learn something about themselves as they study their reflection while contemplating the intriguing design.

For the Vietnam Veteran, The Wall is serene and hallowed ground. A wound, yes, but also a place of healing and remembering, which is so difficult ...no matter how hard one has tried to put it out of their mind. It is a place where it is safe to cry, to talk, to grieve and to recall moments in their lives they have tried to forget. It is a place to reconnect with other Veterans and with strangers--to share friends, relatives, and emotions. It is the only place a Veteran can feel one more time the unmistakable closeness and camaraderie which was formed in combat. The Wall portrays a personal piece of each Veteran's life permanently anchored into the earth and carved in stone---forever.

The Gash in the Earth

For that reason, both my sons and their wives asked me if I would take them to The Wall on one of my volunteer weekends. They wanted to know why I had so completely connected to it and they wanted to know more about me and my service. I was honored. I obliged them on 3 different trips so each had the opportunity to get closer to me and my connection to my past. It meant the world to me to open up to each of them.

As you leave The Wall and look back at it, all you see is the 2 inch wide black scar of granite contrasted against the background of green grass. The scar is supported by the 58,300 names carved in it. *They* are the memorial.

> Although both popular imagination and academic research on the Vietnam War continue to flourish, there is no consensus in sight. Only the U.S. Civil War rivals the power of the Vietnam War to divide and inflame generations upon generations of Americans.
>
> *ANDREAS W. DAUM, America, the Vietnam War, and the World*

The Journey Begins

> The ultimate measure of a man is not where he stands in moments of comfort and convenience, but where he stands at times of challenge and controversy.
> *Martin Luther King*

SOBC Class One-Niner, Ft. Gordon, GA
May, 1969

On January 20, 1969, Richard M. Nixon was sworn in as the 37th President of the United States. He was elected by a majority of the voters because he professed to have a solution to the war in Vietnam and said he wanted to restore peace, harmony and respect for the United States. The hope of many of us was that he would lead the nation out of the deceitful darkness of the Johnson Presidency. Not everyone, however, felt that way about Nixon. For many, civil disobedience continued to be the preferred form of communication with the President.

On his inauguration day, the parade route from the Capitol to Pennsylvania Avenue was alive with protestors chanting, "Ho, Ho, Ho Chi Minh, the NLF is going to win!" Between 13th and 14th streets demonstrators hurled beer cans, bottles and stones at Nixon's limousine as it drove by. It was the first time in the 180 history of our country such blatant hostility had marred the inauguration of a President. The public psyche of the U.S. had reached a new nadir.

At the same time, I received my orders for active duty in the United States Army and to report to Ft. Gordon, GA.

> Let us understand: North Vietnam cannot defeat or humiliate the United States. Only Americans can do that.
> *Richard M. Nixon, 1969*

The First 365 Day Countdown

On April 18, 1969, with my every possession packed into my '65 VW Beetle, I took off from San Francisco on a drive across the U.S. to Augusta, Georgia. My orders read I was to be trained as a Signal Officer at Ft. Gordon in the Officer Basic Course beginning May 1st, continue on with advanced training at Ft. Sill, Oklahoma, and then to Ft. Hamilton, New York for my stateside duty. At the end of one year, I would be reassigned for the second year to USARV (United States Army Republic of Vietnam) for the remainder of my active duty obligation.

There it was in black and white mimeographed print. It had happened. I was chosen to go to war. I was almost relieved I finally had something concrete in my hands with which I could deal. And dealing with it was what I decided I needed to do. On the advice of a recently discharged officer friend, I became determined to make the best of my time in the Army and not spend it complaining and worrying....there was actually nothing good that could come from making me miserable. For whatever the reason, when I truly adopted this simple attitude, there was a significant change in my anxiety level.

After several hot Spring days of driving my un-air conditioned Beetle and getting a heavy dose of our checkered culture and landscape of America, I reported for duty on time. But not before experiencing the shock of the segregated world outside of California. In the Deep South of Mississippi and Alabama I was refused gas because I was a "California Hippie". It didn't matter I was reporting for military duty in Georgia. From their point of view, I drove a foreign car with California plates on it, and that meant I didn't belong on a road in the South. At another stop outside Jackson, MS I tried to pay cash for gas with a Kennedy half dollar and was told it was not accepted currency. These were not playful incidents, the people were still genuinely angry about the passing of the Civil Rights Bill five years earlier, and they didn't want suspicious outsiders in their midst. It was my rude introduction to the ugliness of Civil Rights hatred of the times.

When I arrived at Ft. Gordon, I pulled into the line of "new reports" cars behind the only other Californian according to my scan of license plates. I was looking for friendlies. Clark Struve and his wife of 7 days Toshia were right in front of me and on their honeymoon about to embark on the Army adventure with the rest of us. Both were from the Bay Area and graduates of San Jose State. Oddly, the absurdity of their decision to start their marriage in those incongruous circumstances gave me great comfort. It helped me see the world is not as orderly and logical as I might have imagined. The three of us Californians bonded immediately and we became best friends for life. Clark and Toshia were the first life-time friendships I experienced in the Army...a true gift. We began our journey together on that first day.

Signal Officer Basic Class 19 was composed of young men who were fused together by identical fears. We were no longer pariahs on campus or isolated individuals. We all shared much in common. If nothing else, each of us missed our chance to be at Woodstock that summer. Close friendships were forged easily by our common, if frightful, horizon. Together we discovered an unexpected strength in ourselves. It developed rapidly as our training progressed. We reported as scared and tentative individuals. We departed as promising leaders and close friends.

Woodstock, June 1969

Probably the most common connective tissue for all of us at first was our confused philosophical perspective about the right or wrong of the war. But that quickly became secondary as we focused on learning how to be a leader. The constant training reminders of combat from seasoned instructors underscored the seriousness of why we were there. Leading men into danger was new for all of us and we were each equally unskilled regardless of our backgrounds, educations, or intelligence. We needed the training. Lives were going to depend on us.

A Second Chance

The melancholy of leaving home and separation from Mary for me was somewhat mitigated by the treasure of the new friends I made. They were a welcomed relief from the fractured relationships I had left behind. But they could not truly fill the void in my heart I had for Mary. By being around the married couples in my class, I envied the partnerships they enjoyed. I missed her and I knew I needed her support.

After my breakup with her in October the year before, I realized I had made a serious mistake. By January I had sheepishly fashioned an apologetic rapprochement that she conditionally accepted. We could talk only when she felt it appropriate and with no obligation attached or assumed. Understandably, she was not anxious to get involved with me again. It was marginally okay to just be friends. At my encouragement, we met and talked once a week to stay connected until it was time for me to leave. But after I reported for duty in Georgia, we both missed our weekly sharing. Being single and experiencing the new adventures of military life, I missed her more than she did me. I was still uncertain about whether it was right for us to be serious, but I knew I needed more than haphazard phone calls.

After settling in to the daily training life at Ft. Gordon, I felt the clock moving rapidly towards my Vietnam assignment. It made me realize I had to make the best of the time I had remaining before deployment, so I wrote to Mary daily. Surprisingly, she quickly wrote back to me every day. We became close friends again from a distance. Then her letters were perfumed. I started to call her when I could (no cell phone, just long lines at the post pay phones made it really difficult). I talked as long as I could with an impatient line of G.I.s waiting behind me, and then I'd promise to call again.

When Memorial Day weekend came, our class got a 3 day weekend pass. I decided I would try to squeeze in a trip to San Francisco to see her if she would have it. She said yes. With not a minute to spare, I drove to Atlanta, flew home, spent the weekend with her, flew back and drove to Augusta Tuesday morning just in time to make formation. It was the best way I could show her how much I missed her. We were still in love. The relationship moved to a new level. I had a faint feeling of confidence that if I did things right and kept my head straight I would not lose her again. That felt good.

Even with my improving love life and new found friends, however, other unidentified anxieties returned. I felt myself in constant search of relief from varied and stubborn fears. Alcohol was the acceptable remedy for a soldier's burdens. Drinking was available, socially expected, and supported by the Army. End-of-day drinking with like kind in the Officers Club had a long history in the Army, and I took to it well. I looked forward to the temporary erasure of all worries and fears.

I had never been much of a drinker, but on my own in the military environment, I enjoyed it more than I would have guessed. I became a regular at the O Club almost every day. I could drink more than others. I wanted it more than others. It worked beautifully for me, and I felt accepted by everyone.

Forts Sill and Hood

After Officer Basic at Ft. Gordon, I moved on to Ft. Sill, Oklahoma for advanced microwave telephone communications training. Many classmates from Class 19 did the same. Clark was one of them. The advanced training was to prepare us for a relatively safe communications job which specialized in supervising the running of long range equipment providing civilian-type telephone service to major command centers. It was the type of job which would put me less in harm's way as part of a large well protected operation, rather than in a field communications job at the front lines. It felt a little more secure.

I was also happy getting more Army indoctrination and being with friends like Clark and others from our Signal Officers Basic Class. We had a great time. Our schedule was almost resort-like. We had class in the morning, golf in the early afternoon on the post golf course, and then drinking and cards at night. It almost felt as though I finally was getting my turn at being one of "the chosen" I had envied all my life.

As expected, other Class 19 classmates went in other directions. Some went directly to their duty stations. Some chose to avoid Vietnam and took a European assignment by adding another year to their obligation. I considered doing that, but declined when I thought about going to Ft. Hamilton located in New York City. I was thrilled to be going to The Big Apple. I actually had asked for the assignment on my dream sheet because I thought it "Army logical" to send me as far away from California as possible. So I got it.... until my last day at Ft. Sill.

On the last day, with my duffle shipped to New York, I was called by the company clerk and told my orders had been changed. I was re-assigned to Ft. Hood, TX to be a platoon leader in a NATO communications Reforger battalion which was on call 24-7 for re-deployment to Germany. It meant constant readiness. In the Army readiness means training and field exercises with no let up. Hurry up and wait, day in and day out. I couldn't believe it. My wonderful assignment in New York City had vaporized with Army magic. I was headed to hard work in the Texas desert.

The platoon leader job at Hood entailed babysitting Vietnam returnees who were required to put in their last few months before being discharged. I had to keep them out of trouble (jail, drugs and alcohol) while they waded through meaningless practice deployment exercises. Attitudes were bad, behavior problems plentiful, and my daily personal angst barely tolerable. It was an alternate form of parenting dysfunctional children. Drinking at night in my BOQ along with phone calls to Mary was my daily reward. Our relationship continued to grow closer, but the days at Ft. Hood were filled with impatience and aggravation as I waited to get my final set of orders to go to Vietnam. It was a torturous existence.

Orders finally came in March. I had 30 days to get to Oakland and then to the big Field Training Exercise in Southeast Asia.

Combat Orders

General George S. Patton

"Now, I want you to remember that no bastard ever won a war by dying for his country. He won it by making the other poor dumb bastard die for his country.

Men, all this stuff you've heard about America not wanting to fight, wanting to stay out of the war, is a lot of horse dung. Americans, traditionally, love to fight. All real Americans love the sting of battle.

When you were kids, you all admired the champion marble shooter, the fastest runner, the big league ball players, the toughest boxers. Americans love a winner and will not tolerate a loser. Americans play to win all the time. Now, I wouldn't give a hoot in hell for a man who lost and laughed. That's why Americans have never lost and will never lose a war. Because the very thought of losing is hateful to Americans.

Now, an army is a team. It lives, eats, sleeps, fights as a team. This individuality stuff is a bunch of crap. The bilious bastards who wrote that stuff about individuality for the Saturday Evening Post don't know anything more about real battle than they do about fornicating.

Now, we have the finest food and equipment, the best spirit, and the best men in the world. You know, by God, I actually pity those poor bastards we're going up against. By God, I do. We're not just going to shoot the bastards. We're going to cut out their living guts and use them to grease the treads of our tanks. We're going to murder those lousy Hun bastards by the bushel.

Now, some of you boys, I know, are wondering whether or not you'll chicken-out under fire. Don't worry about it. I can assure you that you will all do your duty. The Nazis are the enemy. Wade into them. Spill their blood. Shoot them in the belly. When you put your hand into a bunch of goo that a moment before was your best friend's face, you'll know what to do.

Now there's another thing I want you to remember. I don't want to get any messages saying that we are holding our position. We're not holding anything. Let the Hun do that. We are advancing constantly and we're not interested in holding onto anything -- except the enemy. We're going to hold onto him by the nose, and we're gonna kick him in the ass. We're gonna kick the hell out of him all the time, and we're gonna go through him like crap through a goose!

Now, there's one thing that you men will be able to say when you get back home, and you may thank God for it. Thirty years from now when you're sitting around your fireside with your grandson on your knee, and he asks you, "What did you do in the great World War II?" -- you won't have to say, "Well, I shoveled shit in Louisiana."

Alright now you sons-of-bitches, you know how I feel. Oh, I will be proud to lead you wonderful guys into battle anytime, anywhere.

That is all."

George C. Scott as General George S. Patton in Patton

When I watched this opening speech of the movie Patton I have to admit I did not really grasp the nuances of what was being said. I didn't make the connection from his words to what was going to happen to me in a war zone, even though I had a strange sense I should be able to. Oh, it was patriotic and inspiring, and was delivered brilliantly by Scott. But his graphic description of how combat is conducted didn't feel like reality to me....it was just a Hollywood representation by some strong character in a film, and I enjoyed it.

I had no context or familiarity with which to process his description of wartime barbarousness except in my imagination. Patton talked in a different time; a different place; a different war; a war with a cause. More importantly, I did not think I was ever going to have to face the raw and sickening realities Patton described to his men 26 years earlier. I was a communications officer not a ground troop carrying a rifle, and I harbored an indistinct hope I would come home unscathed after having missed a few mortar rounds and nothing more working on a big headquarters command base.

Now having lived through combat and with the benefit of time, experience and maturity, I can hear Patton's message more clearly. It is chilling because it strips down war to the savagery it is, and yet it simultaneously captures the mysteries that forever trouble the mind of the warrior.

1. War is about killing people, specifically, killing the other guy. Combat is the act of finding the enemy, closing with him and killing or capturing him. Warriors are trained how to hate and how to kill. There is nothing blameless, romantic or glamorous about it. No matter how sanitized the act of killing is made through the technologies of new weaponry, the objective remains the same, the taking of life. And the act is a life-altering event.

2. Pushed to your limits, you will kill. It is ugly, and the moral damage done to the combatant is permanent.

3. You fight as a team of warriors. You participate together or you die. You fight and kill for the guy next to you and next to him. That's all that matters in the heat of combat, not politics, not causes, not ideals or ideologies. You do not fight, die or kill for causes.

4. There is an exhilaration of combat which will haunt you for the rest of your life.

While I didn't catch the full force of the words of his speech when I saw the movie, Patton's thoughts nevertheless became stored inside me permanently, not to be acknowledged until years later.

To War Alone

"Going to war is a landmark experience in the life of an individual, an episode of tremendous importance. But in the case of Vietnam vets, you learned quickly to repress it, keep it a secret, shut up about it, because people either considered you a sucker or some kind of psychopath who killed women and children."

Bobby Muller,
Founder, Vietnam Veterans Association.

A World Airways Charter to Vietnam

TO WAR ALONE

"I'm leavin' on a jet plane,
Don't know when I'll be back again,
Oh, Babe I hate to go."

One of the unique lessons we learned during the Vietnam War was how poorly we deployed and returned troops to and from the theater of battle, alone--one at time. It had never been done before and it was never done again. An individual's emotional anguish was doubled or tripled because he had to confront his fears alone. He felt no sense of support, security or camaraderie as he would in a full unit deployment. He was alone with his fate and had not a scintilla of confidence he could navigate the fears ahead. He was a body, replacing another anonymous body...maybe alive...maybe dead. Travel to Vietnam was one of the most unnerving and demoralizing experiences in the lives of many of us.

Goodbyes

My orders arrived on time. I was to report to USARV (United States Army, Republic of Vietnam) personnel station on 23 April 1970 to be assigned to a unit once "in country". That meant I would be subject to a duty lottery like everyone else. All the planning in the world could not influence what was going to happen to me or where I'd be assigned when I got there. I had 30 days leave prior to reporting to Travis Air Force Base for an all-expenses paid ride on a chartered World Airways flight to Tan Son Nhut Air Base in the Republic of South Vietnam. Years of anticipation were over.

So I said goodbyes to my company and platoon at Hood, packed up everything I owned in my Beetle again, and drove to California—to be with Mary. We wanted to have a few days together before we told anyone else I was in town and preparing to deploy. It was my way to protect the limited time I had left. And, we needed each other's support for the next steps. We confirmed we were deeply in love; we weren't going to get married before I left;

and we would marry if and when I came home. We spent two days together quietly, and then I went home to my family.

The remaining weeks flashed by. I said goodbyes to a few friends and relatives. I didn't want any attention drawn to me. I was embarrassed to let anyone know where I was going because I was sure they would ask me why I would do such a stupid thing. Fortunately, having been gone for a year, I was off most people's radar.

I made it a point not to connect with any college friends because I didn't want any of that grief either. I hadn't kept up with any of them since I had gone on active duty. And any common ground we once shared had been reduced to a grain of sand because of the time, distance and disagreement over the morality of the life I lived as a member of the military.

For the few people I did see, I remember how awkward the goodbyes were. Each person fumbled for the right words while avoiding saying something politically incorrect like, "Good luck and kill a lotta gooks for us," or, "Hope everything goes well for you and don't get hurt now." I didn't know what to say to them either, other than, "I'm going to miss you." And I dared not show any weakness. I was a warrior going off to war. I didn't want to take the mask off or forget it.

The Last Day

On my last night, Mary and I went to see the movie *Patton*. I couldn't believe such a movie had been made in the politically charged anti-war atmosphere of the times—but it was. It was fantastic and was a sure academy award winner. Oddly, I got strength from watching the film and from Scott's performance of Patton. It was an ironic event for the night before my going to war, but it helped make me feel a little more confident with my decision to serve—even if it meant I might have to sacrifice my life. Somehow, the story made me feel principled in an odd way. Go figure.

When we got back to the house, we stayed up all night talking and holding each other as we waited for the time to take off. In the morning, Mom grabbed me and said a tearful goodbye on her way to work. The poor woman was racked with fears and tears. Through her, I could tell each member of the family was consumed with the thought they might never see me alive again. Her anticipation worsened to unspoken terror in the last minute of our farewell as she broke down completely. I did the best I could to make the goodbye easy for her. It was a poignant moment for both of us.

Dad came up to my room as I was picking up my duffel and he started to say goodbye with a handshake. Then he suddenly broke down and hugged me. He wouldn't let me go. Holding on, I felt him start to cry. I had never in my life seen this Rock of Gibraltar ever shed a tear. I knew I couldn't let it get to me. He was sobbing and speechless so I said, "I'm going to be okay, Dad. I am going to do the best I can, and the rest will have to take care of itself." Resigned to his helplessness in the moment, he nodded and turned away as he said, "Good luck, Tiger."

My sister and her husband Hans said their abbreviated goodbyes the day before. Chris is not very good with things she has to deny from her consciousness, so she usually clips them short and turns them over to God. Hans wanted to talk, but didn't know what to say. He had come so close to going, I think he felt a twinge of guilt. My brother called and gave me a cursory good luck. I hated him.

The Long Walk

It was time to go. Mary was my arranged transportation, so we took off. She cried the entire trip across the Bay Bridge. When we got to Travis Air Force Base, there were no bands playing, no crowds cheering or waving flags, no one but Mary with me to give me some emotional strength to face my journey. And it was no different for every other troop who boarded the plane with me. We felt like cattle rotating in stockyard pens and then herded into the chute to face The Man.

Mary hung with me to the last moment. We said one more passionate goodbye then I spun towards the plane and walked out onto the tarmac.

I didn't look back. I couldn't. I felt bad for her and everyone else. The weight of being alone and afraid was heavy on my shoulders. Even in the bright sunshine, it was as though I was walking down a dark tunnel with no light at the end and absolutely no idea where it would lead. All the feelings of security I ever had in my life vanished. Every step was momentous. I had to concentrate on my movement and nothing else just to get to the stairs of the plane.

As I boarded, I felt an eerie calm slowly take hold of me. It was such an odd feeling that I remember thinking there must be something wrong with me. 'Do you actually feel good about this?' Incredibly, the answer was yes. I felt relief. It must be the same relief a condemned man had when he finally mounted the stairs of the gallows. The fear, anticipation, and anxiety of the unknown began lifting. After years of agonizing and hoping it would never happen, it was. And I was at the point of no return. I had to deal with whatever fate would hand me instead of perseverating about it. I was ready.

The flight was packed with enlisted replacements. I think I was one of 3 officers on the plane. It didn't matter. The equalizer for all of us was our inexperience, not rank. No one had any combat time: no lifers, no extendees. We were all cherries. The enlisted were in their bright new fatigues and I was in my tropical weight khakis with a National Defense Ribbon pinned over the pocket. It was regulation, and I felt like a dorky poser. I never wore the uniform in Vietnam.

The men cut their tension and fears by harassing the flight attendants who were all battle-hardened professionals and could take anything thrown their way, literally. I was not in a playful mood so I tried to sleep as best I could. I just wanted to get there and get started with whatever it was I was going to do.

The "flight" was a long set of flights. Travis to Hawaii; Hawaii to Wake Island; Wake to Guam; Guam to the Philippines; then finally to Tan Son Nhut Air Base outside of Saigon—almost 24 hours for the trip and I was completely disoriented in time and location when we finally got there.

At about 5000 feet of altitude on final approach into Tan Son Nhut my stomach and sphincter started to tighten up when I looked out the window and saw puffs of smoke around the landing field. I had no idea what they were from, but to me they were all the evidence I needed to be convinced it was enemy fire directed solely at me. I felt a tightness grip me. 'Get this airplane down and get me outta here!' I kept mumbling. We finally touched down hard....like on an aircraft carrier catching the restraining cable.

Wheels Down, Vietnam

We were off-loaded in double time so the plane could re-fuel, load, reposition and get off the runway before being mortared. As soon as I stepped into the doorway to get off, I inhaled my first breath of the smothering Southeast Asian tropics. The stench of the air and the suffocating heat and humidity hit me like a brick in the face. I had never been sickened by anything like it. The inside of a used sweat sock had a better smell and feel. 'Never mind, get moving.' I thought.

We got hustled into steel reinforced buses for the ride to the 90th Replacement Battalion at Long Binh for in-processing (a euphemism for the Assignment Lottery game). The buses looked like the ones they use to transfer the hard core criminals from San Francisco City and County Jail to the Federal Penitentiary at San Quentin. It took me awhile to realize the MP escorts and the steel reinforced windows were to discourage any little fellows from hitting us with bombs or grenades while we traveled through their neighborhoods.

The streets were jammed with mopeds, people, animals, cars, garbage, scatological waste, peddlers, bicycles, rickshaws, hookers, and anything else you could imagine in a Third World environment. Street peddlers sold gasoline in old Coke bottles with no cork or stopper which was really handy because they doubled for Molotov cocktails in a pinch. The smoke from the mopeds was so thick you could barely see across the roads. Pavement was intermittent.

The Vietnamese population was an odd mixture of people in black pajamas with coolie hats and others in cheap gaudy western dress. People relieved themselves as they walked down the street. The women had a particular technique which was clever. They pulled up a pant leg of their black pajamas and aimed at a heap of garbage. It worked.

It was Saigon, and it was a very rude wake-up call. 'What are we trying to save here?' I asked myself in my calloused American mind. 'This place is a dump of monumental proportions, and *this* is supposed to be the good part of the country? What are we doing? No more discussion,' I thought. 'You're here now and you have 365 days, so deal.'

The bus let us off at the 90th Replacement hootch in Long Binh. Officers went one way, enlisted another. I checked in with my orders and was told by the clerk it would probably take 2-3 days to get me assigned because my MOS (Military Occupational Specialty) was so rare and the Signal Corps was picky about where their men got assigned. Wow, that sounded like good news. I told the clerk to take his time while I went to the officer quarters to wait it out.

Long Binh Replacement Depot Recreation. My kind of war

Long Binh Post had paved streets with such amenities as streetlights, hot showers & flush toilets, electric utilities, a fire department, and a dog catcher.

Most of the steel office buildings were air conditioned. It had dental clinics, large restaurants, snack bars, Post Exchanges, swimming pools, basketball & tennis courts, a golf driving range, University of Maryland extension classes, a bowling alley, many nightclubs with live music (officer, NCO, enlisted), a Chase Manhattan Bank branch, laundry services, and a massage parlor. This is a war zone? It was better than Ft. Hood and probably safer. Maybe I could get stationed here!

I think I'll have a drink at the O Club....this might not be too bad.

Close Calls

> "The mark of the immature man is that he wants to die nobly for a cause, while the mark of the mature man is that he wants to live humbly for one."
> *Time Magazine*

Yikes!

Throughout my young life, I had a deep seated fear of dying prematurely in some unnatural way: an accident; a fatal disease; a snake bite; an enemy alien; or even in war. Maybe it was because early on I had too many close and fearsome calls which really scared me. Even though at the times they occurred, I didn't realize their seriousness or significance.

Being the youngest, I was always conscious about shaking off physical pain so as not to be accused of being a slacker or a sissy. But calamity always seemed to be right over my shoulder. And because it was, I was prone to getting into trouble unexpectedly. I developed a habit of being on the lookout for an oncoming fatal event. I ran scared a lot but lived to tell about the ordeals. I can now see how my early traumas probably laid ground work for a future bout with Post Traumatic Stress Disorder.

CLOSE CALLS

Now that I am a grandparent and see what the younger generations call trauma, my near-death deeds look and sound downright fatal by comparison. I have to admit I don't have a good enough perspective about any of this to give sound guidance to young parents like my children. The incidents I considered as average scars of my growing up and navigating life are now the stuff of institutional grants and diagnostic research.

On one occasion, when I was 3 years old I wandered off from the summer vacation house the family was renting. I couldn't talk, but I was very curious. I ended up blocks away at the police station where I had the officers in a panic because I couldn't give them a clue as to who I was or where I should be. Remember, I still didn't talk yet. So they had no idea what to do or to whom I belonged. Hours later with an ice cream cone in hand and the duty officer's hat on my head, Mom and Dad arrived. They were there to report my missing status and were consumed by the fear I had been abducted or run over by a car. I remained oblivious to the trouble I had caused while I finished off the cone.

One of the most gruesome and lasting traumas I witnessed happened when I was a third grader. Like all young city boys, whenever there were the sirens of fire engines, I would chase them down with friends to see what exciting things were happening. One day while outside playing in the streets, I heard the sirens come close to my house. I ran less than a block to find the action and, sure enough, there they were down the street in front of my friend's house. Full force flames licked out from every front window, just like in a movie. Firemen chopped in the roof and front door while water poured on them from the pumper truck and hydrants. The action was very exciting.

A crowd had gathered across the street to watch in horror as the front door was demolished and 3 firemen pushed through it with a hose blasting them. In a minute or two, steam flowed from the front windows when the flames were extinguished. The crowd went calm and one of the firemen came through the rubble shaking his head and yelled something to his Captain below which I couldn't make out. Then the other two firemen came through the steaming front door and down the front stairs carrying something large wrapped in a tarp of some kind to a waiting ambulance.

I heard people in the crowd murmur, "Oh no!" as the firemen struggled to force the awkward load through the back doors of the ambulance. Not old enough to effectively consider what was happening, I ran to the back of the ambulance (before the days of yellow crime scene tape) to get a look. I got there just in time to see the Captain pull back the tarp from the charred body of my friend's mother. She was as stiff and lifeless as a charcoal black mannequin. It was suicide by self-immolation. Uncontrollably, I got violently sick in the street and ran back to my house in tears. Nightmares were with me for months, and I can still see her blackened body.

I had lots of injuries too, sometimes bad ones. More stitches than most other kids. From the 56 needed to repair my face, forehead and eye socket when I fell straight onto a broken bottle I had dropped on purpose, to the 36 needed to re-fix the same eye socket when my brother accidentally hit me with a golf club. The family used to say we should have had a reserved parking space at the emergency hospital just for my visits.

I always felt I was just not as tough and immune to pain like my brother. Fearlessness and courage were not strong traits of mine. Jim was amazing, and he always made me feel inferior. But what are little brothers for if not to intimidate? I was genuinely afraid to get into a fist fight. I didn't want to box or wrestle other kids because it hurt. My intimidating Uncle Shoulders always called me a girl because I wasn't tough like my cousin John or my brother. That hurt in more ways than one. So I was constantly conflicted with a desire to be seen as brave and rugged but I had an aversion to pain and discomfort which I tried to hide. Consequently, I could easily be shamed into situations in which I knew I shouldn't engage.

For instance, I tried to learn how to swim in the churning currents of the Russian River at 6 years old. I was terrified of the water, but was told the time had come for me to learn like my brother and sister had at my age. My brother was to give me a lesson. "Jimmy will be with you," they said, "there's nothing to be afraid of." I obeyed, even though I was petrified. Jim was a good swimmer and twice my size, so what could go wrong? Off we went. At his command, when I swam a few strokes into water where my feet couldn't touch bottom, panic struck like lightning. I went down for the count, breathing water through my nose and mouth in successive gulps while Jimmy watched and screamed, "Float! Float! Float!". 'How?!' I wanted to scream but was consumed with inhaling water. Fortunately, my cousin watched all of this unfold and rescued me at the last moment. I remember laying on the sand spitting up water for an eternity. I didn't try to swim nor go near the water again until I was 12. My fear of the water seemed sealed tight. I was ashamed.

Rio Nido Beach at the Russian River
Note the current

Some years later after I learned how to swim, I got enough confidence to think I had the water thing down pretty well.

Dad had treated himself to a small sailboat during my high school years, so I took up sailing on San Francisco Bay....even though I routinely got sea-sick as a kid. In fact, I was the only one in the family who got sea sick, air sick and car sick. How could that be in a Sicilian fishing family? Sailing somehow took care of my problem, and I eventually got good enough at being around or in the water to become overconfident.

One September Saturday afternoon just before I started college, Dad, a friend and I went sailing in the Bay. We raced around in our sporty sloop when we were unexpectedly caught in a violent wind shift just off of Candlestick Point which swamped us in a matter of seconds. The all wooden boat completely sunk out of sight in less than a minute. Suddenly, we were in the middle of the Bay with no lifejackets or flotation in the blustery late afternoon. Remarkably, I kept a cool head and swam around (those swimming lessons eventually paid off) and picked up anything that floated out of the cockpit for flotation and paddled back to the other two. I had both hang on to my sweatshirt while I figured what to do next.

Completely oblivious to time, temperature, weather conditions or anything else, I had to concentrate on keeping both Dad and my friend calm because they were preparing to die right there and then. So we all kicked together towards the closest buoy. Fortunately, we were rescued about an hour and a half later by a first-time boater in his big power cruiser. He thought we were scuba divers waving at him and he almost chewed us up with his twin props as he hauled us aboard.

When we got back on land, we found out the harbor master was about to call the Coast Guard for a body search. Water temp was 50 degrees. Another 15 minutes, we were told, and we would have been overtaken with hypothermia. Another near death escape, and I was not even 18. That's too many to count for a full life

And then there were the other times when I would take huge risks just to see what would happen or because I had some kind of latent death wish. Before I could even speak as a baby, in my crib I would habitually unscrew the light bulb in the wall lamp above me and stick my finger in the socket to get a shock. I was mystified by the invisible buzzing jolt I got. I always wondered about the buzz while I tried to shake the vibration out of my hand. Lucky I had little fingers.

Or when I was 15, and routinely took our jalopy-like '50 Chrysler Imperial out of the garage and drove it around Lake Merced where I pretended I was racing in the Indy 500. I would drive it at top speed risking whether or not it would hold together or disintegrate. My being under age with no license or permit added to the thrill. And so did the possibility of being stopped by the police. Crazy.

Behind this early life mosaic of near-death episodes, I privately suspected I was living life every day on borrowed time and the clock would run out on me sooner than a normal person. Most people didn't get as many chances at life as I had. So as I neared military duty, it was perfectly logical for me to obsess about my own mortality. I had to conceal the terrorizing thought that my time in Vietnam might be my Final Call. Now it seemed due. But the closer it got, the more I didn't want to face the death of others or have it happen to me. I had navigated the draft and ROTC just so I could have some control over my destiny, but that truly didn't guarantee me any peace of mind. There was too much unknown.

I kept wondering, 'Would I do anything and everything in my power to save myself even if it meant groveling, cowardice, or dishonor? Or would I accept whatever fate was going to convey, regardless of the potential danger or outcome?' I didn't know. So with all my energy and concentration, I remained committed to being an officer and a leader. I refused to allow myself room to consider doing anything other than what I was expected or ordered to do, no matter how I felt.

Vietnam might well be payback time for all of my close calls. But it was too late to re-write the earlier chapters of my luck and my gambles.

My Rendezvous with Destiny

> This war has already stretched the generation gap so wide that it threatens to pull the country apart.
> *Senator Frank Church. May, 1970*

The 101st Airborne

Long Binh Base looked better than okay to me at first glance. It seemed to have everything necessary to make life bearable in a war zone. I was relieved I would get a couple of days to stretch out from the long set of flights while the Army figured out how to use my highly sophisticated skills and training. So I found myself a bunk in the officer BOQ and started to unpack. I was getting ready to put on some civvies and lounge by the pool when, in no more than 20 minutes, I thought I heard my name over the loud speaker system. I couldn't imagine it was me, but I went back to the admin clerk and asked. Sure enough, he was looking for me. "Okay, lieutenant, we've got you assigned to a slot with the 101st Airborne." The blood ran from my face, and my knees weakened.

"Oh no, there's a mistake," I pleaded. "I'm not jump qualified, so I can't go to a jump unit."

"Oh, you don't need to be jump qualified anymore for the 101st, they're Airmobile now. They're gonna train you in their SERTS School when you get up there. There's a C123 gonna take off in about 20 minutes right out there," he pointed out a filthy window to a runway. "I just got you on the manifest, so don't miss it."

The ride to my destiny

"Wait. Wait! Wait!!! What does Airmobile mean? Where's the 101st? What the fuck is SERTS? Who can I talk to about this? Something's wrong here! I worked for SEARS! I could be a supply officer or something else. I'm not a killer, I'm a CIVILIAN! I need a different assignment." The groveling had begun. The rest of my life suddenly looked very short.

With a "you-gotta-be-kidding" huff he said, "Airmobile means you move by helicopter and you rappel out of it. SERTS is Screamin' Eagles Replacement Training School and they're gonna teach you how to work with choppers and rappel when you get up there. The 101st is up on the DMZ…they just came off of Hamburger Hill," he said with a bit of menacing delight. "You can talk to the colonel if you want, but he ain't gonna change nothin'."

"I want to see him, please"

He was right. The Lt. Col. Personnel Officer listened impatiently as I whined about what was happening to me and how wrong it was. He waited until I was finished and said, "Okay, Lieutenant, let me tell you something. Today's Army is an Army of choices, so here you go. See that C123 out there? It's taking off in about 15 minutes and you can have your ass on it *or* you can wait here for the next bus over to Long Binh Jail. It's your choice."

My fear was now instantly divided between coward-like insubordination to save my life or of following orders to what I thought to be an almost certain death. Neither choice was attractive. So when in doubt, follow orders. "Yes, Sir," I threw on a set of jungle fatigues, re-packed my gear and hustled out to the plane as it was warming up. The loadmaster asked me if I was the guy going to Phu Bai. I shrugged. "The 101st?" he yelled over the deafening sound of the engines hitting full pitch. I nodded. I couldn't speak I was gagging so much on near tears and vile stench while in a state of disbelief. He smiled and gave me thumbs up. We took off quickly with Vietnamese civilians on board with their goats, chickens, and ducks like a flying Noah's Ark. This was really happening to me!

As we flew north, I looked out at the odd terrain below: coastline, flat rice paddies, huge dark green mountains to the west touching the clouds. There was not a 2 story building to be seen anywhere—just flimsy shacks for living made from grass and used cardboard boxes along with indiscriminately dug round graves of '68 Tet Offensive casualties. It was an uncivilized mess and impossible to imagine why we were spilling our blood here. Out of the corner of my eye I thought I could see flashes and then puffs of smoke popping intermittently on the ground, some areas more intensely than others. I didn't want to look or sound stupid, so I pointed them out to the load master without saying anything but with an obvious questioning look on my face. "Mortars and artillery!" he shouted. I swallowed hard and decided not to look any more.

About 45 minutes into the noisy flight, he came back to where I was sitting and yelled in my ear, "We can't land at Phu Bai 'cause they're taking too much incoming. We're gonna drop you at Evans. "Oh. Where's that?" as if it would make any difference even if I knew its location. "It's a little further north, just about on the DMZ." The nightmare was getting worse.

Cushy Camp Evans, 3rd Brigade HQ,
Home to 2/506th Curahees, 101st Airborne

We finally landed at Evans on a PSP landing strip like the ones on Okinawa or Tarawa. It was a god-forsaken old Marine base camp about 6 km from the DMZ. There were no dental clinics, restaurants, swimming pools, basketball courts, driving range, bowling alley, or Chase Manhattan Bank. This sure wasn't Long Binh or Kansas, Toto. It was the logistical support base for the northern part of I Corps along the DMZ out to Laos, and was intentionally maintained as a tough, minimalist outpost of the 101st for good reason. It was routinely attacked.

From the air as we landed, I could see Camp Evans was well dug in and sandbagged with a high berm and triple concertina wire. In fact, it was considered cushy by 101st standards because it was a brigade headquarters. It had tents and cots for sleeping rather than a poncho liner and bunker but no running water and no toilets. There were Claymore anti-personnel mines, Foo gas (napalm) barrels, and triple trenching with concertina razor wire around the perimeter. 'Maybe this will be my base,' I thought. My hopes were dropping steadily with the changing geography and the degrees of perceived safety.

After the C123 jerked to a fast stop to avoid being mortared, I jumped out as fast as I could. The plane spun around and took off in a cloud of dust. When the prop-wash debris settled, waiting for me at the end of the airstrip was a jeep and driver. He pulled up alongside of me and asked if I was Lt. Baffico. He was there to drive me down Highway 1 to Camp Eagle to report. I asked him if it was safe to drive on this infamous road (snipers, ambushes and roadside bombings happened almost every day). My imagination was in high gear.

He laughed and said, "Yeah, sure. It's just about 20 miles. I brought you an M16, just in case." Twenty miles through unprotected, wide open rice paddies did not seem like a pleasure ride to me, but I had no choice. I grabbed the rifle and pointed it outside the jeep as I checked magazines and ammo. I tried to remember the basic stuff about using it. I felt a moment of slight relief when I found the selector switch and put it on full automatic. No single shots for this trooper!

The ride down Highway 1 was tense. My head was on a swivel as I looked for areas of potential ambush, assessed every Vietnamese and every water buffalo (water buffalo could bite me as far as I knew) with an eye of mistrust and suspicion. I was too wound up with fear to keep up with the driver's chit chat as he tried to make conversation.

After about 15 minutes of intense observation, I saw the driver suddenly lunge forward and grab thin air, "Awww, SHIT!" he screamed. I heard something snap above my head. My index finger went to the trigger, thumb on the selector. We screeched to a halt, and he jumped out and walked back down the road very carefully. Instinctively, I got out and followed in his footsteps like a little brother. I couldn't figure out how to look cool with my rifle while being scared out of my mind. So I did one of those macho Terminator moves walking backwards behind him while sweeping my rifle from side to side.

"Shiiiiiiiittt!" he screeched. "Look here L.T. It must be a dud round 'cause I know I hit that wire hard." I looked down at the side of the road and saw what he was pointing at. There it was. A 105 howitzer round packed in mud connected to the trip wire we had just hit and aimed to blow the jeep to pieces. I swallowed hard and couldn't say anything. I was so scared I couldn't separate reality from the terror in my mind. 'Did that just happen to me, or was it some sort of fear-induced hallucination?' I kept shaking my head as though I had just taken a hard punch. But the silence of the driver told me it had really happened. He was finally scared too. I thought no one would ever believe me if I told them I was this lucky on my first day in country. You just never heard those stories...you only heard the ones about guys trying to find a piece of an unlucky buddy's body to confirm his KIA status on his first day or week. I was silent and wobbly the rest of the ride to Camp Eagle. My thoughts were out of control, 'What am I doing here? Get home! I can't do this!'

When we arrived at Eagle, I was dropped off at the A Company, 501st Signal Battalion Orderly Room to report for duty. It was called a hootch and was a plywood hut with a tin roof and triple sandbags 360 degrees around it. The heat, humidity, crude conditions and the stench of burning shit was asphyxiating. I wondered how anyone could survive it all for a year.

The morning burn

Groveling

Still shaking, I tried to compose myself enough to look cool and to report to the Company Clerk properly when a tall Airborne Ranger 1st LT came popping in and extended his hand, "Hi, I'm Jack Hopke. Welcome to the 501st. I hear you had a little excitement getting up here. Don't worry, that's not normal. It's actually pretty secure around here as long as you stay inside the wire." 'This guy must be a lifer and nuts too,' I thought. I had little trust in lifers.

"Yeah. Mmmm. Thanks. I'm having a hard time believing I am here, let alone being booby-trapped on my first day."

"Yeah, well it could get worse. I have a feeling you are going to get assigned to the VHF platoon as their platoon leader, and that would not be good. We burn through those guys pretty fast. So when Capt. Gray calls you in today, tell him you'll do anything but VHF"

"What the hell is a VHF platoon? I have an MOS for heavy duty long range microwave. Isn't that why I'm here?"

"Don't think so, but do anything else but VHF. It's a bad deal. These guys are on choppers with the Infantry every day, all day placing this new phone technology in the bush so they can talk to us over secure phone radio. It's new stuff and the 101st is the only unit with it. Trouble is you have to go everywhere the action is, and air assault in. It's bad shit."

"Oh fuck!" I screamed, "This can't be happening to me! I was a lousy ROTC cadet! Look at my records, you assholes! I don't know anything about this shit, and I am not a fucking lifer like you are! They can't do this to me. I'm not trained. I am a lousy reserve officer!" More pleading on my part and it didn't work. More weakness in my knees. Hopke never lost his smile as he said, "Hey, I'm ROTC too out of Dartmouth. This place *is* fucked up, but you can do it. I hear you're from California. That's a big plus here because you aren't a Yankee and you're not a Red Neck. They're going to love you and respect you. That's big. You'll be okay."

I regained a modicum of composure and thought, 'Maybe I should listen to him. He is obviously smart and knows his way around. And he knows how to talk to me. I think I like him. At least I'll stay close to him until I get my feet on the ground.'

"Lemme show you to your hootch," Hopke said. "You can get unwound while you wait to talk to Gray." He led me down the hill and told me he would take care of getting my paperwork squared away.

In my hootch writing home the week I reported to the 101st

The junior officers' hootch was dug in and sandbagged like all the others, but stark and dreary. It was for cherries (new reports), and I was more than qualified. I was the only one in it. Other officers had been there long enough to have staked out much better living arrangements. It was called "time in country". I had one day, so I picked out a bunk and dropped. I was hot, exhausted, and tight. I lay there wondering how I would be killed and how long it would be. I couldn't help tallying up my chances for survival while I waited for my sentencing from Captain Gray. Hopke had unequivocally warned me. Flying on helicopters was dangerous living. Your chance of being shot down and killed was three times greater than an Infantryman on the ground. 'This can't get much worse. I'm going to have to beg for mercy or disobey orders', I thought.

Two hours later I was summoned to the Orderly Room by Gray. I did the best begging and groveling I could muster. But in short order I was assigned to be the VHF platoon leader. Neither argument nor dramatized pleading had any effect with Gray. He was a career soldier who had made his way to Captain through the enlisted ranks. I am sure he took delight in seeing a college ROTC boy sweat profusely and beg for reason and mercy. But I didn't care my cowardice showed. "You'll be replacing Lt. Steadman, and he'll show you the ropes tomorrow. We have a chopper coming in at 0600 to take you out. Get some rest. You'll need it."

I went back to the hootch and lay on the bunk staring at the tin roof. I thought of my choices. It was hard for me to believe I was going to live through a daily existence hoping to make it mission by mission, but it was the unvarnished truth. It was demoralizing, to say the least. But, I thought, I was not going to embarrass myself or disobey orders my first day in war…

Sleep was out of the question. I wasn't tired but I was exhausted. I wasn't hungry…there was nothing to eat anyway. I wished I had a little alcohol, but it was out of the question. My fear wouldn't subside. After all my unexpected brushes with death up to this point in my life, I couldn't believe I had been so swiftly ordered to an almost certain one. I began to tally my life vs. death balance sheet to mathematically conclude that the time for my dying had likely arrived. The irony was more than I could process.

Darkness fell. The exhaustion from my obsessive thinking finally overtook me. I dosed off in my underwear only to be awakened by successive explosions and the sound of shrapnel hitting every hard surface around me. The concussions continued to get closer and the sound of tinkling on the tin roof increased to golf-ball sized hail. I heard "Incoming!!!!" being yelled as sirens went off all around.

Completely alone and enveloped in my own panic, I instinctively flipped out of the rack onto my belly and low crawled below the sandbag line to get to cover outside. I found a small hole to crawl into. I remember digging with my bare hands trying to get lower while I held my bowels as tight as I could. I couldn't bear the thought of dying and being found in soiled underwear. Mom told me it would be the worst embarrassment I could ever suffer. That's how twisted my mind was.

The attack was over in about 10 minutes. I came out to find guys laughing at me as I dusted off. "What?!!" I spit back.

"They weren't that close," one of them guffawed, "Didn't you hear them walking the rounds towards us? We had plenty of time. You'll get used to it, and you'll eventually be able to tell incoming from outgoing," another said. Not sure I wanted to acquire the skill. I was shook up.

101st airpower at Eagle: Serious Airmobile

At daylight on my way down to the helipad for my first day of flying, I looked around to see what damage had been done. Impaled a good 6 inches into a nearby pole was a piece of corrugated tin roof which had been blown off. The pole was also riddled with fleshette nails from our own anti-personnel rockets. One of the enemy mortars had scored a direct hit on a fully loaded Cobra attack helicopter on station about 200 yards from us. The Cobra blew to pieces and all his armament cooked off over the base camp. Pilot and co-pilot killed and many injuries all around. Not so funny and not so routine. It didn't help my frame of mind or reduce the tautness in my body as I prepared to make my first combat assault. My mind couldn't stop racing. I wished I could have a drink.

'I'll never make it. Too much, too close, and too soon. I'm dead.'

Real or imagined, a scene replayed in your mind every day.

MYTH VS. FACT

> The great enemy of the truth is very often not the lie -- deliberate, contrived and dishonest, but the myth, persistent, persuasive, and unrealistic. Belief in myths allows the comfort of opinion without the discomfort of thought.
>
> *John F. Kennedy*

President Johnson and Secretary of Defense McNamara

Our country has struggled for decades with the culpability for Vietnam. For various reasons, it is the result of many controversial issues, the principal one being the never-ending moral debate about the essential rightness or wrongness of the war and whether or not the deaths of 58,300 Americans were necessary. The debate has been characterized by false assumptions, misinformation, faulty history and reconstituted lies. What are usually missing are the facts, and those have been traditionally hard to uncover. Why? The lack of a thorough and unbiased diplomatic analysis of the situation combined with an expedient political justification for our involvement in the war in Vietnam gave rise to dishonesty in White House communications that later became endemic.

Faulty reasoning on the part of presidential advisers both civilian and military in the Kennedy White House was the conspicuous characteristic of an arrogant and uninformed U.S. diplomatic policy during the Kennedy segment of the Cold War. The Bay of Pigs Disaster, the pusillanimous U.S. reaction to the construction of the Berlin Wall, the humiliation of Kennedy by Khrushchev, and the Domino Theory are a few examples of major blunders. Today Vietnam stands alone as a unique and continuous catastrophe in U.S. history which was principally caused by politics, hubris, egos, lies and the lack of a rigorously honest assessment of the goal or mission beginning with Kennedy and enduring through the Johnson and Nixon Administrations. Subsequent efforts to suppress the lack of exactitude began a torrent of misinformation which has never been rectified.

Taylor

Lodge

Bundy

Westmorland

The condition was exacerbated by the outright dishonesty of the powerful political and military leaders of the times: Lyndon B. Johnson, Robert S. McNamara (Secretary of Defense), General Maxwell Taylor (Presidential

Military Advisor; Chairman, JCS), Henry Cabot Lodge (U.S. Vietnam Ambassador), McGeorge Bundy (National Security Advisor), and General William Westmoreland. A steady diet of their deceitfulness was fed to the American public through a manipulated media. Add to this, the pugnacious and antiquated advice of General Taylor and the bickering Joint Chiefs of Staff juxtaposed with the lack of a clear mission-specific strategy, and the formula for a world-stage sized embarrassment was complete. The poorly veiled misinformation and skullduggery employed by each administration throughout the Vietnam Era amplified the ugly underpinnings of a U.S. military and diplomatic humiliation which will never be forgotten.

For all these reasons, what little people do know today about the U.S. involvement in Vietnam is generally incorrect. Most of what they claim to know is either made up of old sound bites left over from the myth and folklore of 60's, or just malformed stories passed through generations. Unfortunately, Hollywood has filled the historical void about Vietnam with movies and drama which exploited the war for artistic interpretation and commercial gain while offering little truth or fact.

U.S. involvement in Vietnam deeply scarred many people, understandably. The stain on the country's proud history cannot be removed. Actually, if one looks closely, the pathology which was born as a result of the diplomatic, political, military and communication transgressions during the Vietnam War continue to both inform and plague every sitting President since.

One thing which must be genuinely improved is the accurate teaching of the history of this tragedy, which is a significant imperative for our culture in light of the still somewhat volatile facets of the narrative. And it becomes more difficult to assess the facts forensically with each passing year.

Our education system was initially intimidated by the controversy of this war, and there were few if any real efforts to learn it correctly until recent years. But the perceived similarities of the Vietnam War to our country's latest wars almost demand it. Unfortunately, the points of accurate reference about Vietnam for both are limited.

For over 30 years, however, The Wall has silently been setting the record straight through the vigilant work of the Vietnam Veterans Memorial Fund and its dedicated volunteers. The Wall is primarily a living memorial, but it also represents a source of facts. The rangers and the docents who man the Memorial are fiercely proud of the accuracy they bring to this history. To that end, each ranger and docent carries the following information when they work. The facts have been compiled by volunteers Allen McCabe and proofed by Dan Arant through hundreds of hours of tedious work. Most volunteers have every line memorized so as to not hesitate when asked a question. It is included herein not to overwhelm the reader, but to point out how the powerful and simple symbolism of The Wall masks profound and somber information enclosed in the presentation of the names.

> No event in American history is more misunderstood than the Vietnam War. It was misreported then, and it is misremembered now.
> *Richard M. Nixon, 1985*

History / Important Dates / Background

by Allen McCabe with proofing by Dan Arant

1. French Indochina – had been under French control since 1882 (except Laos – added 1893). French began initial conquest of the area in the 1840's.
2. French defeated at Dien Bien Phu after 6-week siege, 7-May 1954. (2 U.S. pilots flying for 'Civil Air Transport' (CAT) died in plane crash from anti-aircraft fire while ferrying in supplies to French during the siege). Not on The Wall–Civilian. French did not fully leave Vietnam until 1957.
3. The 1st 128 U.S. Advisors in 'French Indochina' (MAAG/I) arrived 17-Sep 1950 in support of the French – training on U.S. equipment only – no active role in combat. Truman administration. U.S. elects to support France in our fight against Communism (domino theory – China fell to Communism in 1949, South Korea attacked 1950)

4. The 1st 'official' confirmed death – Richard B. Fitzgibbon Jr.: 8-Jun 1956 (added 1999 – Panel 52E, Line 21) (Fitzgibbon was murdered by a fellow USAF SSgt – who died in Vietnam but name is not on The Wall). Fitzgibbon's son, Richard, also died in Vietnam 7-Sep 1965 - LCPL Marines (in 'correct' chronological order on 2E, Line 77)
5. 2nd 'official' death, added later to The Wall – Harry Cramer, died 21-Oct 1957 - debate on whether or not a training accident. Wall initially started with deaths from enemy fire – Dale Buis & Chester Ovnand, killed 8-Jul 1959. Buis and Ovnand were the only 2 who died in 1959, 3rd name – Maurice Flournoy – died 21-Feb 1960.
6. 12-Feb 1955 / 1st advisors for South Vietnam – pre MAAG/V. MAAG/V: 1-Nov 1955 (earliest official date of eligibility)
7. Geneva Peace Accords (never signed) 21-Jul 1954 finalized division of 'French Indochina' into Cambodia, Laos, North Vietnam, South Vietnam. North/South Vietnam division was supposed to be only 'temporary' until July 1956 elections
8. Gulf of Tonkin; 2 and 4-Aug 1964. USS Maddox attacked on 2-August by North Vietnamese gun boats. Defense Secretary Robert McNamara, in 2004 documentary 'The Fog of War' says 'It never happened' (4 -Aug attack). Gulf of Tonkin Resolution' (7-Aug 1964 passed, 10-Aug signed) permits President unrestricted authority to wage war on North Vietnam. Senate vote 88-2; (Wayne Morse & Ernest Gruening oppose); House vote 416-0 in favor of the resolution.
9. Mayaguez Rescue: 13-15 May 1975. 23 USAF killed on 13-May en route to staging area from Thailand base. The last 18 names on the Wall were killed in battle on 15-May 1975 on/near Koh Tang (island) – Cambodia. 41 of the last 42 names are Mayaguez- related deaths (23+18). The crew of the Mayaguez totaled 40 – all rescued.
10. Peak U.S. Troop strength (in country) 30-Apr 1969 543,482 The last ground patrol 5-Aug 1972, by Delta Company, 3rd Bn., 21st Infantry
11. Last Combat Unit out 23-Aug 1972: 3rd Bn., 21st Infantry. Next to last out: 1st Battalion, 7th Calvary, 1st Calvary Division, 22 -Aug 1972

12. 16-Mar 1968/ My Lai 2-Sep 1969 Ho Chi Minh dies Battle for Hue/31-Jan thru 26 Feb 1968 (142 Marines killed, 75 Army)
13. 30-Apr 1970/ Cambodia invasion – this lead to: 4-May 1970 Kent State ('4 dead in Ohio' sang Crosby, Stills, Nash, and Young) + 2 killed at Jackson State, 14-May
14. 1-Jan 1972 / down to 133,000 total troop in country; 27-Jan 1973 Paris Peace Accords 10-20 May 1969/Hamburger Hill/ A Shau Valley / 101st Airborne/70 KIA
15. 'The 10,000 day war' – from 26-Sep 1945 – 15-May 1975 (10,848 actual) (Peter Dewey - Mayaguez).
16. 29-Jul 1967 – USS Forrestal – 134 killed. Panels 23E-24E (Senator John McCain was a Naval aviator on the Forrestal)
17. 1st regular U.S. military ground troops into Vietnam: 2 battalions of the 9th Marine Expeditionary Brigade (MEB), 8-Mar 1965 – Da Nang
18. 627 civilian women served with the American Red Cross' 'Supplemental Recreation Activities Overseas' (SRAO) program from 1965-1972. (aka 'Donut Dollies') logged over 17,000 miles monthly by helicopter during year-long tours to play diversionary games, visit hospitals, and staff rec centers as respite for troops. 4 died in Vietnam.
19. Panel 3E – Ia Drang Valley – 1st Major battle between U.S. and NVA forces. 14-18, Nov 1965. 234 1st Cav killed over 4 days. 'We Were Soldiers Once, and Young' Authors – Reporter, Joe Galloway and LTG, Hal Moore. Movie does not show the 4th day, when losses totaled 155 of the 234. Galloway, a civilian, later awarded the Bronze Star with 'V' device for heroism.
20. Actor Chuck Norris' brother, Wieland Norris (Panel 9W, Line 5) and Buffalo Bills' pro football player James Kalsu (Panel 8W, Line 38) died with 101st Airborne at or near Firebase Ripcord, A Shau Valley - summer 1970. This major battle kept secret/classified for many years – it occurred right after Kent State.
21. Shea and Nystul - Marines (Helicopter crashed in South China Sea) and McMahon and Judge – Marines killed during rocket attack on

Tan Sun Nhut airport outside Saigon. All 4 died 29-Apr 1975 - The last 4 '*Vietnam*' deaths on The Wall (1W, Line 124)

22. William Nolde (1W, Line 112) often called 'last killed in the war' – killed 27-Jan 1973 (day of Paris Peace Accords)
23. The Draft/Lottery – First Draft Lottery (by birth date drawing) on 1-December 1969 (took up to #195). Before then, a local Draft Board would select. Last lottery for Vietnam on 2-February 1972 for men born in 1953. None called up. 1971 lottery took up to #95. 1.7 million drafted overall during the war years (not all went to Vietnam).
24. Air Campaigns: Operation 'Rolling Thunder (N. Vietnam targets): 1965-68. Operation 'Linebacker' (N. Vietnam targets) Spring – Fall of 1972 Operation 'Ranch Hand' (Defoliants): 1962-71 (19 million total gallons of herbicides, includes 11 million of 'Agent Orange'). Operation 'Linebacker II': December 1972 Operation 'Arc Light' (B-52 raids, primarily S. Vietnam targets) 1965 – 1973

Casualties / statistics

About 1.5 - 2.0 million Vietnamese died during 'the American War' Estimated 800,000 - 1,100,000 North Vietnamese troops (including Viet Cong); 300,000 + South Vietnamese troops; and up to 400,000 civilians (North and South).

25. Over 153,000 U.S. soldiers were wounded in Southeast Asia from 1955 – 1975 (requiring hospital care) Approx. 220,000 Purple Hearts awarded in Vietnam.
26. Roughly another 150,000 listed as 'wounded', but not requiring hospital care. Approximately 23,000 wounded considered 100% disabled.
27. 3.4 million U.S. servicemen and women served in Southeast Asia from 1955 – 1975. This includes slightly over 500,000 Navy - South China Sea.
28. 9.1 million men and women in U.S. Military service in total from 4-Aug 1964 (Gulf of Tonkin attack) to 28-Mar 1973 – last POW's released.

29. Numbers vary on total U.S. Military women who served in Vietnam. 8,500 is close. (Diane Carlson Evans' number). NPS says about 10,000. About 85% nurses.
30. Vietnam War Unknown Soldier: Michael Blassie, 1 W, Line 23. Exhumed 14-May 1998, identity confirmed. Reburied in St. Louis 11-Jul 1998
31. Maj. Charles Kelly, 1E/52 of the 57th Medical Detachment, call sign 'DUSTOFF', killed 1-July 1964. Later medical evac operations took the name 'dustoff' from Kelly.
32. The youngest killed - Dan Bullock (23W, Line 96), on 7-Jun 1969 at age 15 - USMC. Next day - Sharon Lane, only U.S. military woman killed by enemy fire.
33. *Oldest to die in Vietnam*: Kenna Taylor, 7W, Line 82 (62 years old). *Oldest to die of wounds*/died 2002-added 2003: Luther Huddleston, 16E, Line 109 (68 years old)
34. Average Declared Dead/MIA per Day in 1968: 45 Average per day 1959 – 1975: 10 Average per day during 7 worst years (65-71): 22
35. Average declared dead/MIA's per day in WWII: 290 (19,000 dead/ missing at Battle of the Bulge, over 12,000 at Okinawa, over 6,500 at Iwo Jima)
36. The Women: Sharon Lane 23W 112; Eleanor Alexander 31E 8; Hedwig Orlowski 31E 15; Pamela Donovan 53W 43; Annie Ruth Graham 48W 12; Mary Klinker 1W 122; Carol Drazba 5E 46; Elizabeth Jones 5E 47 Deaths vs. Served: 1.7% (58,282/3,400,000) 2.0% if Navy excluded
37. Drazba and Jones, the first 2 women, died together on 18- Feb 1966 in helicopter crash, piloted by Charles Honour.
38. Mary Klinker died in C-5A plane crash 4-Apr 1975 during Operation 'Babylift' – orphan evacuation from Saigon. 155 on plane were killed.
39. Worst Day: 31-Jan 1968 / 246 'Declared Dead/MIA' (35E L84 – 36E L44) ; Worst Week: 5-11 May 1968 / 616 'Declared Dead/MIA'
40. Declared Dead/MIA / by Branch: 38,264 Army; 2,564 USN; 2,585 USAF; 14,862 USMC; 7 USCG

41. Declared Dead/MIA / by Year (worst 7) : 1968: 16,594/ 1969: 11,624/ 1967: 11,156/ 1966: 6,154/ 1970: 6,085 /1971: 2,359 / 1965:1,863
42. Declared Dead/MIA / Officers/Enlisted: Total officers: 7,904; Enlisted 50,378
43. Declared Dead/MIA / by Enlistment: 34,671 Regular, 5,810 Reserves, 101 National Guard, 17,700 Drafted (30.4%) Nearly 70% enlisted
44. Declared Dead/MIA / by State (top 7): CA / 5575; NY / 4120; TX /3416; PA / 3143; OH / 3097; IL / 2935; MI / 2655
45. Declared Dead/MIA / Race mix: 81.1% Caucasian; 12.5% African American; 5.2% Hispanic; 1.2% othe Frequently Requested
46. Declared Dead/MIA / Religion mix: 64.4% Protestant, 28.9% Catholic; 6.7% other/none
47. Declared Dead/MIA / Officers (non-Navy): Maj Gen/5; Brig Gen/6; Col/232; Lt Col/333; Maj/733; Captain/18821st Lt/2021; 2nd Lt /1788; WO/1274; 629 Navy including 1 Rear Admiral and 26 Captains.
48. Declared Dead/MIA / Last Name (5 most frequent) : 667/Smith; 526/ Johnson; 406/Williams; 383/Brown; 350/Jones
49. POW's: 771 total captured. 114 died in captivity or are still listed as MIA. Last prisoner released 1-April 1973.
50. Average age of those declared dead/MIA was 22 years 9 months old – not 19. Draftees averaged 19 years old – but they were only 30% of the total.
51. Declared Dead/MIA / African American represented 12.5% of total; while African Americans in total U.S. population of draftable-age was 13.5% (1964-1973)
52. State with highest percentage 'declared dead/MIA': West Virginia, with 84.1 of every 100,000 males. National average 58.9 per 100,000.
53. Longest held POW (from any American war in history)– Capt. Floyd 'Jim' Thompson, U.S. Army 'Green Beret' from 26-Mar 1964 thru 28-Mar 1973. 9 years, 2 days. Died 16-Jul 2002 in Key West, Fl.
54. 246 Medal of Honor recipients from Vietnam -154 of them awarded posthumously. 91 lived to be awarded the Medal. 155 Medal of Honor recipients on The Wall.

55. 57 men on The Wall are listed as 'Canadians' in the directory. The Canadian Vietnam Veterans Memorial (called The North Wall) in Windsor, Ontario, lists 103.

The Memorial – The Wall, 3 Servicemen, Women's Memorial, In Memory

56. 58,282 names are on The Wall as of Memorial Day 2012 (10 names added May 2012). Font: Digitized version of Optima. Lettering is .53 inches high
57. 507 MIA's have been changed to declared dead since The Wall was dedicated (including 12 in May 2012) – dropping the total MIA count to 749. VVMF say 1,256 MIA were listed on The Wall when dedicated in 1982. 137 Lines on the tallest panels.
58. Panel 1E covers period from 8-Jul 1959 thru 6-June 1965; Panel 1W covers 15-Apr 1972 thru 15-May 1975 Angle of walls: 125 degrees, 12 minutes
59. 9 years covered on 1E and 1 W. Other 7 years – 138 panels. 1968 alone requires 72 of 140 panels – last 37 east and last 35 west.
60. Panel 70E ends with Jesse Alba, alphabetically the first casualty on 25-May 1968. Panel 70 W begins with John Anderson, 25-May 1968
61. '3 Servicemen' statue sculpted by Frederick Hart, local DC artist - deceased. Dedicated Veterans Day 1984. Weapons – M-60, .45, and M-16.
62. Spare black granite panels are stored at Quantico Marine Corps base in Virginia. They are blank. *Wall temperature recorded at 1430 hrs on 25-Aug 2007: 150 degrees*
63. Granite is from Bangalore, India. – and was used because of its deep colour and consistency. 5 ft. panel weighs 875 lbs. 10 ft. panel weighs 1750 lbs.
64. The Wall represents a 'cut' or 'gash' in the earth, as 21-year old Maya Lin envisioned the hillside being peeled back to

65. 59 U.S. Civilian women died in Vietnam – 37 of them in plane crash with Mary Klinker. No civilians 'officially' listed on the Wall – but 1 listed by mistake.
66. 'In Memory Day' previously held on 'Patriots Day', 3rd Monday in April, (19-Apr 1775 was battle of Lexington and Concord), honor those men and women who died as a result of their service in southeast Asia whose names were not eligible to be added to The Wall.
67. 'In Memory' plaque dedicated 10-Nov 2004. 24 x 36 inches, black granite. Authorized by Congress April 2000.
68. All of the names on The Wall were read aloud – in chronological order - during dedication, on 10th (1992), 20th (2002), and 25th (2007) anniversaries.
69. The Wall is 246 feet, 9 inches long in both east and west directions. 10 feet, 6 inches tall at apex.
70. Name additions, spelling corrections, and MIA to 'Declared Dead' status done by James Lee of 'Engrave Write' of Colorado – generally done in May of each year.
71. A diamond is 'declared/presumed dead' – either KIA or death from other causes (10,786). About 900 'declared dead' on The Wall are 'body not recovered'. Some groups consider these men still 'missing'. Slightly less than 1,700 bodies not recovered from Southeast Asia, but DOD does not consider them all 'missing'.
72. A '+' symbol is 'missing in action/status unknown'. There are no circles around any '+' symbols as no missing has ever been found alive.
73. Good example of a name addition for visitors is Billy Smith on 1E, line 42. He was seriously wounded 8-Nov 1963 and died 7-Oct 1995. He was added prior to Memorial Day 1999 – and was placed as close to those men he served with in 1963 as possible. Note lighter colour/ less weathering.
74. 343 names added since 1984 - 110 added in 1986 - most were airmen flying combat missions from Thailand, but President Reagan ruled them eligible. 68 added in 1983 – most were Marines killed in plane crash in Hong Kong on R & R.. The other 165 were mostly men who

were accidentally left off or died after The Wall was dedicated from combat wounds. ** E. Alan Brudno (5E, Line 2) – was a suicide in the States. Brudno had been a POW from 18-Oct 1965 thru 28-Mar 1973 (7.5 years)

75. Estimated - 38 men were mistakenly listed on The Wall at dedication who were still alive. These names are not listed in the directories, but are in the total count.
76. Memorabilia left at The Wall is stored in a climate-controlled warehouse in Landover, Maryland, managed by Park Service. Flowers and perishable food are not kept. Over 130,000 items are cataloged. Some items are on display at 'The Price of Freedom' in the Smithsonian's National Museum of American History.
77. The flag base contains the emblems of all 5 branches of service including Coast Guard.
78. 2003 law requires the POW flag to fly at all national military memorials – including Korea, WWII, and Vietnam and national military cemeteries.
79. The names of Maya Lin, Jan Scruggs, 1982 members of the VVMF board, advisors, and architect Cooper-Lecky are engraved on the top, back side of the memorial.
80. Vietnam Veterans Memorial Fund founded 27-April 1979 by a group of Vietnam Veterans led by Jan Scruggs.

TAKING OVER

While the rest of the world wondered why, the Screaming Eagles fought and died in some of the fiercest battles of the Vietnam War. In just under seven years, the 101st had twice as many casualties in Vietnam as it did in WWII.

Learning to rappel at 101st SERTS School at Camp Evans, Vietnam

Highway to the Danger Zone

After being assigned as VHF Platoon leader and getting the lay of Camp Eagle, the 101st base camp, I was sent to Camp Evans for a week of training in the SERTS Airmobile School: rappelling, weapons, tactics, Division Standard Operating Procedures, Division Rules of Engagement, more weapons training and Division uniform protocol. Because I had gone through formal Vietnam training twice in the States, I thought the third time would be a waste of time. But after my first day in country surviving booby traps and incoming mortars, it was obvious I needed every minute of any extra training I could get.

Lasting approximately a week, Veteran 101st cadre instructors imparted hard-learned lessons orientating green troopers like me to the rigors of jungle warfare and the tactics of the cunning enemy. Strenuous physical training and running exercises were mixed in, more so to acclimate and condition us to the brutal tropical weather in hopes of reducing heat prostration cases once we got into real live action. I also realized being with a group of professional killers was probably the best thing that could happen to a city boy like me who had never hunted a rabbit or killed a mouse. These guys were *serious*. They were good and they stood above and alone when compared to other units.

Our uniform protocol was an interesting example. The 101st was the only American unit in Vietnam authorized to wear their Screaming Eagle unit patch in full color. All other units and branches had to wear subdued olive drab color for better camouflage rather than standard color patches. Not the 101st Airborne. No sir. They wouldn't think of hiding behind a camouflage patch. Why? It was simple. Because they don't hide from anyone or anything--any time. So there it was, our perfect bright Screaming Eagle on our left shoulder.

It was said most North Vietnamese had never seen a bald eagle, so they called the 101st soldiers "Chicken Men" or "Rooster Men." Viet Cong commanders were rumored to regularly include in their briefings strict instructions about avoiding confrontation with the "Chicken Men" at all costs, as they were sure to lose. This legend has remained a source of fierce pride among all 101st. Veterans to this day.

After a demanding week of SERTS training, I went back to Camp Eagle to officially take over my platoon. Steadman had gone home, and the platoon was mine to lead with Staff Sargent Bob Minteer, a career Non-Commissioned Officer. Bob was from Harrisburg, PA on his second tour and was a hardened, well-regarded NCO. He knew how to do his job and had a good rapport with the men. His professionalism made my job a lot easier.

Our VHF platoon ran equipment which gave any friendly ground commander full secure wireless telephone communication with all his higher command and support needs: tactical air support, artillery support, Division HQ, and logistics. While crude and cumbersome, the equipment was the first experimental stage of what eventually evolved into cell phone technology. However, it required 2-3 men to set up and keep it operational 24-7. It was a vital communication advantage, so we were always in heavy demand.

There were usually between 15-25 active locations where my teams were positioned. The number changed because we moved with any friendly Infantry, and they moved in pursuit of the NVA. Most installations were Fire Support Bases (firebases) carved out on remote mountain tops in the middle of treacherous triple canopy jungle terrain. On the firebases there were heavy artillery batteries supporting the ground troops who fought NVA troops infiltrating on the Ho Chi Minh trail from Laos. Access to these critical installations was by helicopter only, and missions flying over the ongoing ground battles were perilous. Firebases were intentionally located in the middle of the major NVA concentrations, so contact with the enemy was daily and unusually heavy. Air assaults gave us the ability to helicopter into and place artillery and communications equipment in the middle of enemy movements and then move out quickly if the situation dictated. The 101st was the only U.S division who operated with this kind of mobility, training, communications and firepower.

1st Lt. Baffico, VHF Platoon leader
B Co., 501st Sig. Bn., 101st Airborne

My major responsibility as the platoon leader was to keep my men ready, mobile, fresh, informed, fed, protected, reasonably happy, and marginally healthy in the hostile environment. To me, that meant I had to make myself available to them and check their daily lives routinely. There was only one way I could do that. I had to helicopter out to their locations as often as possible and bring them what they needed or relieve them for some stand down time.

My approach was a marked change from Rich Steadman. He was a good enough manager, but not a leader. He did most of the job from the rear. Rich was consumed with being shot down or stranded in enemy territory, so he protected himself by hanging back. The men did not appreciate it. He was known as Lt. REMF (Rear Echelon Mother Fucker) to the platoon.

After SERTS training, my perilous first day reporting, and a week of flying combat assaults, I realistically began to consider that, 'I'm probably going die here and there is nothing I can do about it no matter what training, defense, or weapon I want to load up on. When it happens it happens. It's fate. Worrying about it might make me crazy and my chances worse, not better. With the responsibility of sending men into danger, I probably shouldn't think any other way.' This consideration helped me to face my fate with my own style of bravura and to hope for good outcomes.

As strange as it may seem, the rationale helped me settle down. In hindsight, it was my first harsh risk-assessment test. It forced me to learn how to face risk, develop priorities and to direct people under pressure, in real time.

By the second week of flying missions, I felt less scared and a dash more confident. I had gotten along well with the men I met, and they responded positively to my grip-and-grin style of working with them on their turf. The grueling, pressurized, long hours of activity were hard, but they made me feel like I contributed. I didn't focus exclusively on me, and it was satisfying to know I could be of value to the hard working warrior. For my first two weeks of flying I managed to keep my mind off the dangers and risks I encountered--until I was confronted with my first life or death mission.

The Silver Star

As dawn broke on the morning of May 6th I was called to Division Tactical Operations Center (the Situation Bunker) and told Firebase Henderson was under heavy attack and partially overrun. It had started as a night sapper (sneak) attack. Now the ammo dump was hit and cooking off. My three man team had been mortared. Two were dead and one medevac'd out. The battle was at full peak and the only working communications for the entire firebase was the Pathfinder radio (LZ air traffic control). I was ordered to get a new team and equipment ready and get them re-installed within 45 minutes regardless of the situation. I was not to leave the firebase until the new team was in place and the equipment back on the air.

I hadn't visited Henderson in my first set of fly-arounds, so I didn't know the three men or the terrain of the firebase. I had no time to figure out where

Henderson was, who the men were, or even grieve them. I had to move fast. I had just 45 minutes. Minteer put a new team together and we ran for the helipad heavily armed and loaded with new equipment. As we waited for the chopper to land, the fearful grim looks in the faces of the replacement team spoke volumes to me. This was not going to be a social visit. Minteer stayed behind to run things. I had to lead the assault. Those were my orders.

At the pad, Captain Connelly, a lifer and the battalion Operations Officer, joined us. He was on his second Vietnam tour getting his career "ticket punched" as a 101st officer. Steel pot, flak jacket, M16, bandoliers of ammo, and a 45 pistol, he looked ready to go. I asked Connelly what he was doing and he replied, "I'm gonna get me a Silver Star. The place is being overrun, and this is my chance to be a hero." I have to admit I felt some relief to have Connelly's rank and experienced company riding along with me. I thought he was kidding, but had no time to process it because the chopper came in on short final approach and landed.

As the team threw their gear on board and nervously jumped in, Connelly and I stood on the skid while the pilot asked me where we were going. "Henderson!" I shouted over the whine of the transmission. "No way," he yelled back. "I just saw my best friend shot down in a Medevac at Henderson. There is no way we can get in, and I'm not going to risk it."

I froze for a moment...unsure what to do or how to handle a conflict of orders. The mission versus the lives I was putting in danger...I was just too new. I looked to Connelly for direction and support. He was the ranking officer. He looked me in the eye and yelled, "You gotta go." Conflict over. I was stunned. This was it.

It was pure reaction on my part as I looked back at the pilot and screamed, "Look, I'm a 1st Lieutenant and you're a Warrant Officer. I can give you a direct order to go or you can do it on your own. I gotta get out there and insert this team!" The pilot turned away and got on the radio for about 30 seconds before he turned back to me and shouted, "Okay, we'll go. But, I am going to call for all suppressive fire when we get close....which means door gunners open up and the firebase will fire everything they have. Don't fucking panic. IF we can get in, I'll give you 30 seconds, max, to get your men and your shit off 'cause I'm pulling out before they mortar us. Got it?!" I nodded and gave him thumbs up.

I started to jump in with my men when Connelly grabbed my arm and said, "Good luck, Lieutenant. I think I'll stay here. You don't need me." I couldn't believe what I heard, and I had no time to sort it out. Cowardice? Sure death? Rank has its privilege? I didn't know and I needed to go. The only words I had were, "Let's get the fuck outta here," to the door gunner as I gave thumbs up and jumped into the cargo compartment.

There was complete silence and dark looks on board as we lifted off. Normally there was shouting and nervous chatter over the ear-pounding cacophony of a full load take-off. Not that morning. We all had thoughts of our last minute of life. There were a million thoughts in seconds of time at 1500 feet altitude—over and over. The most nagging was, 'How will I die?'

As we got close to the burning battle scene, I saw the pilot hadn't exaggerated the severity of the situation. Black smoke was billowing from the firebase-- the perimeter was half overrun and fires were burning all over. There were flashes of exploding artillery rounds from the burning ammo dump. It looked impossible to get in, but we had no choice but to try as the pilot positioned us to land on the only working LZ. On cue, the door gunners opened up, and friendly suppressive ground fire erupted. The deafening sounds of small arms, machine guns, grenades and artillery rounds faded from my hearing as I concentrated feverishly on getting the men and equipment off-loaded safely. A landing helicopter is a huge vulnerable target. All of us wanted to jump off from 10 feet we were so anxious for cover. But I held everyone back to wait for my hand signal. The pilot flared and started the bird down as fast as possible.

We were about 3 feet off the ground when the men bailed out and ran for cover. I positioned myself facing out on the skid so I could throw off gear as we touched. At the same time, I saw a bare-chested blond guy nonchalantly walk towards the chopper yelling something at me. He looked surreal he was so calm in the madness of the dissonant action around us. My attention was split between him and my men. He yelled to me over the gunfire and whoosh of the main rotor, "I'm the Pathfinder. Are you Baffico?" I nodded a big yes. "Okay,

I'll take care of things from here," he yelled in my ear. "I know how to set your equipment!" I couldn't be sure I heard him right but there was no time to clarify.

At the same moment, the pilot yelled at me over his left shoulder, "Get the fuck off!", and gave full pitch to the main blade with the collective and pulled hard for maximum lift on the cyclic. The time for clarification about anything was gone. We started to take off backwards. I was still faced out with my heels hooked onto the skid...absolutely thunderstruck. As we lifted off, I watched the landing zone shrink between my boots. I had to get safe--fast.

By the time I got spun around enough to try to get back into the cargo compartment, it looked like we were 150 feet off the ground and gaining altitude fast. Green and red tracers flashed everywhere. Thoughts were running through my head at the speed of light but everything I saw was in slow motion. I knew I was a perfect target hanging on to the outside of the chopper as I steadied myself on the skid and reached for anything to help me get back in. Door gunners were busy firing protective fire. At the same, time I tried to get the proper grip on my rifle but couldn't, so I let it fall. As it dropped away, I remember it looked like one of those divers going off the cliffs at Acapulco in slow motion. I clawed until I finally grabbed a cargo ring on the floor and pulled myself up and in.

Henderson After-Action Damages

Inside the chopper, I heard the barrage of small arms fire everywhere. The blasts of the door gunner machine guns were constant and thunderous. I had no idea where shots came from, who was shooting or what was hit. I just knew I was down to the last seconds of my life. I envisioned rounds piercing the floor or a RPG (rocket propelled grenade) hitting us squarely in the engine. My life flashed by as I lay balled up in a tight fetal position waiting to be hit with no weapon except my lousy 45 pistol. And that was to shoot myself if I needed to. I shut out the earsplitting sounds of gunfire all around as I thought about Mom and started an Act of Contrition, "Oh my God I am heartily sorry for having offended thee……..."

After about a minute of top speed flying and gaining altitude as fast as possible (I have no idea of the time except it felt like an eternity), it was finally safe enough for me to uncurl and sit back on the floor. No bullet holes I could see or feel—no RPG had hit us—we were flying okay. I couldn't believe it. I ached all over. I lit up a cigarette and tried to clear my head. I couldn't calm down or fathom I was still alive. 'This must be the other side of the Valley of Death,' I thought. I was dazed and had no idea if the Pathfinder was real, imagined, competent or corrupt. 'How did he know my name? Why did I trust him? Did I do the right thing? Am I a coward for trusting him? What about my men? What did they think?' I would find out later.

About 40 minutes later we hovered over the 501st helipad at Eagle. I spotted Connelly from the air waiting for us to land and the instant I saw him adrenaline released in me like a burst water pipe. I girded my mind for a confrontation. His presence told me he was there to tell me they didn't make it. 'Shit. I can't do that again.' I thought. When we touched down, I kicked my gear out and shambled towards him while fighting to stand up against the force of the main rotor wash.

The chopper took off and left me with Connelly in the silence and stillness of the suffocating morning heat. I was so spent and weighted down from my gear and the tension of the mission that he had to hold me erect as he blurted out, "Man that was unbelievable. They're back up on the air already and we're beatin' the gooks back. Man, you're gonna get the Silver Star! I already talked to the colonel about it. It's all approved. This is unbelievable."

Exhaustion and frustration pushed the anger up my throat and out my mouth like rancid bile before I knew it. "Captain Connelly, fuck you and your Silver Star, and tell the colonel to get fucked too," I screamed in his face. "Two of my men were killed out there today and one wounded who probably won't make it. Give them the Silver Star, you asshole." I threw my ammo bandoliers to the ground and said, "I need some water." I stumbled over to the potable water blivet to saturate my head and thirst while I collapsed to the ground. Connelly departed quietly without another word. I didn't care what he thought or reported about me. Completely dehydrated, my body did all it could to loosen up and calm down in the smothering heat. I couldn't stop drinking water.

I drenched my head under the spigot and re-played the action over and over. I had made it. I couldn't believe it and couldn't stop trembling. The intensity of surviving was overpowering. I had lived through the most terrifying moment of my life…the one I had always feared. I faced death straight up and came out alive...not for glory….not for a medal or recognition…not for a cause…but because it was the mission. Others were being killed and needed us. For whatever reason, fate had spared me on this mission.

Mysteriously, the chaotic action of combat and the death defying ballet on the skid of the chopper were both perilous and yet exhilarating. Although exhausted, I never felt so alive. I couldn't sort out the confused emotions. But as I began to calm down and collect my thoughts, a feeling took over that surprised me. I was proud of what I had done. I felt a sense of accomplishment for overcoming my own fear and weakness. I didn't recognize that I had experienced a life-changing breakthrough which would be with me for whatever life I had left.

Combat stirs up an emotional cocktail which you can't process sensibly in the moment. My body tension continued to subside as I guzzled water and my mind slowed down. Would there be more dangers ahead? How could I know? I did know I would be more willing to face danger if I had to. I began to understand why you might sacrifice your life for the sake of others. Suddenly, it made sense to me in a very forbidding and uncanny way.

The mission had ignited flickers of self-confidence. Sitting there alone, I realized I had unexpectedly moved into the ranks of the elite warrior team called the 101st Airborne as a genuine, full-fledged member. And I didn't have to have any fanfare or medal to prove it. The Silver Star was not important to me. The milestone of the passage was experiencing the enigmatic act of sacrifice for others. My perspective was to be forever altered by the revelation....sometimes consciously, mostly unconsciously.

Henderson also taught me why Patton was absolutely right in his combat orders. You are a part of a team who fights for each other, not causes or politics. In the intensity of battle, you will know what to do or your cowardice will consume you. Combat has a seductive and everlasting texture to it. Finally, make the other guy die and move on. That's the job.

The charred remains of artillery on Henderson

FSB Henderson Official After-Action Report

At 060505, FS/OB HENDERSON received RPG, small arms, satchel charges, recoilless rifle fire and mortar fire, followed by a well-organized and coordinated ground assault by the 8th Bn, 66th NVA Regt. Fires ignited by the flamethrowers employed by the NVA caused approximately 1000 rounds of 155mm artillery ammunition to explode. Defending forces supported by ARA, cannon artillery and gunships, accounted for 29 NVA killed. The enemy withdrew at 0720. Total US casualties were 32 killed, 33 wounded, and two missing in action. ARVN casualties were 19 KIA and 45 WIA.

JOINING THE BAND OF BROTHERS

Shifty Powers, an Original Brother of the Band

After I was home from the war for a few years, I tried watching a movie about Vietnam more out of curiosity than anything else. I wanted to see through the eyes of Hollywood what they thought my Vietnam time might have looked like. So I agreed to try *Coming Home* with Jane Fonda, Bruce Dern and John Voight. It was a big mistake. I had little if any emotional strength to process the garbage about Vietnam which was pumped out of La La Land.

For years thereafter, I refused to see others. No *Deer Hunter*; no *Apocalypse*; no *China Beach, Full Metal Jacket, Hamburger Hill, We Were Soldiers Once;* no more *Victory at Sea* either. When people would ask me cautiously if I had seen one of these gems, I would simply respond, "No". The conversation inevitably ended abruptly or the subject immediately changed. I felt strongly I was paid ahead in my life on war and on camping out. My sons were never going to be Boy Scouts nor would they enjoy a camping vacation with me fighting off filth and vermin all night at some remote campsite. Furthermore, I wanted no part of telling war stories at VFW or American Legion hangouts. Finally, the 101st Airborne Association was never going to hear from me no matter how many solicitation techniques they tried.

This denial formula worked until 1987 when the older of my two sons, Jon, was 13 and the movie _Platoon_ came out. By then, enough time had passed for Hollywood to sensationalize another story about Vietnam. It caused quite a stir because it was an Oliver Stone creation. It was apparently his turn to opine about Vietnam. His work generally masquerades as "interpretive history" or "docudrama" so it sells as if it is a type of "journalism" which appeals to a broader audience. But it is no more than his platform to make social statements by conveniently and loosely interpreting a few facts.

In the mid 80's, video games got into the pretend world of glorified combat by providing more action, faster games and more sophisticated special effects. Video games like _Street Fighter_ and _Metal Gear_ took over the industry by replacing _Asteroids_ and _Mario Brothers_ as the leading entertainment medium for young kids. Embellished violent actions and competitions became a steady diet of entertainment for many. _Platoon_ played into the trend.

Even though there was an unspoken understanding in our family that I never talked of Vietnam, Jon had apparently taken it upon himself to boast to his classmates about my being a Vietnam Veteran who could put _Platoon_ through some kind of truth screen to determine its believability. I was honestly flattered by this kind of talk about me. After years of living in silence about Vietnam, I was taken back a little because he had the courage to ask me to take him to see it. And even though I didn't want to see the movie, I didn't want to miss the opportunity to share something important with my son.

I took some time to explain to both Jon and younger brother Jeff why I had reservations about the movie and the subject matter, glamorizing and romanticizing war, unrestrained special effects for sensationalism, pointless graphic carnage, and manipulating truths to make them fit a story; etc. I didn't go into any personal details. My explanation was, perhaps, more a clumsy attempt at releasing some of the latent anger which was buried inside me. I was unsure of how I would react to the film but I wanted to help Jon. So we decided to see it together.

We went off for the Saturday matinee screening at our local theater. The place was packed. The movie had received pretty good reviews, but then so had most of Stone's work. This one was supposedly the stuff of Oscars. We settled in for a good look while I braced for a potential avalanche of flashbacks. But I didn't have to worry. The movie was an awful piece of fiction. It was nothing more than a poorly constructed compilation of worn-out exaggerated Vietnam combat stories made into violent vignettes peppered with every hackneyed expression and phrase of the time in an attempt to provide the scenes with a modicum of authenticity.

I think Jon was mortified to think I might have witnessed such excessively graphic barbarism. I was concerned he was overwhelmed by the dehumanized rawness. I worried about him and how to explain my view of what I had seen in the film.

It was easier than I thought. When we came out into the sunlight, I saw he was a little teary from the interminable violence. And, he seemed worried about my reaction. He said he was okay and wanted to know what I thought. It was a good moment for me to try and open up, so as we rode home in the car, we began to talk.

> In WWII the average soldier saw 40 days of combat in 3½ years of war.
> In Vietnam, the average soldier had seen 204 days of combat in one year.
> *Author Unknown*

I gave him my assessment. Overall, fierce. . .yes, that's how combat is. That part Stone got right. The rest was misleading garbage. But I thought it important for him to learn a larger lesson from seeing the film. War has no romance or glory. I wanted him to realize war is ultimately about death and destruction no matter how it is dressed up in action, effects, color or story line. And it is final. Unfortunately, our culture likes to commercialize it because it is a flashy, easy sell. But the target in war is another human life. And to actually kill someone is something from which you never recover. No film, game or book can replicate the finality of taking another life because it isn't a game. War bestows upon each participant the lasting lesson of the inhumaneness of killing which any reasonable person would never want to repeat.

I told Jon I thought the film would win awards because it satisfied people's hunger for information about Vietnam. Most people knew very little, but Stone presented his version as if it was fact. It would presumably lead people to feel they were better informed about a piece of history which had caused the country so much pain and so little satisfaction. But I explained that real factual information was generally locked up inside those of us who had participated. And, unfortunately, there was no safe ground for any one of us to have a dialogue without causing more enduring pain and disagreement.

I was glad we had seen it together and we had taken the time to talk about something so deep in me and meaningful to my son. I, frankly, had never considered that he had interest in my history with Vietnam. It was the only brush with my memories I shared with any family member until a few years later.

Then it was Jeff who stepped forward. He had missed his 8th grade class field trip to Washington DC because of a bout with the flu. We decided to go on a weekend DC trip ourselves so he wouldn't miss any class time. We were careful to make our itinerary the same as the school field trip. Of course, it included a trip to the National Mall. As we worked our way through the usual sites, the Smithsonian Air and Space, Supreme Court, Library of Congress, etc., I was caught off guard when Jeff asked if we were going to stop by The Wall. "Sure. Of course," I said.

I didn't know Jeff had any information or interest in The Wall, but I could tell when we got there he was a little ginger confronting the uncharted territory the Memorial presented to both of us. I was quiet and probably radiated a painful expression. Being a gentle soul, Jeff carefully asked, "Did you know anybody on the Wall, Dad?"

"Unfortunately, yes. There were five." I said.

It was troubling for me to process the feeling of pride I felt being at the Memorial with one of my children contrasted with feeling the guilt for the loss of my men and the thousands of others who didn't make it back...the memory of the lives lost weighed against the new lives we survivors brought into the world was difficult to reconcile. 'Why me,' I thought. 'How?' It was unsettling for me and Jeff could tell. But he pressed on. "Do you know where they are?"

Jeff at The Wall pointing to Mike Bohrman's name

"Yes, you're standing right in front of two of them." I pointed to Mike Bohrman's name. "I'll take your picture pointing to it if you want to show it to your class." Ever the pragmatic thinker, I guess I thought he would need proof of the trip.

We took the picture and I said, "Let's get out of here." I didn't want to be embarrassed or open up any more than I had. I simply didn't know how to handle the feelings--his or mine. I tried to comfort Jeff so he didn't feel he had done anything wrong. Fortunately, he was fine. So I mentally slammed the door shut on Vietnam for another long period of time. Some years later when Jeff was in college at Marquette, he took a class on Vietnam. Then I waited quietly to see if he would ask me anything. He asked if I had any pictures I might share with him. I gave them to him, but found myself not able to talk about them at all. Years later it was Jeff who again, gently prodded me to recall my experiences.

During a period of estrangement from both sons because of my divorce from Mary after 30 years of marriage, I tried occasional phone calls or coffees to stay in touch with them. Frankly, the three of us were uncomfortable with each other. Mostly, I was trying to figure out where I fit in in their lives. The divorce had caused normal relationships to become shadowy possibilities. But by the second Christmas of separation, we decided to try a day of gift exchanging apart from the normal calendar celebratory week so their holiday schedules weren't burdened with split loyalties. It was their idea and a good one. We all got a chance to heal a little and to feel closer.

Jeff's gift to me was a DVD set of *The Band of Brothers*. I vaguely recalled hearing about the HBO series. I was living a very distracted life at the time, and I didn't spend much of it watching TV, so I felt badly I didn't know about it. He told me he thought I might really like it because it was about my old unit, the 101st Airborne in WWII. I politely thanked him and put the gift on a bookshelf for later. I had no intention of ever watching it. More garbage, I thought.

Months later during another visit, Jeff asked me if I had had a chance to watch the series. I sheepishly admitted I hadn't, but promised I would take a look. I was living alone and had little to do in the evenings except read or watch a little TV when the mood struck me. I really didn't want to take time to process more Hollywood detritus, but I needed to fulfill my obligation to Jeff. So one night I pulled out the package of DVDs and with some hesitation started Disc 1.

From the moment I saw the opening scene of basic training at Taccoa, I was gripped. I can't say why, but I found myself feeling an empathic pride which I had no idea I possessed. 'I did this too,' I thought as I watched. I remembered the good and the bad of being put through rigorous physical and mental toughness training. Of feeling the pain and coming close to quitting, while at the same time building my strength and confidence through small personal accomplishments, especially in the company of others you could absolutely depend on...your brothers, so to speak.

It felt as though I had found a piece of my past which had been stuffed away somewhere. I even recalled times in Vietnam when I thought things were tough, our battalion Sargent Major Smith would say, "You think things is tough here, L.T., you should have been at Bastogne—things was *tough* there—this place here is for pussies!"

The Original Band of Brothers

Wow. I felt the dots connect! Smith had been at The Battle of the Bulge with the Band of Brothers, and I had been with Smith in Vietnam. It made me feel as though I was part of a continuous thread to the original warriors. I had to learn more.

I watched the entire series the first night. I related to every scene and feeling. They were all the same feelings I had never permitted in my consciousness or had ever shared with anybody. Easy Company's was a different time and a different war, but exactly the same experiences and emotions. I realized then, that combat imparts identical burdens on each participant regardless of age, color, place of birth or background. And it creates an unfathomable lifetime bond among warriors, regardless of when one served. I felt duty-bound to connect more dots.

I went on a tear reading everything I could get my hands on about Easy Company, 2nd Battalion, 506th Infantry Regiment: biographies, autobiographies, interviews, articles, and internet information. I bought books and devoured them. I researched some of the after-action reports from the Library of Congress files so I could walk in their steps.

I had to go to Normandy. So I did, to Utah Beach, Omaha Beach, Carantan, Bastogne, and Foy so I could see and feel what they did. When I stood where they stood and looked at the same terrain, I related my old fears and terrors to theirs. Omaha in particular was overwhelming. To look into the cliffs and emplacements and realize death was staring you in the face. But your men, your mission and your duty carried you forward. It was Henderson all over for me. I didn't feel so alone any more…I didn't feel like some anomalous human who had to prove I was really normal. Others had done the same and much more long before I did. They remembered and I could too. It finally felt okay for me.

I came home from Normandy and joined the 101st Association. I felt I could be a part of it with honor. Now I was proud to have served with an elite unit. I found out our battle on Ripcord was honored at the 101st Memorial in Arlington Cemetery alongside other 101st battles of distinction in their history: Bastogne, Market Garden, and Hamburger Hill.

Thanks to Jeff and seeing *Band of Brothers,* I had a defining moment in my Vietnam history and an important personal breakthrough. It led me to my own insides and the realization that my story needed to be talked about and brought into the open rather than buried. It helped me open up to the possibility I needed help to process my thoughts.

I was particularly touched by the interview vignettes with the real brothers at the end of each episode. Their humility, pride, sense of duty, heroism was exemplary. And their pain was genuine. The lives they went on to live spoke volumes about the strength of character each had. There was not a loser in the bunch. I developed a heroic veneration of the men of Easy Company because their story helped me unlock my story.

One volunteer weekend at my hotel in Washington I had the pleasure of meeting Shifty Powers, one of the original Band of Brothers. I had my 101st patch on my volunteer shirt from working the Wall and was invited to sit in on an autograph session with him. He was as genuine and humble as he had been portrayed. It was a personal thrill for me.

I have also been fascinated with the life of Lt. Buck Compton. He has an incredible story before, during and after his time with the Band of Brothers. I wanted to know more about him, so I bought and read his book, *Call of Duty*. When I finished it, I felt compelled to write him a letter of thanks and to tell a little of my story. I also gave a copy of the letter to my sons so they could understand a little more about what the unlocking of my past meant to me. It was good to share it.

Dear Buck:

I just finished reading your book, Call of Duty, and felt compelled to write to you to say thanks for writing it, for your service, leadership, courage and wisdom throughout your life...and for your part in making The Band of Brothers.

My name is Paul Baffico, and I am a Vietnam Veteran of the 101st. I was a University of San Francisco ROTC Signal Platoon leader with the 501st Signal Battalion. I made 206 combat assaults supporting all 3 Infantry Brigades of the 101st during my 1970-71 tour. I was actually most proud of supporting the 2/506th in their defense of Firebase Ripcord in a now historic battle.

Like you, I returned to civilian life in San Francisco a few days after I came home. I went right into graduate school to try to put the horrors of war out of my mind as fast as I could and to get back to life as I thought I understood it.

I quickly found myself on a corporate career rocket ship ride for the next 30 years ending up as the President of the Sears Automotive Group and the CEO of Western Auto. I am absolutely convinced my success was predicated on the good sense of applying my army combat lessons to corporate life. After having a great run and tons of fun, I was able to retire in 2001 when I was 55 years old.

Shortly after leaving Sears, my youngest son asked me if I had seen The Band of Brothers. He knew I did not talk about Vietnam, nor would I ever see any Vietnam movies, no matter what the reviews. Somehow, however, he knew intuitively I had a silent but strong pride and respect for the people I had served with in the 101st. So he took the chance of gifting me a DVD set of Band.

It took a while for me to open it, but when I did, I was absolutely gripped. It was the first time since I had come home, I actually allowed myself to recall the confusion, frustrations, sorrows, pains and fears of combat which all of us have experienced. My memories and emotions were exactly the same as what I was watching in The Band of Brothers: the loss of the lives of my men, the surreal actions and instincts of combat, and on and on. I even recalled my Sgt. Major and First Sgt. were both Veterans of Bastogne. They used to kid me about how tough Bastogne was by comparison to Vietnam!

As I watched the series over and over, my mind started to open up to my own memories I had so fitfully locked away when I came home 33 years before. Gradually, I started to feel it was okay to remember; to mourn my men; to recall the agonizing feeling that I was destined to die in a god-forsaken land; to recall the funny things; and to even recall the friends I had made in the unit.

Eventually, I just had to go to Normandy to trace the steps of the 101st in the D-Day operations: to Brecourt Manor; to Vierville; to Sainte-Mère-Église; to Carentan, I stared at Omaha and Utah for hours trying to comprehend the incredible sacrifices which were made. I went to Foy and Bastogne and thought of my Sgt. Major as a kid fighting in the Ardennes Forest. I even went to the road block defensive positions leading into Bastogne and tried to imagine what it was like to have been there during the frigid winter with no food, ammo or supplies. I was in awe.

Walking in those footsteps helped me realize the shame and guilt I had endured as a Vietnam vet was very misplaced. My service and my call of duty were not any different than yours or others who have served our country. Gradually, a pride crept over, which I had not experienced since battle. I finally was able to see how those of us who answered the call at different times in history are all cut of the same fabric.

I certainly wasn't appropriating the special code of the original Band of Brothers. I was beginning to feel I am part of a continuum of men who have stood up and been willing to offer themselves for a country and value system which has given so much. I am now proud to be considered a part of the 101st.

Buck Compton

So, thank you again for your book, your Easy Company contributions, your fabulous career, and your courage to consistently stand and deliver for what you believe in. You are remarkable.

And thank you for helping make The Band of Brothers. It was inspirational for many. For me, it provided the first light I needed to look into a part of my life for which I had felt deep shame and guilt for a long time. Now I can feel proud. Thank you again.

Sincerely,

Paul A. Baffico
1LT, 501st Sig. Bn, 101st Airborne

This is the Job

"We discovered in that depressing, hellish place where death was our constant companion that we loved each other. We killed for each other, we died for each other and we wept for each other. And in time we came to love each other as brothers. In battle our world shrank to the man on our left and the man on our right and the enemy all around. We held each other's lives in our hands and we learned to share our fears, our hopes, our dreams as readily as we shared what little else good came our way.

General Hal Moore

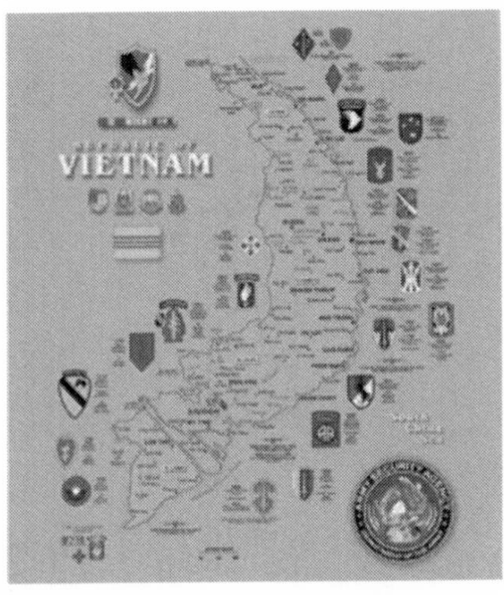

101st Airborne Area of Operations

Fate Is the Hunter

The Henderson battle and the loss of the three men in my first 3 weeks left a permanent imprint on my mind and soul. I didn't realize how deep or lasting it was until I was far removed from it. But as a leader going forward then, I accepted that I had little to say about when, where or why anyone might die. Henderson made me recognize there were things I could and could not control in order to do my job and simultaneously maintain some sanity. There was no explanation as to why I made it back from the mission, why the Pathfinder unexpectedly helped me, or why others lived and my men died. The living or dying part was out of my hands. I got it. *Fate* was the hunter. And by acquiescing to this reality, I accepted that the men, the mission and those we supported had to be the sole focus of my attention. Nothing was more important. So I committed myself to being the best leader I could possibly be for all concerned. Survival, personal pride, and awards immediately took a back seat to the mission and well-being of the men under my command.

Each day brought different requirements: discipline problems, equipment, battles, weather, family emergencies, fading morale, new firebase installations, rotations home and cherries reporting in. I threw myself into each task and always scratched hard for the best outcome. I liked the feeling of making decisions and of making a difference. I found out I was comfortable leading men in the remote hell we had to endure together. Platoon leadership in combat taught me an invaluable life lesson. It is that there is a very distinct difference between being a leader and being a manager. It was an enlightening discovery learned through simple tenets I could not possibly have gleaned from a book or in a classroom.

1. Lead by example.
2. Make decisions firm, fair, and fast.
3. Evaluate a situation fast and efficiently: OODA=Observe. Orient. Determine. Act.
4. No matter how much data and intelligence you may have, no decision is ever perfect.

5. Always remain flexible: Semper Gumby.
6. Listen to your team: 1+1=3.
7. Maintain high morale.
8. Keep proper separation between leader and followers.
9. A good sense of humor is critical to everyone's sanity and performance.
10. Always praise publicly and criticize privately.
11. Watch your back and the backs of those you lead.
12. Don't take yourself too seriously.

The pride in the platoon improved steadily as the men responded to this leadership model. An unexpected blessing was the great mix of men I had who wanted to be the best. They developed their own unique esprit de corps and moved to a higher level of performance. Morale got better. Sick call numbers went down dramatically. Camaraderie improved. Drug abuse subsided as heavy users were dealt with firmly and without hesitation. Volunteerism improved. Competition for positive attention became intense. Humor was a critical success element in which everyone participated.

"Arc Lights"

The terrain outside of Camp Eagle being bombed by B-52s

I personally developed a fierce 24/7 work ethic which distracted me from my nagging preoccupation of not going home alive. It made me focus on the job and the day in front of me. I lived in the moment. I learned not to attach to anyone or anything. I learned that fatigue is an enemy. I did the best I could for my men. And each day hoped to live just another day.

These psychological contrivances kept my fears at bay during the day. They cloaked a dark internal perspective which I would not allow anyone to see. My private and fatalistic view of survival would reveal itself only at night, when I was alone and tired, and trying to put some perspective on the day. I soothed myself with a tumbler or two of Drambuie and Coke. It worked. It made me feel better, and it was the only way I could fall asleep. Routine drinking put my poltergeists back in the closet temporarily so I could try to be ready for another day of flying assaults. I never considered that the alcohol that worked so well would ever cause me any harm or problems. I had no time to care about it, and I had no perspective on it.

Vietnamization

The rotation and deployment of my men into action was a full time job. The platoon activity was tied directly to every friendly ground deployment in our AO (Area of Operations). That meant 101st units, ARVN (Army of the Republic of Vietnam) units, Special Forces (both U.S. and Vietnamese) and others. My job was to check on as many as 6 to 7 locations per day for defenses, performance, maintenance, equipment and personnel needs. Most of the flights were to very active firebases, and a few to static and safe installations like inside the walled Citadel in the city of Hue or out to Eagle Beach where routine stand downs were held for ground troops so they could recharge after combat time in the bush.

The AO was exceptionally large and active with NVA. We were spread thinly across triple the amount of territory a regular division would normally cover. The terrain had previously been held by two Marine Divisions and one Army Mechanized Infantry Division. But because we were Air Mobile and the elite 101st, we could cover three times more ground than conventional ground forces. We were equipped with the best trained personnel and technology, which allowed us to deploy efficiently and rapidly by helicopter assault. We would fight hard and smart, and then move expeditiously to the next battle. The 101st has a long tradition of being called on to do more in impossible situations. They are a superior unit who pride themselves on being the best. It is in their DNA.

My Daily Taxi Ride, Courtesy of The Comancheros
The 101st Assault Helicopter Battalion

During my tour in 1970-1971, the White House had to accelerate the "Vietnamization" phase. It represented the tactical definition of Nixon's '68 campaign promise to the American voter to end U.S. involvement. It was not a new or intricate idea. The concept was to expand, equip and train South Vietnam's combat forces (ARVN) for their larger role in the fighting for themselves so the number of U.S. troops could be reduced. It was *the* singular element in the formula for U.S. troop withdrawal that began in 1969.

But in Nixon's first year and a half in office, Vietnamization had not made much progress for various unspoken reasons. By March of 1970, the fall elections were on the horizon, and he needed to convince the world the U.S. was pulling out or risk the possibility of losing control of Congress in the mid-term election. He had to demonstrate proof the ARVNs were prepared to fight for their own cause. It required them to engage the enemy, which they were not accustomed to doing.

As a result, the 101st became responsible for not only the larger geography of the entire I Corps terrain, but also for the basic training of the 1st ARVN Division. It meant we had a dual mission: to make them competent enough to take over from us while we were simultaneously leading the day to day prosecution of the war. That was Vietnamization-speak and the political concept that would hypothetically enable the U.S. troop draw down to be a reasonably safe possibility.

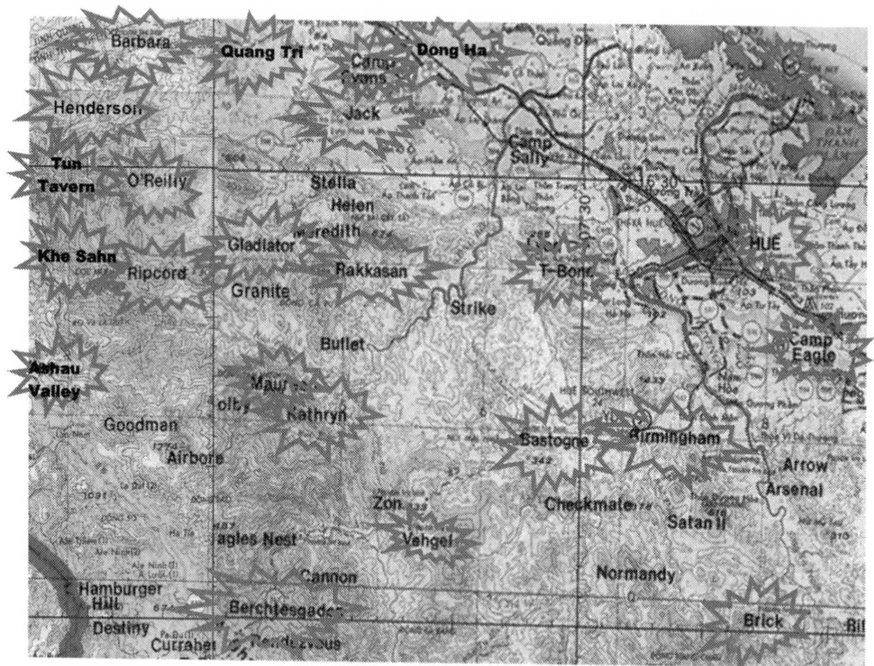

1970 Firebase Activity for the 101st Airborne

A U.S. Cambodian Invasion had been devised to give the ARVNs enough breathing room to get trained and ready to fight during the middle phase of Vietnamization. By aggressively attacking the NVA inside Cambodia on May 1, 1970, the U.S. Army's 1st Cavalry Division achieved much needed time and terrain by truncating supply lines before they reached into South Vietnam. They blunted steady Northern aggression on the Trail with the surprise attack. But just as the Cav made significant progress, Nixon ordered them back. The unannounced invasion across the Cambodian border appeared to the rest of the world to expand the war and be counter intuitive to the concept of Vietnamization. Global opinion exploded into an uncontrollable demand for U.S. troop withdrawals.

The severe back blast of negative opinion which erupted was completely unexpected by the insular President. A shocked Nixon struggled mightily with the bad press and hostile reactions. Public outrage at home boiled over into the streets and on campuses unlike anything in our history. The White House immediately reacted by suppressing all news and curtailing combat reporting. The media was evacuated from the battlefield and prohibited from reporting to the world on Vietnamization status or of the significant risk such a tactical ballet created. There were three distinct reasons for this move.

National Guard Troops at Kent State: At the Ready for National TV

First, three days following the Cambodian Invasion, four innocent students were killed by Ohio National Guardsmen at Kent State University. The incident unleashed an all-out anti-war/anti-U.S. sentiment throughout the world. It ignited smoldering antipathies which had steadily built during the anti-war movement. The killing there and at Jacksonville State ten days later underscored a political and social barbarity the severity of which had not been seen since the Civil War. It was the ugliest of public exposures. To have witnessed the killing of our own, by our own, during freedom of speech demonstrations was unconscionable to all Americans. More war coverage would heighten already raw emotions. Moreover, the unintended consequences of the shootings were far-reaching. The North Vietnamese had exactly what they needed to prolong the war, strengthen their case against the U.S. aggression, and continue to manipulate the Peace Talks to their advantage.

Next, with the fall 1970 elections about to get under way, the Republican Party line continued to be that Vietnamization was a success. The war was being handed over to the South Vietnamese, so it was said. But the public saw it as the lie it was. That, in turn, promulgated legitimate White House fear that factual exposure of the lack of progress of Nixon's solution would be a fatal political embarrassment for Republicans and significantly jeopardize any possibility for his re-election in 1972. Consequently, all media was banned from any combat action. We who were fighting in Vietnam had no idea these changes had taken place and that our activity was suddenly and inexplicably classified. All we knew was there were no more body counts for public consumption.

Finally, as previously mentioned, from April to July, the Curahees, the 2nd Battalion, 506th Infantry Regiment of the 101st, were in a long siege on Firebase Ripcord atop the mountains which formed the Ashau Valley. The 2/506th was the same unit who had fought on Hamburger Hill 12 months prior. The infamous battle there on Hill 937 had been covered in great detail and gave the media sensational material to be highly critical of the strategic importance of taking 937 versus its high casualty rate. The battle created a journalistic feeding frenzy which dominated headlines and broadcasts. Troops had been interviewed during the battle for the evening's 6 o'clock national news. A year later, the siege at Ripcord would have easily been portrayed as a repeat of "bad military judgment" by the same unit. However, Ripcord was an entirely different situation at a critical time in the war. Regardless, no military official wanted to defend Ripcord's strategic and tactical significance in the court of public opinion after the tragedy at Kent State. The world had seen and heard enough about the 2/506th and Vietnam.

Determined to fight the current of overwhelming national dissent, Nixon went on national TV to assure the country all Vietnam actions were proceeding according to plan so more Americans would soon be pulled out. It was his calculated attempt to keep the American public calm in the face of an indefensible situation. A pitifully corrupt and hopeless South Vietnamese government combined with an ineffectual and equally corrupt military protracted the stalled peace talks (they had moved beyond the shape of the negotiating table by then). National Security Advisor Kissinger had made little if any progress. The ARVNs were a dangerous liability and the North knew it. Unfortunately, from the 101st vantage point these facts were hideously obvious.

Nixon Explains How Well Vietnamization is working to a National TV audience

In just under three weeks on assignment, I had seen major US casualties suffered at FSB Henderson, a combined ARVN/101st firebase. It was easily overrun by NVA sappers and regulars through a maladroitly secured ARVN sector. My platoon suffered 3 dead because the firebase was so poorly defended. My men and 64 other U.S. casualties paid the ultimate price for

ARVN incompetence. I had absolutely no confidence Vietnamization would succeed no matter how much training was devoted to the ARVNs. My baptism of fire at Henderson had removed even the slightest trust I might have had in the government or the Army of the Republic of Vietnam. Regrettably, things were about to get worse.

> Television brought the brutality of war into the comfort of the living room. Vietnam was lost in the living rooms of America--not on the battlefields of Vietnam.
> *Marshall McLuhan*

Tun Tavern

The May invasion into Cambodia by the 1st Cav might have been spectacular if it hadn't been abandoned after the initial success. It did, however, push the NVA supply line north on the Ho Chi Minh Trail through Laos, and it forced an NVA retreat directly into a 101st blocking force partially covered by FSB Ripcord. Fighting was fierce. More interdiction was needed, however.

On June 1st, I received orders to provide VHF support for an assault by the 54th ARVN Regiment to a remote and isolated firebase only a few kilometers from the Laotian border and northwest of Ripcord. Fire Support Base Tun Tavern was an abandoned U.S. Marine sister firebase to Henderson which had provided artillery support to Khe Sanh during the siege there in 1968. It was in the middle of the North Vietnamese re-supply area adjacent to the Ho Chi Minh Trail along Route 9. Its remote location in very difficult terrain guaranteed trouble. Intelligence reported Tun Tavern was surrounded by 2 NVA battalions. Ground and artillery cover of 101st was too distant to be of any value. The only source of reliable support was the 101st 2/17th Air Cav unit (Cobra Assault Gunships) who had reported numerous contacts for 2 weeks in and around the area.

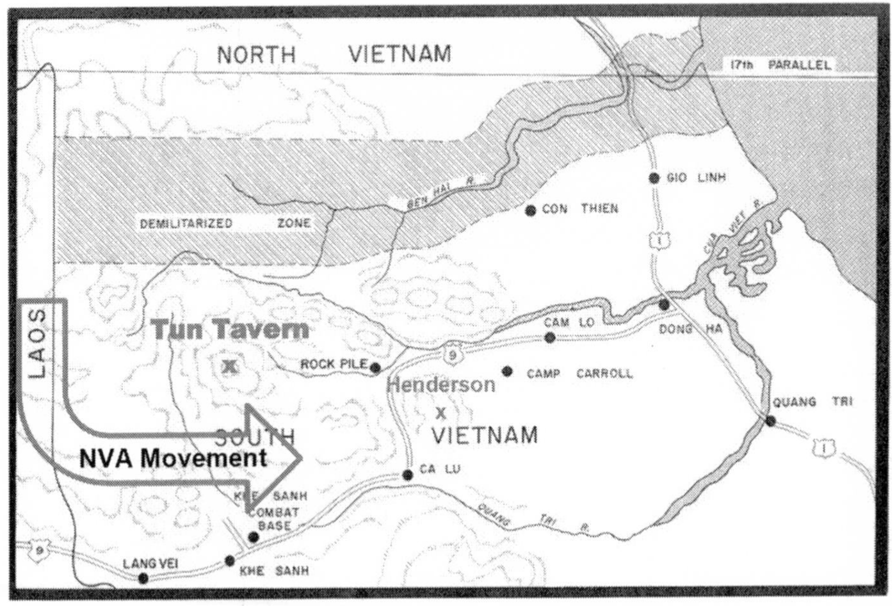

At this time, the ugly truth was that Vietnamization was not much more than a throwaway phrase which had little to no credibility on the battlefield. A quick logic test of the Vietnamization theory would expose a raw undeniable fact: there was no reason for the ARVNs to fight when the most powerful armed force in the world was so willing to do it for them. We who were fighting the war sensed that and lived with it every day. But, the embarrassment at Henderson the month before had to be overcome. This mission would be a way for the ARVN leaders to display some evidence that Vietnamization was viable. But it was a ridiculously bad idea.

Unfortunately, geography and the lack of nearby support made Tun Tavern a suicidal operation. Nonetheless, politics and continuing troop withdrawals demanded that the ARVNs make some attempt to satisfy the Nixon promise. The odds of it happening successfully were extraordinary long. The all-ARVN Tun Tavern assault mission spoke volumes about the untenable stage of the war at that point.

The only Americans who had to support the insanity were the men of my platoon because of our unique technological capability. A few Australians were attached for advisory support and they were equally shocked when I received the order. I ran to the Division Tactical Operations Center (DTOC) to argue that it was a suicide mission for us. It was too inaccessible, isolated from covering fire, and clearly in enemy territory. I argued vehemently that the ARVNs were simply not capable of fighting from such a disadvantaged position. It was far too big a leap for them, and there was absolutely no reason to waste any lives on such an ill-conceived plan. But in Vietnam, ARVN military wisdom was always in short supply. Everyone in the DTOC agreed. The order stood. I was ordered to back down. I had the sick feeling I should have pushed harder with a different approach, but I didn't.

I hurried back to my bunker to plan the mission. Minteer and I talked over who we would send and how we should support it. He suggested we ask for volunteers. He knew it would be dangerous and wanted to make sure those who went would be mentally prepared. I agreed. Minteer said he would personally insert the team and get them positioned on the firebase safely, determine their needs and defenses, and come back to report. I was relieved Bob volunteered to take them out. I didn't have the courage in me to do it, and I think he sensed it. He told me I was more needed running the show from base camp. We put out the word to men waiting for assignment or ready for rotation back to the bush. Two volunteers came forward unexpectedly, Mike Bohrman and Ken Luttel.

Bohrman had been a great soldier and wanted to see more action after his time running our R&R site at Eagle Beach. He said it was too much for him to be in a cushy rear job when he knew guys had their lives on the line. He had voluntarily extended his tour by 6 months knowing he would go back out if he wanted to or he could stay in the easy job in the rear. He really wanted to go, and I felt he could handle it. I also understood his guilt of being in the rear. It was common for many.

Luttel had just been assigned to us. His fatigues had not even faded he was so new. I tried to talk him out of it—I wanted him to get a few more weeks before going out. Get the drill down. No need to rush into a tough assignment. He wouldn't hear of it. He said, "I didn't come over here to sit on my butt." I cautioned him more but made no headway. He was determined.

Eagle Beach, the 101st In-Country R&R Installation

I decided to augment the team with Sgt. Bob Woodall, a combat hardened, fearless team chief from North Carolina who could provide additional firepower and support—probably more for my own guilt and peace of mind than anything else.

I had a haunting feeling I should have gone with the team to assess the situation, but I just couldn't bring myself to do it. I was too scared by the thought of being shot down going in and having no support from the ARVNs. I felt like a coward, but rationalized by recalling my luck at Henderson in addition to future opportunities to lose my life I would undoubtedly face after Minteer rotated home. 'Plenty of time for more heroics,' my mind said. My reasoning was temporary, however.

Fully loaded with equipment and heavily armed, I saw the team off from our helipad at 2 pm. Minteer was back by 4. The chopper inserted the team and received no contact. I should have gone with them. But Minteer's grim look said it all.

I asked for his assessment. "It don't look good, LT. They're way out there and they're not dug in very well," I could only hope they would make it until we could get back out the next day to help them dig in.

But at 5:45 am the next morning, I was called by the company commander to tell me Tun Tavern had been overrun on all sides at 4:30 am. Luttel and Bohrman were dead. They had been hit by a mortar round, lost limbs and couldn't get on a medevac because so many ARVNs were jumping on to save themselves. One of my men, I don't know which one, bled out and died going back during the panic, the other was killed instantly. Woodall was badly wounded and was dusted off to the evac hospital. The Australians were wounded but no KIAs. In addition to my men, 50 ARVN KIA, 119 WIA, 81 NVA killed, and 1 POW in less than 18 hours. The base was evacuated in the afternoon before dark. It was a complete waste of lives and resources.

Minteer and I went to the evac hospital to pin the Purple Heart on Woodall's pillow. He was groggy but awake when we came in. The first words out of his mouth were, "You should have been with us, LT, you fucker." I momentarily froze. I felt in my entire being that I knew what he meant, and his charge pierced my guilt with laser-like precision. 'I knew I should have gone!' I thought. I left Woodall's bedside numbed with more shame and anger than I could absorb. Minteer drove us back to Eagle so I could once again send the gear of dead men home to their families. My guilt enveloped me in a depressive silence. Their deaths were devastating. I had sent them. Why hadn't I found some way to stop the mission or refuse the order?

Platoon SSgt Bob Minteer and I conferring

Packing Bohrman's belongings into his duffel was sickening. Each item was such a physical confirmation of his vibrant young life, which had been terminated just hours before. I was shattered and wanted to cry when Minteer came into the hootch and said, "Woodall don't know what he's saying, LT. Don't you think about breaking down. We need you to be okay. The other 28 men need you real bad, so don't give in. It don' mean nothin."

Bob Minteer was a good platoon sergeant and he had it right. There were others who needed leadership and direction. I was the one to provide it, with and through Minteer. I had to re-orient my mind and press on. That's what you do. Compartmentalize and minimize it so it won't occupy your mind space. Otherwise you are useless and dangerous to the men and the mission. No time to grieve.

Drinking the pain away that night helped a little. It anesthetized my mind so I didn't have to think about my dead men. The alcohol allowed me to float through the ugliness of violent deaths again. I was unaware at the time exactly how much I needed the sensation of a numbed mind, distancing myself from any and all feelings. I had to move through it as though it never happened. My personal anguish could not be dealt with at the moment. Our A.O. was extremely active. There were missions to fly and more to accomplish.

Official After Action Report

Significant Activities: At 020430, at TUN TAVERN, the 2nd Bn, 54^{Regt} (ARVN) received an attack from all sides of the firebase by the 9th Bn, 66th NVA$^{Regt.}$ employing 82mm mortar, 75mm recoilless rifle, RPG and small arms fire. The enemy penetrated the perimeter and was able to occupy bunkers on the east side of the firebase. The situation was static at 0645 hrs. A sweep of the contact area revealed 81 NVA KIA and one PW. Three US soldiers from the 501st Sig Bn (AMBL), in support of the 1st Bn, 54th Regt (ARVN) were casualties. Two were killed and one wounded in action.

Australian After Action Report, Captain Bill Dean, AATTV Advisor
Events on Tun Tavern spiraled out of control. The disgusting eagerness of the ARVNs to Medevac themselves (officers and enlisted) after they had received the slightest wound with their complete disregard for those more seriously wounded soldiers was unbelievable. By the time the first Dustoff arrived, about 20 seriously injured, some with limbs missing, were lying on stretchers or ponchos beside the helipad. By the time the advisers had helped WO Birdie on board (a badly wounded AATTV adviser) and had returned with a stretcher borne U.S. soldier, the Dustoff was crowded with ARVN soldiers who had been able-bodied enough to board the Dustoff of their own accord while those more handicapped were unable to get help. In the event, the wounded U.S. soldier had to be thrown across the ARVNs on the floor, and he died on the return trip.

Missions Accomplished

In the next 3 months I surprised myself. Every mission was accomplished with no more casualties. I qualified for 2 Bronze Stars, 8 Air Medals, the Army Commendation Medal, and the Vietnam Gallantry Medal and turned down the Silver Star. I flew 206 combat assaults and had two forced landings, both at dusk. On one of them, we had to spend the night on a remote ARVN firebase. That's when I had to deal with another ugly personal shock.

Late in the day while flying a routine mission, we lost control of the steering mechanism of the chopper (a hydraulics failure) after a heavy takeoff. It forced us to hurriedly look for a friendly place to land with little time to set down easily. Firebase Jack, an all-ARVN location, was close so we landed hard while the pilot still had some control. There was no help that could get to us until daylight, so we had to set up a night defensive perimeter. With the disabled Huey sitting on the LZ, there was a good chance we could be attacked in the darkness. It was too tempting for enemy mortars. I quickly assessed our situation. There were 8 Americans to count on if we got hit. There was my team, the chopper crew and me. The rest of the troops were ARVNs making it another possible ugly ARVN crap shoot. We didn't feel secure at all.

Shortly after getting set up in our positions, my team chief came to me almost crying. His camera had been taken by one of the ARVNs who refused to give it back because the camera hadn't been properly secured. In the Vietnamese belief system, the camera had become the property of the "thief". The difference in the Vietnamese culture between theft and "finders-keepers" was tenuous at best.

Firebase Jack

I found the guilty ARVN troop and asked him to give the camera back. He refused and claimed it was his. Impatiently, I insisted he give it back immediately. He refused again. Impulsively and without hesitation, I ripped the helmet off his head, flung it into the wire, put my rifle on full automatic and fired half a clip into it like some street gang thug. Next, I lifted him up by his shirt in one hand and put the hot muzzle of my rifle under his chin and said, "That's your fucking head. Give it back."

"Okay! Okay! You number 10!" he gasped. Number 10 in broken Vietnamese meant I was the lowest of human beings on a scale of 1 to 10. I cared little about what he thought. The argument was over.

I went back to my position, curled up tightly and began to groan quietly. I couldn't believe my torrential rage. I couldn't believe I was ready to pull the trigger. I couldn't believe I would have blown his head off without hesitation.

I couldn't believe his life meant absolutely nothing to me. I couldn't believe I was no longer me.

My momentary loss of control felt as though it was the nadir of my life to that point. The ugliness of the war had penetrated my defenses and I was ashamed and dazed. I had always tried to be a decent human being, but suddenly and uncontrollably, decency was gone. The thought of invalidating the preceding years of my life, the education, training and civilized structure which made me who I thought I was because of an impulsive act of rage and hatred was a disgraceful revelation. The evils of war and living in a state of primitive survival had sucked me in. 'Was my moral compass permanently damaged? When will I rage again?' Those were questions I extinguished instantly.

But the imprimatur of the moral injury was indelible. In the solitude of my own conscience, no matter how much I would rationalize my loss of control then or in the future, I had to face the fact that my own evil had almost overtaken me. I was ready to take a life needlessly, and I didn't care. War and hatred had left their mark. I didn't know it at the time, but the injury would be with me for life. I feared the return of the evil and resolutely vowed to keep it from the view of others...forever. My remedy going forward was to detach and execute; stay calm and hold tight my bearing rather than succumb to emotions. My men expected it. I needed to rely upon it.

Firebase Kathryn

All told, I counted 5 separate times when I could have been killed. Besides the everyday dangers of flying and combat, I had to talk men down on two separate incidents while the barrel of their weapon was pointed at my chest. Both were stoned silly on drugs. One went to jail. The other was one of my own men. The platoon took care of him for me. He was an exceptionally good soldier after they got him straightened out.

I was pleased with what the platoon had accomplished during my time. In six months, we had installed or moved over 72 installations with just 33 men. On-air reliability was unmatched. Every unit commander we supported had nothing but praise for the men. Considering the equipment, protocols, and procedures were all experimental and unique to our Division, it was an amazing performance.

As the time passed, I had become comfortable with the job and comfortable in my own skin even with the conflicting thoughts and emotions combat imparted on me. I developed a little swagger in my step and an edgy, aggressive attitude. I wore my white t-shirt as my symbol of being a citizen soldier not a lifer. But I was very proud to have been accepted by the warriors of the 101st Airborne. In my own way, I became one of them, and that gave me a completely different perspective on things for the rest of my life.

Hawaiian R&R

In August, Mary and I met in Hawaii for R&R. I had been encouraged by my company commander to take a shot at getting a standby seat on a military R&R flight so I could catch a break from the action. To my surprise, it worked. Mary flew over a day after I arrived. We had a spectacular time together. It gave us a chance to organize our thoughts about our future.

We thought about getting married while we were there, but decided it would be untimely and selfish. We simply enjoyed each other and the tropical beauty of Oahu with its welcoming attitude towards the GI that included special prices, hotels, meals, tours, etc. Hawaii still has a special place in my heart because of the incredible relief it provided then. It was beautiful, safe and friendly. The memory of Pearl Harbor is inextricably woven into the Hawaiian culture and history. There, I didn't have to be ashamed of wearing a uniform. Not only was it expected, the Hawaiians made you feel proud and special to be a member of the Armed Forces. It was a remarkable contrast to the Mainland.

While Mary and I enjoyed the freedom and beauty of Hawaii, we decided I would try for an early release from the Army to attend graduate school. Because of the continuing withdrawal of U.S. troops, enlisted personnel were being allowed to apply for an early out for school rather than go back to a short useless assignment in the States (eliminating the kind of headache platoon I had at Ft. Hood). There was nothing in writing about officer early releases---no precedent to which I could refer, but I thought it was worth the effort to try. Admission to school from a distance was going to be thorny, so Mary happily agreed to help with the application logistics. I had absolutely nothing to lose.

Over the pilot's shoulder on approach to Khe Sanh.

After a revitalizing R&R with the love of my life, I flew back to Vietnam with a plan in my head which fostered a little more hope about making it home...and maybe early at that. The time in Hawaii felt as though I had sampled a priceless piece of the Good Life at a time when I least expected it. The rich and vivid respite felt more wonderful than I could have ever imagined. Even with the fear of resuming combat, I felt more alive. I had 8 months left on my tour.

THEIR WAR--OUR AGONY

"I am tonight announcing plans for the withdrawal of an additional 150,000 American troops to be completed during the spring of next year. This will bring a total reduction of 265,500 men in our armed forces in Vietnam below the level that existed when we took office 15 months ago."
President Richard M. Nixon, April, 1970

The wreckage of South Vietnamese Choppers abandoned and destroyed on LZ Sophia during Operation Lam Son 719

Unwinnable

During my time in Vietnam, the viability of the Vietnamization strategy deteriorated progressively as the withdrawal of U.S. troops resulted in less offensive firepower and additional danger for us remaining forces. Territory which had been secured by U.S. troops in the previous years of the war continued to be steadily surrendered by the incompetent ARVNs and the ever-changing government of South Vietnam. The North Vietnamese maintained an indomitable patience waiting out the U.S. withdrawal. As previously stated, the Cambodian Invasion would have paid huge dividends if it had not been stopped short early into the incursion. Unfortunately, less than 6 months after the Invasion, a re-built and re-supplied NVA force was ready to attack South Vietnam from Laos instead of Cambodia.

By January 1971, the ARVNs were under enormous pressure to validate their self-defense legitimacy. So they devised a plan to attack across the Laotian border into a suspected NVA logistical hub near the village of Tchepone, Laos. Operation Lam Son 719 was an all-ARVN operation (719 was named for Highway 9, the primary road to target and 71 represented 1971, the year of battle). The objective was to stop the expected NVA advance into South Vietnam along Highway 9 in Laos before crossing into Vietnam and to the populated cities of Quang Tri, Hue and Phu Bai.

Like Tun Tavern before, 719 was designed to demonstrate that the ARVNs on their own were capable of engaging and defeating the NVA in hotly contested territory. I had done some of the scout work at Khe Sanh for the operation and was frustrated with the futility of another dangerously flawed mission. And because the Cooper-Church Amendment prohibited U.S. ground forces and advisors from entering Laos, the 101st was designated as a reinforcement and decoy unit, and only if necessary. It wasn't necessary.

Lam Son 719 proved that the South Vietnamese Army was no match for the NVA. In heavy contact after minimal initial success along Highway 9 and into Laos, South Vietnamese troops ran from any contact in a panic and deserted. The costly ground for which American troops had fought so hard for 5 years was abandoned to the NVA in a month because of the humiliating cowardice, disorganization and political in-fighting of the ARVN commanders. The operation, an utter calamity, served as incontrovertible proof that the ARVNs were incapable of defending themselves and it was a precursor to the eventual fall of the South.

At the same time, the Paris Peace Talks continued as a meaningless P.R. play. Le Duc Tho played Henry Kissinger for the ego maniacal fool he was, as he preened in front of the world community. Tho was confident the North could outlast the U.S. bombing while Nixon was convinced bombing would bring the negotiations to a conclusion. Tho held steadily to his strategy of Victory by Attrition—the attrition of American troops, not NVA.

By the time of Lam Son 719, I was at the end of my tour and it had become painfully clear to me that the time I had spent risking my life with other American troops was absolutely worthless. Five of my men had been sacrificed for Vietnamization needlessly. The thought of more American lives wasted to support the cowardly disaster of 719 felt enfeebling. My hate, anger and resentment of the Vietnamese and the entire U.S. involvement in their war became very permanent. To come home with a feeling of ineffectuality is still frustrating to me. The war was unwinnable and a major disaster. All I wanted for me and anyone else who wore our uniform was to survive in one piece and get home. Vietnam could be defined only by only one word, futile.

Kissinger with Phan Van Dong, North Vietnamese Prime Minister in Hanoi

Live with Hope

In the agony and futility of fighting what had become an unwinnable war, we learned to live day to day on a trickle of manufactured hope. It was this trickle of hope that kept most of us in a state of resolve to do our jobs. I know that I couldn't have made it through my tour without the support I received from Mary and my family. They helped make survival a possibility. The mail--letters to and from, cassette tapes and occasional care packages--made life bearable. Each parcel represented care from home I could physically touch and be reminded every day that I had something to live for. They stimulated a feeling of hope, no matter how faint.

Occasionally, I could even talk to them on a crude phone system. As one of my extra duties, I was in charge of the MARS (Military Auxiliary Radio System) station for the Division. It was a short-wave radio that connected manually to a phone in the States by an amateur short wave operator. To help pass time, I would work the airwaves with the enlisted radiomen throughout the night. During my shift, I tried to drop a call back home so I could hear familiar voices and to have them to hear mine. It was a timed 3 minute call made clumsy because you had to say "over" at the end of a sentence. But it was enough to get a feeling of family love and attention by hearing their voices. Yet giving them any detailed news about my daily existence was out of the question.

All conversations were intentionally vague so no one actually knew what I did or what my assignment was. I felt strongly there was no need to have them worry about things over which they had no control. The image of Dad holding on to me the day of leaving was lodged in my mind, and it made me careful about what I said or wrote. Even when I made cassettes to send home, if there was enemy fire that was heard in the background, I always claimed it was outgoing so as not to worry them. For whatever the reason, I felt compelled to assure everyone I was safe and fortunate to be with a tough unit like the 101st who knew how to fight. I think only Dad got the drift of that.

The Unpredictable Miracle

This hope which kept me in the game and doing my job every day eventually paid off. I got lucky in October. My 6 months "in the bush" were finished. Monsoon season was approaching and our activity typically slowed down in the mud. Coincidentally, the Division was assigned a new General and, as is traditional, all available officers were ordered to attend the change of command ceremony. I thought it was an insane idea to pull everyone in for some ridiculous military pomp and circumstance charade. I couldn't believe the lunacy of the United States Army, but I had been there long enough to know it was best to just follow orders. So with everyone else, I fell into the officer formation.

As General Hennessey, the outgoing commander, walked in review he stopped in front of me and said, "Lieutenant. Baffico, I understand you might be the luckiest 1st Lieutenant in the 101st. You have done an outstanding job and I want you to know I appreciate it."

"Yes Sir. Thank you, Sir." I thought, 'Does this guy have me mixed up with someone else?'

"Lieutenant, I want you to tell Col. Smartt I said you could have any job in the Battalion because of what you have done for us."

"Yes Sir. I will, Sir. Thank you, Sir"

I almost peed my pants right there. I couldn't believe what I thought I just heard. My job was over? My flying days were over? I could really have a safe job? It was true. The Division Commander, a MAJOR GENERAL said it. There were witnesses. Colonel Smartt was right next to me and he heard it too. After the ceremony, Smartt told me Hennessey really meant it. I was delirious and couldn't wait to pick my new job.

The choice was an easy one. I wanted to be the Battalion Adjutant, the Battalion Commander's administrative assistant.

It called for the rank of Captain, but in recognition of my performance, I got it. It was the perfect REMF job for me. There was a large desk, a safe bunker; and no more combat assaults. All I had to do was push paper, listen to complaints, and keep the shitter stocked with magazines for the colonel to read every morning. Best of all, I got hot water, a decent hootch with a fan and only one roommate. I finally had time to think about something other than getting killed all day long.

The Bob Hope Show December 1970

As soon as my assignment change was official, I told the colonel I wanted to try for an early out to go to grad school. He tried to talk me into an Army career and the lure of making the rank of general…I blushed and said no, hoping I hadn't finessed myself out of the chance for an early drop. He told me to put the paperwork through and he'd sign it. I couldn't believe I had managed to get a little closer to going home.

It was October. School started in January. I was originally scheduled to rotate home in April. There was no time to dither. No officer had ever been granted an early out from the 101st. My chances seemed dim, but I was willing to try. Mary got the paperwork for school and helped get transcripts and other details arranged. I walked the paperwork through Division Personnel with a case of scotch for the clerks. At that juncture, I had a relatively safe job and nothing to lose.

A new kind of waiting began in earnest.

We were the children of the 1950's and John F. Kennedy's young stalwarts of the early 1960's. He told the world that Americans would go anywhere, pay any price, and bear any burden in the defense of freedom. We were the down payment on that costly contract, but the man who signed it was not there when we fulfilled his promise. John F. Kennedy waited for us on a hill in Arlington National Cemetery, and in time, by the thousands, we came to fill those slopes with our white marble markers and to ask on the murmur of the wind if that was truly the future he had envisioned for us."

General Hal Moore

General Hal Moore at The Wall

<u>We Were Soldiers Once and Young</u>

Never Forgotten

> There is no such thing as closure. My son lives in my heart. I see him in my other children.
>
> *Annie Gray*

One Saturday in April, I was working at The Wall along with the usual weekend volunteer team. Our group always works the crowds in a setup so each one of us covers about every 40 feet of Wall space. It is our unofficial but routine "formation" for duty. It makes it easy to summon each other if the need arises. On this particular day, I was in front of my panels. Others had taken up their specific positions, and we worked the steady stream of visitors.

Allen McCabe had just given his ranger talk to a group and was walking down the West Wall to fall into position when a young couple stopped him and asked if he would look up some names. Allen carries a small hand-held device which holds the records, so he can do it much faster than others who carry the large directories. I don't carry anything because I enjoy simply greeting visitors as they walk by me. The other volunteers enjoy looking up names.

I was waiting to work with my next visitor when Allen excitedly called me over to meet the young couple. I saw the military haircut on the young man, so I greeted him with, "Thank you for your service!" He looked at me quizzically, but then said, "Oh, the haircut?" I confirmed and asked his name. "Justin Butler," he said, "and this is my wife Kelley." I was about to get more personal info from him when Allen interrupted and said, "Wait. Let me tell you who this is and what he just did with me. This has to do with the 101st!"

Justin had asked Allen to look up three names and do rubbings for him. As Allen was completing the third rubbing, he said, "Gee, all three went Missing In Action on the same day." Justin proudly replied, "No they're not. I found them last month." Dead silence from Allen. Dead silence from me when he repeated the story.

Allen smiled and said, "Meet Justin Butler. He is a Marine Captain who is in charge of a Joint POW/MIA Accounting Command (JPAC) team. His team found the remains of these three last month in your old Area of Operations. They went missing at the time you were there. He wanted to get a rubbing with the crosses by their names, and then will get them after they are changed to diamonds. Did you know about these guys?" I suddenly realized what a treasure of information and history this young Marine represented to all of us.

"No, I didn't know them, but what can you tell us, Justin?"

Young Capt. Butler explained the three men were a 1970 101st Long Range Recon Patrol (LRRP) who had been ambushed just off of Highway 9 near the Laotian boarder. The location is close to firebase Tun Tavern where Luttel and Bohrman were killed. I knew the site. My stomach knotted and felt the hair on the back of my neck stand up as I flashed back to the primitive location. It is an almost uninhabited area, so it made a great place to cover the movement of the NVA. The landscape is perilous and the weather conditions even worse. That part of The Ho Chi Minh trail snaked directly to the northern cities of Quang Tri, Dong Ha and Hue and was also the area where Lom San 719 was supposed to blunt NVA infiltration. It was notoriously unfriendly terrain and territory then and now. My mind raced furiously as Justin described the mission and the ultimate recovery of the remains of the three LRRPs.

It was almost surreal to hear the first hand details of a recovery in a location I knew and could clearly remember from 40 years before. It was amazing that JPAC could identify a location and start a search there because the vegetation is thick and the mountains are overwhelming. Justin confirmed it was the most challenging recovery site he had ever worked. He said his JPAC team searched for almost 30 days when they finally uncovered a piece of poncho. As they dug deeper, three sets of remains which had been wrapped in ponchos were excavated. The NVA who had ambushed them apparently disposed of the bodies by wrapping and burying them. The discovered remains were sent to Hawaii where they were positively identified.

The terrain around the recovery site

This was the first time any of us volunteers had ever spoken with a JPAC member, let alone a bright team leader of Justin's caliber. I asked if he and Kelley had time to talk with all of the volunteers so we could share the wealth of his knowledge. He graciously agreed to fill us in, so we called everyone over. He did a wonderful job explaining how JPAC worked, and where it did most of the searching. He told us engrossing stories of finding missing remains from as far back as WWII in European battlefields as well as in the waters of the Pacific and Atlantic. It sounded like a fascinating assignment. Kelley was also delighted to be an integral support of her husband's work.

In our volunteer duties, we routinely reference and explain the JPAC work. After our visit with the Butlers we could recite concrete personal facts and first-hand knowledge to our visitors. It was an illuminating hour of conversation.

The JPAC command conducts global search, recovery, and laboratory operations to identify unaccounted-for Americans from the Vietnam War, the Korean War, World War II, and the Cold War. The work is designed to support the Department of Defense's personnel accounting efforts. Headquarters is located in Oahu, Hawaii and it is the home of The Central Identification Laboratory, the largest and most diverse forensic skeletal laboratory in the world.

The core of JPAC's day-to-day operations involves researching case files, investigating leads, excavating sites and identifying Americans who were killed or went missing in action and were never brought home. The process involves close coordination with U.S. agencies involved in the POW/MIA issue. JPAC has 18 Recovery Teams whose members travel throughout the world to recover missing Americans. In order to ensure mission success and the identification of unaccounted-for Americans, it routinely engages in technical negotiations and talks with representatives of foreign governments to promote and maintain positive in-country conditions wherever their teams deploy.

The recovery missions can be extremely dangerous and can last from 35 to 60 days. Unexploded ordinance and unfriendly locals are just a few of the dangers of the job. Reaching a site can be problematic in itself. Team members routinely walk through jungles; traverse difficult terrain in 4x4 vehicles; rappel cliff-sides; climb mountains; and ride on horseback, boats, or trains to reach sites. The most common method of reaching remote sites is via helicopter. Depending on the location, terrain and nature of the recovery, a team of dedicated specialists of up to 30 people from forensic archeologists and medical technicians to ordinance specialists and engineers are deployed.

How and when JPAC teams deploy to a recovery site is directly affected by various logistical concerns. The 3 LRRPs whom Justin found, were the result of a project that lasted 60 days and was almost terminated because of the fast-approaching Monsoon season. In addition to the factors of terrain and site accessibility, the cooperation of non-hostile locals had to be taken into account because the location was remote and treacherous.

Personal effects are a special category of material evidence which complement identification. Every effort is made to recover all personal items (such as a ring, watch, comb, etc.) from the excavation sites since these items aid in identification and are treasured mementos for family members.

Laotians hired to assist U.S. sift and move tons of dirt.

A technician sifts through airplane wreckage.

When the recovery effort is completed, the team returns to Hawaii. All remains and artifacts found during the recovery operation are then transported to JPAC's Central Identification Laboratory there for analysis. Once the identification process is complete, they are sent back to families and loved ones.

In honor of the sacrifice made by those individuals whose remains are recovered during a mission, JPAC holds an arrival ceremony with a joint service honor guard and senior officers from each service. Veterans, community members and local active-duty military often attend the ceremonies to pay their respects as the remains are transported from a U.S. military plane to JPAC's Central Identification Laboratory.

In addition to the thrill of hearing the details of the recovery, all of us were deeply impressed and oddly proud of the young Marine Captain and his wife. In our eyes, they represented not only the best of our country's youth, but the best of today's military family. It was satisfying to be proud of them, their work, and their dedication to each other.

I was even more delighted to learn both were graduates of Indiana University and had been students about the same time as Jon and wife Tiffani. Addionally, Justin had come out of the I.U. ROTC program. We had a lot in common, and revelled in the closeness we felt for each other. It was more Wall Magic and a great encounter.

Although Justin rotated out of this exciting job shortly after we met, we stay in touch via email. His youthful outlook and enthusiasm for his work was infectious and continues to be a treasure for all of us.

U.S. Navy divers working with JPAC plant an American flag on the site of a crashed WWII aircraft in the South Pacific

As a final footnote to the JPAC recovery by Captain Butler's team, the following year two of the three names of the LRRPs whom he recovered were converted to "Found" from MIA status in the Memorial Day ceremony. The third name continues to be designated MIA. The family did not want the remains identified. Grief presents itself in many forms.

Coming Home, Bittersweet

Each young man who went to war had an individual tour of duty, 365 days, and then home, on his own, with no effort on anyone's part to prepare him for the shock of return, to help him make the transition from war to peace, from privileging of violence to its prohibition, from the sharp edge death brings to the life of a soldier to the ordinary daily life of a civilian, which denies death altogether.

Marilyn R. Young

The Vietnam Years

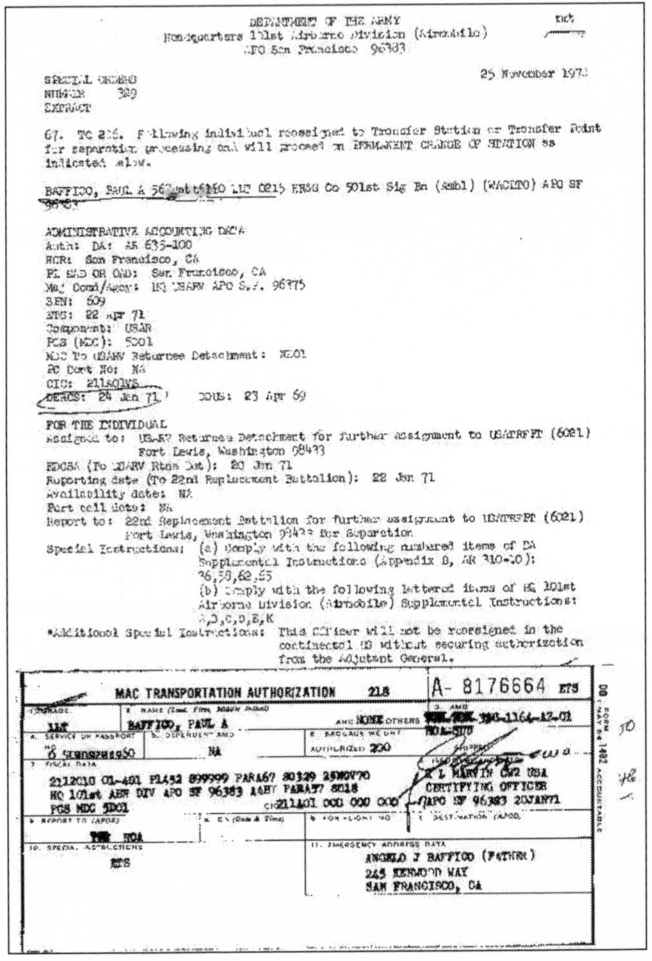

DEPARTMENT OF THE ARMY
Headquarters 101st Airborne Division (Airmobile)
APO San Francisco 96383

25 November 1970

SPECIAL ORDERS
NUMBER 329
EXTRACT

67. TC 236. Following individual reassigned to Transfer Station or Transfer Point for separation processing and will proceed on PERMANENT CHANGE OF STATION as indicated below.

BAFFICO, PAUL A [illegible] 1LT 0215 HHSC Co 501st Sig Bn (Ambl) (WACLTO) APO SF 96383

ADMINISTRATIVE ACCOUNTING DATA
Auth: DA: AR 635-100
HOR: San Francisco, CA
PL EAD OR OAD: San Francisco, CA
Maj Comd/Agcy: HQ USARV APO S.F. 96375
SEN: 509
ETS: 22 Apr 71
Component: USAR
PCS (MDC): 5D01
MDC To USARV Returnee Detachment: 5E01
2C Cert No: NA
CIC: 211A01VS
DEROS: 24 Jan 71   DOUS: 23 Apr 69

FOR THE INDIVIDUAL
Assigned to: USARV Returnee Detachment for further assignment to USATRFFT (6021) Fort Lewis, Washington 98433
EDCSA (To USARV Rtnee Det): 20 Jan 71
Reporting date (To 22nd Replacement Battalion): 22 Jan 71
Availability date: NA
Port call date: NA
Report to: 22nd Replacement Battalion for further assignment to USATRFFT (6021) Fort Lewis, Washington 98433 for Separation
Special Instructions: (a) Comply with the following numbered items of DA Supplemental Instructions (Appendix B, AR 310-10): 36,58,62,65
(b) Comply with the following lettered items of HQ 101st Airborne Division (Airmobile) Supplemental Instructions: A,B,C,D,E,K
*Additional Special Instructions: This Officer will not be reassigned in the continental US without securing authorization from the Adjutant General.

MAC TRANSPORTATION AUTHORIZATION 218 A- 8176664 ETS

1. GRADE: 1LT
2. NAME (Last, First, Middle Initial): BAFFICO, PAUL A AND NONE OTHERS
3. AMO: [illegible]-1164-17-01
4. SERVICE OR PASSPORT NO: [illegible]
5. DEPENDENT AMO: NA
6. BAGGAGE WEIGHT AUTHORIZED: 200
7. FISCAL DATA: 2112010 01-401 P1452 899999 PARA67 SO329 25NOV70 HQ 101st ABN DIV APO SF 96383 AAHY PARA37 SO18 PCS MDC 5D01 CIC 211A01 000 000 000
R L MARVIN CW2 USA
CERTIFYING OFFICER
APO SF 96383 20JAN71
9. REPORT TO (APOE): TMR HOA
10. SPECIAL INSTRUCTIONS: ETS
11. EMERGENCY ADDRESS DATA: ANGELO J BAFFICO (FATHER)
245 KENWOOD WAY
SAN FRANCISCO, CA

DD FORM 1482 ACCOUNTABLE

My orders home with flight manifest approval

A Hard Farewell

It worked. I couldn't believe it. My early out orders came through in November saying I had received a release from service to go to graduate school. My ETS (Estimated Time of Separation) was officially moved from 23 April 1971 to 24 Jan 1971. I DID IT!! I DID IT!! I was almost home.

The days moved more sluggishly as the date drew near. I was cautious about everything I did and every place I went and I began to lose my swagger. I didn't want to risk missing anything and yet I knew I had to be vigilant about everything.

For some strange reason I couldn't explain, I wanted to go out on a few more chopper rides, but men from the platoon always talked me out of it. I had done enough dangerous things to that point, and I didn't need to do more without thinking through the possible consequences. For instance, one night I watched the motor pool being blown up by mortar rounds landing closer and closer to me before I realized I needed to get down and protected. That's an example of the insanity of war. Life becomes so expendable you even lose perspective on your own. You experience enough close calls to get a feeling of insuperability, but you need to be careful not to test fate too much. I had to remind myself I had something to live for, especially as my time became shorter and shorter. Then the thoughts of going home became otherworldly.

I was finally one day short of going home but there was one last ritual before leaving. It was the traditional 101st officers' goodbye party the night before. It was a hard drinking goodbye. Ceremoniously, an outdoor dinner was held around the officers' hootches. After dinner, everyone poured you a shot or more into an 8 oz. tumbler of what they drank. You had to chug it... at least I thought you had to. The last thing I remembered was falling backwards off the bench I was sitting on.....and that is all I remember.

Unfortunately, the morning of my scheduled departure the next day, I woke up strapped down in my bunk stark naked and in so much pain I was barely able to move. My head hurt so much I could hardly open my eyes. I couldn't keep anything down and I couldn't stand up. I could only lay flat on my back. Worst of all, I didn't remember a single thing except putting the first glass to my lips and falling over backwards. I was speechless with pain and my lack of recall.

Apparently, with the continuing aid of my fellow officers, I got so drunk I had to be restrained. My hootch-mate, Roger Dwyer, told me I was so completely out of control that I stood on a rock and fired a full clip of my M16 on automatic into the air like I was some kind of delirious insurgent rebel announcing to everyone I was going back to "The World". My profligate enthusiasm made it very hard for others to restrain me, thus the tie down to my rack.

Obviously, my "merriment" was more a release of anger and rage than it was of joy and relief. Both emotions had been severely repressed for many months (or maybe even years) which made me as dangerous to myself as I was to others. But my behavior was so aberrant that rather than lock me up, my mates got control of me and with some effort calmed me down. They also forgave me. I have no recollection of what happened. I had to believe whatever Dwyer told me. The throb of my body was evidence he did not exaggerate. By the time I was able enough to hear what he said, I couldn't process it properly anyway.

That had never happened to me before, and I recall thinking this genie could not be let out of the bottle in the civilized world. But now I just wanted to get home as soon as I was physically able to make the trip. Consequentially, the pain and sickness were too much, and I was in no condition to move from the horizontal position. So there I was, on my official day of departure, my supposed *last* day in Vietnam, so hung over I couldn't get in a Jeep to catch the ride to my Freedom Bird...I had to stay longer.

By the following day I was able to hold down some aspirin and was lucid enough to focus on what I needed to do to get on my way. As a driver waited to take me to the helipad, I made my goodbyes. But the seemingly mundane departure formality elicited unforeseen emotions. In my heart I was reluctant to go. A frog stuck in my throat as I shook hands, saluted and looked in the eyes of each of my men and fellow officers. So much is communicated by eye contact. The emotional pull was powerful.

It was supposed to be a happy farewell, but the kaleidoscope of feelings was all-consuming. I had never experienced the closeness, trust, suffering, fighting, loving, and sacrifice for others as I had in that nightmarish place. Somehow I suspected I never would again. To go home while those I cared for had to stay seemed selfish. The empathy and conflict the leaving provoked was stirring. And the things I left behind, a part of myself, the proud 101st and the unfinished war, the deep pride and loyalty I felt, the men I would miss and never see again all tugged at me. Much of me had been re-shaped over the 10 determinative months I had spent with the 101st. I had earned a prized membership in their exclusive brotherhood. But on that day of separation, I involuntarily had to surrender my membership. I felt a brother no longer. I began to tear up with the leave-taking.

I finally left Camp Eagle a day late even though I was lime-green sick and had to endure a jostling jeep ride to my re-scheduled flight. But one-way travel alive and *out* of Vietnam on a big twin rotor Chinook helicopter was a child-like fantasy, like flying in a house above the fray with the pilot sitting on the front porch in control. It was a new thrill. Eagle to Phu Bai. Phu Bai to Danang. Danang to Tan Son Nhut Air Base. 'I *never* have to see this God-forsaken place again,' I thought as the Chinook lifted off. It felt like an out of body experience. At Tan Son Nhut, we were processed quickly and were hustled onto a waiting World Airways charter flight. There was no time to think, just to move fast. The End was at hand and the civilian jet looked absolutely beautiful, no olive drab!

I will never forget taking off from Tan Son Nhut on the first leg. Once on board, we buckled in fast. The tension was thick and overbearing by the time the door finally slammed shut. It was then that all of us simultaneously realized there was no way to escape or to run for cover. Our emotional pressure peaked as we hurriedly taxied into position. We instantly became a sitting target waiting to take off. There was a deafening silence, not even PA announcements. Everyone's hyper-vigilance was red-lined. We jerked to a stop. Engines came to full power and the 707 vibrated violently with restrained thrust. The brakes finally released and we burst forward with a startling rumble. Picking up speed, we could feel a slight lift. Sweat rolled down my face and armpits. Eyes were shut. I gripped the arms of the seat. Every person stayed focused intensely on one single thought. 'Get up! Get this fucking thing off the ground!!!' I demanded of God.

The nose of the plane finally picked up gently and we began to gain a little altitude. Uniforms were soaked...and not from the heat. Eyes still shut tightly, '...God, please...just one more time...' When the landing gear double-thumped against the underbelly of the plane, a raucous roar broke out as every man spontaneously celebrated "The End" with high fives. As though rehearsed, a slow and guttural, "IIIIIIIIIIIIII......*hate* this fuckin' place", bellowed out of our lungs in unison followed by terse outbursts of, "Fuck you, Vietnam!!!," either shouted or mumbled by each of us. We were finally out of range on our way back to The World...nothing was ever so sweet. Even though we were going home as individuals, we all felt subliminally bonded for life. We had lived to tell about our time in Vietnam, and we were proud of it.

The flights home, as those we took to Vietnam, were agonizing and nerve-racking. Tedious travel through Yakota, Japan; Anchorage Alaska; McChord AFB in Washington; and finally to Travis AFB in California punctuated the journey. It was a long ride in many dimensions. It gave me a lot of time to think.

I had survived the ordeal of combat and had completed my obligation. I did more than was expected of me, and more than I believed I could do. I had learned much about myself; about others; about leadership and teamwork; about tragedy; about evil; about war; about morality; and much more. But I was so flooded with the joy of going home, it was impossible to comprehend much of it at the time. Mine had been a highly compressed maturation few people ever have to navigate. It would take the rest of my life to unpack, validate, accept and appreciate it as more than just a time in my life fulfilling an obligation.

I couldn't appreciate how I had changed. I knew I felt a strong sense of satisfaction and accomplishment. I was more confident and mature than my chronological years. And I was deeply proud of having served with the 101st. It was a feeling which was absolutely unpredictable the year before. I felt I had earned a place of honor and respect in the eyes of family and friends. But the hard-earned lessons and achievements which had been permanently implanted in me and would serve as sources of confidence in my life were not in clear focus the day I came home. They became deep reserves, personal, private and eventually very influential.

Home at last!
Travis AFB greeted by Mary

Re-Entry

At Travis Air Force Base, our Freedom Bird taxied to its assigned parking space and powered down. As soon as the door popped open, I smelled the fresh air of California that evoked a sense of familiarity. I was home. It felt great.

A loadmaster came to the doorway and took charge by saying, "Alright, welcome home. When you go down the stairs here to go into the terminal, just stay on the yellow line and DO NOT DEVIATE from it. It will lead you directly into the terminal where you will get your instructions. If you have family waiting for you, they will be able to meet you outside the building on the other side, once you process with your orders. Again, I repeat, DO NOT DEVIATE from the yellow stripe. It will lead you through a cyclone fence tunnel which is there so the protestors can only spit on you and jeer you. DO NOT STOP AND ENGAGE THEM. Okay?"

'Oh, yes. Welcome home to California', I thought, 'This ought to be funny.'

I fell in the conga line behind the guys in front of me and descended the stairs. The yellow line did, indeed, lead us through the fenced corridor. As we walked through it, we were spit on, had water, paint and urine thrown at us and were called fascists, pigs, murderers, and any number of vile invectives that came from the mouths of the protestors. Some guys jeered back as we moved through, but I didn't. I thought about how much sicker the Anti-War Movement had become while I was gone. The soldier had become the one to blame. He was the killer and the enemy. That was new and unexpected. But most of us had been hardened enough to shut out our feelings. We had experienced enough hatred to ignore it and stay in our own zone. Besides, we were so happy to be home on our own dirt that no amount of incivility could ruin the day.

Welcome Home. We're proud of You, Pig.

I knew Mary and Dad were waiting because we had talked on a regular telephone when I got into McChord to let them know when to expect me. I didn't know what was going to happen with my discharge details, but I also didn't expect there to be anything I couldn't get through or to stop me from meeting up with them. There were no problems. I waltzed through.

Outside the terminal, there they were. Mary and I embraced as Dad clicked away with the Instamatic for posterity. There were hugs, kisses, a handshake, and Dad's great big arm around me that felt so good. I didn't know how much I missed a warm and friendly touch. In Vietnam I had to condition myself to stay detached from others.

We got in the car and headed to San Francisco. It might sound peculiar, but I had to strain to make conversation. With almost a year gone and the sensations of a safe haven filling my head, I felt oddly uncomfortable. After our usual family courtesy of asking about friends and relatives, I was at a loss for words. There was nothing I could or wanted to tell them. I knew I was tired and spent, but I felt badly. I thought the discomfort would pass when I got back into the rhythm of civilian life.

Right there and then, though, the balminess of being home and safe was heady. The California sun was warm and gentle. There was no oppressive heat or stench. Cars and people moved in a smooth pattern on the roads. I didn't have to look for cover or worry about hiding places for snipers. I realized how much I had taken for granted before and got a hint of how much I had learned living in a Third World country. Everything looked so good I had trouble taking it in. I couldn't help but think I didn't deserve it, 'Why did I get to come home and not others?' Not for me to answer. I had a life full of hope ahead, and I needed to keep that thought in my head.

I was also startled by the bumper stickers on almost every car like Free Huey, Stop the Bombing, Impeach Nixon, Free Tibet, Save the Whales, Whales are People Too, The Life of an Illegal Pet is No Life at All and more. I felt compelled to ask, "Does everyone here have a cause?" The bumper politics and morality were intimidating. They easily extinguished any pride I might have indulged in on the plane ride home. Now I felt like an alien in my uniform. I wanted to get out of it and on with life.

On the way to the house we stopped at the Sears Mission Street Store where Mom worked. I surprised her on the sales floor with hugs and kisses. There were tears of joy and congratulations for both of us from her co-workers, most of whom had known me since I was born. It was a big relief for me also to see Mom okay and happy. I had worried dreadfully about her every day I was gone, often thinking of the pain and sorrow she would suffer had I been killed or gone missing. I'm not sure why, but mothers and lovers are at the top of every soldier's mind in combat. With the burden gone, it was so good to see her smile and happy.

That night at our house, as would be expected, Mom had prepared an Italian feast for a gourmet. Hans, Chris, Dad, Mom and Mary (Jim called in his welcome home from Michigan) all gathered around the sacramental meal to give thanks for my safe return. More food than I had eaten in a month, and even though I had grown unaccustomed to its richness, every bite reinforced my gratitude. I was finally safe and in warm, friendly and familiar surroundings. I was home.

"THE WORLD"

For over a thousand years, Roman conquerors returning from the wars enjoyed the honor of a triumph - a tumultuous parade. In the procession came trumpeters and musicians and strange animals from the conquered territories, together with carts laden with treasure and captured armaments. The conqueror rode in a triumphal chariot, the dazed prisoners walking in chains before him. Sometimes his children robed in white, stood with him in the chariot, or rode the trace horses. A slave stood behind the conqueror, holding a golden crown, and whispering in his ear a warning that all glory is fleeting.

George C. Scott, Patton

A 1971 Album Cover

"No News...

My time in Vietnam was spent living under the naive impression the world would somehow stand still while I was gone. I was unaware of any of the changes taking place. Fearing for my life 8000 miles from comfort or shelter was gut-wrenching drama. The facts were that I had lived through 10 months of civil war; no one could be trusted; the language, ethics, customs, and living conditions were completely foreign, as were U.S. troops; and it took every ounce of my being to just survive. It's no wonder there was no time keep up with "The World". Furthermore, the only emancipation from the untenable situation came from alcohol and limited contact with loved ones. Both helped me dream about what I had left behind. My imperatives there were to do my job as best I could, get home in one piece, and then figure out my life.

We called home "The World" because it was the short hand way to refer to that which had been familiar to us. It was where we were comfortable, accepted, and safe. To the intruding U.S. soldier, Vietnam was definitely not a part of "The World". "The World" was where we were good at navigation, had hope, and understood the language. Each man had their own private version of it. Unlike today's deployments which provide soldiers with email, Skype, or cell phones to connect on a daily basis to home and friends, our information from the U.S. was carefully parsed and filtered. In truth, most of the news which was frugally apportioned to the 101st was carefully re-constituted so you couldn't get a genuine feel for what was happening. That was probably for safety and morale purposes. Too much news could have been dangerously distracting. Mission and survival had to occupy all of your mind space.

Even though the ubiquitous *Army Times* was routinely distributed to the far reaches of the battlefield every week, it contained processed news which was partially manipulated and censored. AFVN TV broadcasts (if you were in a place which could receive them) were formatted to look roughly similar to what we were accustomed to at home. They were packaged nightly news from home followed by *Bewitched* or some other sitcom. Vietnam Top 40 radio programming played the "latest" rock hits 3 months delayed, usually followed by a replay of old Yankees or Red Sox games. Entertainment and news were basically synthesized military propaganda formulated as a palliative for your attitude. No provocative real life information was allowed. For example, The Smothers Brothers Comedy Hour, an uproariously hilarious and cutting political lampoon of White House antics, was never shown on AFVN even though at home it topped the rating charts. It was deemed too controversial and too close to the truth.

Meanwhile, "The World" back home continued to mutate into more indecent stages. The massive and chaotic social change of the 60's had continued unabated. Growing disillusionment with government; advances in civil rights; and an increased influence of the Women's Movement framed a potentially rude welcome home for many. The myriad of "radical" ideas which had been proffered in 1969 had gained wider acceptance in 1970 and then became mainstreamed into life by the start of 1971.

The changes, the continuing social realignment, the Machiavellian presidential drama and the anti-war activities looked like a battle of extremes to the Vietnam returnee. Moreover, the pace of change was mind-boggling, and in some instances intimidating to many of us. Shockingly, we had no concept of what "The World" of 1971 would look like. None of us who had risked our lives in a pitiless war had participated in the culture that unfolded in our absence. Although gone for less than a year, the cultural fissure appeared almost insurmountable to me.

Combustible Discontent

The Nixon White House had inevitably proved itself to be as bad, if not worse, than its predecessor. Nixon became pathetically obsessed with his approval ratings and did everything possible to trick the voting public into thinking all was well. He manipulated, lied, and cajoled anyone and everyone about innumerable controversial issues operating on the maxim that the end justifies the means. He concocted any number of sinister plots to hold on to office. White House taping became routine. Hints of the Watergate scandal began to simmer. The Ping Pong diplomacy in China was contrived to mask trouble at home and in Vietnam. Henry Kissinger was Nixon's surreptitious agent in the tomfooleries. But the American public was not fooled. The public demand for truth simply increased.

Then bold terrorism shockingly surfaced on March 1st. A bomb exploded in the men's room of the Capitol Building. The Weather Underground Organization claimed responsibility for the direct attack on the government. The tenor of discontent and rebellion had intensified seemingly overnight. Anti-war protesting took on a significantly larger profile in the media. It replaced the combat footage Nixon had exorcised the year before as he sought to reduce the headlines littered with carnage and body-count statistics. The U.S. Supreme Court ruled the Pentagon Papers could be published, rejecting government injunctions as unconstitutional prior restraint.

> The most massive leak of secret documents in U.S. history had suddenly exposed the sensitive inner processes whereby the Johnson Administration had abruptly escalated the nation's most unpopular and unsuccessful war.
> *Pentagon Papers: The Secret War*
> *Jun. 28, 1971*

The mistrust between Nixon and the American public would have bordered on the comical had it not been so tragically serious. The people wanted their voices heard. The government refused to listen. Nixon was too busy performing political sleight of hand tricks. When the Pentagon Papers ruling and public references to the stealthy Plumbers were exposed, his psychotic paranoia hit its apogee. It was then that Nixon and his Administration developed a picture-perfect bunker mentality for the world to see.

Protests became bigger and closer to the power center. They were more effective as credible people stood to be heard. On April 22, 1971, John Kerry was the first Vietnam Veteran to testify before the Senate Foreign Relations Committee in the Fulbright Hearings on proposals relating to ending the war. He was still a member of the United States Navy Reserve, holding the rank of Lieutenant Junior Grade. Wearing green fatigues and service ribbons, he spoke for nearly two hours. Kerry began with a prepared speech, in which he presented the conclusions of the Winter Soldier Investigation, and then went on to address larger policy issues.

The day after his testimony, he participated in a demonstration with thousands of other Veterans in which he and others threw their medals and ribbons over a fence erected at the front steps of the United States Capitol building to dramatize their opposition to the war. For more than two hours, almost 1000 angry Veterans tossed their medals, ribbons, hats, jackets, and military papers over the fence. Each Veteran gave his or her name, hometown, branch of service and a statement. Kerry threw some of his ribbons as well as some given to him by other Veterans.

> I'm not doing this for any violent reasons, but for peace and justice, and to try and make this country wake up once and for all.
> *John Kerry*

As a newly decorated Veteran who really didn't care about the medals I had won or the continuing controversy about the war, I did, however, feel ashamed of Kerry's emblematic act. I was dumbfounded by the disrespectful grandstanding of a fellow officer of the United States Military. For the other 1000 participants, I had some empathy. But as I watched Kerry speak, I couldn't discern whether the act was treasonous, for protest, personal gain, or all three. I eventually concluded it was an act of contrived self-aggrandizement which could do major things for his political aspirations. I thought the use of others' anger for the sake of his personal gain was contemptible.

The next day approximately 200,000 peaceful protesters gathered in the nation's capital to demonstrate against the war. At the front of the demonstration was a new group, the Vietnam Veterans Against the War (VVAW) led by Kerry, their new trusted and articulate leader. Then numbering about 20,000, VVAW was considered by some, including the Nixon Administration to be an effective, if controversial, component of the antiwar movement.

The Jarring New World

By the time I came home, vulgarity and offensiveness had become the identifiers of change. They were heavily marketed in behaviors, fashions, and news. Revolution was mainstreamed as marketers packaged and promoted it in various forms in everyday life. "Revolutionary" was *the* new way to sell cool.

The Drug Culture moved beyond the infant stage as more addicted combatants came home and new varieties of drugs hit the streets. Drugs augmented alcohol as a part of the culture and social scene. The drug overdose deaths of Jimi Hendrix, Janis Joplin and Jim Morrison in the course of the year offered a strong barometric reading on the cultural progress of drug acceptance moving across the landscape. Their deaths were mourned by the masses, not small splinter groups.

Patriotism and loyalty were disdained and derided as more post WWII behaviors were summarily jettisoned. Civil disobedience was no longer confined to big cities. Rebellion against authority moved up a notch in intensity. Prisoners at the upstate New York correctional facility in Attica took thirty hostages in a stand-off which lasted four days. The rebellion ended when state troopers and sheriffs stormed the facility. Ten guards and 32 prisoners were killed. Horrified viewers watched the rebellion on TV as it exposed a level of heinous hostility never before seen by most of the population. The action was highly criticized as an example of state and federal mismanagement, use of excessive force, poor planning, and hyper-aggressive action. There was little attention paid to the violent ignition of the riot by the inmates. Not surprisingly, The Establishment was assigned the blame for the catastrophe.

The Attica Riots

In fashion, designs represented provocative social statements. The color palate of fashion had turned completely psychedelic. Styles of big bell bottoms, longer hair, jeans for every day, high healed klunky shoes, wide belts, heavy metal, suits and sport coats with big lapels and patterns, hot pants, bare midriff all made bold fashion statements. Everything seemed to be a symbolic way to say, "In your face!" …or worse.

TV had become an ethnic battleground with *All In the Family* and *Sanford and Son* leading the charge. Presented as comedic entertainment, the aberrant language, racism, and bigotry in living color was like nothing ever seen before. The black and white days of *Donna Reed* and *Leave it to Beaver* were ancient history. The last Ed Sullivan Show aired in 1971.

The 1971 Cultural Landscape of "The World"

Music moved from Folk, Soul, Surfin', Beach Boys, and Mo Town to the weird hard hitting, ear piercing, head pounding acid rock of Alice Cooper, Jethro Tull, The Doors, Black Sabbath, David Bowie and more. Loyalties to anything traditional were considered weaknesses or treasonous to the new Cultural Revolution. The bitterness of the divisive Boomer Generation grew exponentially and overpowered every major element of our social structure. Attacks on anything that smacked of the previous generation became fashionable and trendy. Standards and traditions were changed pugnaciously as clamorous disagreement ranged from Nixon, Kissinger, and Danielle Ellsberg down to the union vs. non-union food which was put on the dinner table. The collective conscience of the Boomer Generation was all-consuming and undirected. Priorities for a national discussion of resolution were a dim hope.

Some of the other landmark events of 1971 which captured headlines and changed the cultural landscape produced compounding and confusing shockwaves. Mandatory busing in Boston led to violence and disruption of the educational process. The 26th Amendment was ratified allowing

18-year-olds to vote. The first Gay Pride march was held in New York City beginning the modern GLBT movement. A ban on radio and television cigarette advertisements went into effect in the United States. On March 31, 1971, Lt. William Calley was sentenced to life and hard labor at Fort Leavenworth for My Lai. The next day, Richard Nixon ordered Calley transferred from Leavenworth prison to house arrest at Fort Benning pending appeal. The leniency was protested by Melvin Laird, *Nixon's* Secretary of Defense. The prosecutor, Aubrey Daniel wrote, "The greatest tragedy of all will be if political expedience dictates the compromise of such a fundamental moral principle as the inherent unlawfulness of the murder of innocent persons.

On July 10, 1971, at the founding of the National Women's Political Caucus, co-founder Gloria Steinem delivered an address to the women of America which became one of the most memorable speeches of the era. The speech, was delivered at the height of the Women's Movement, and is today considered one of the 20th century's greatest. Not only did the speech address the issues of sexism and misogyny, but also those of racism and social class.

> "This is no simple reform. It really is a revolution. Sex and race, because they are easy, visible differences, have been the primary ways of organizing human beings into superior and inferior groups, and into the cheap labor on which this system still depends. We are talking about a society in which there will be no roles other than those chosen, or those earned. We are really talking about humanism."
> *Gloria Steinem*

Gloria Steinem

As I headed into civilian life in San Francisco after fulfilling my 2 year military obligation, it was all I could do to digest the changes that had taken place while I was absent. I was in such a state of disorientation, I didn't know if I wanted to integrate. I didn't feel as though I would have a place in the new World unless I could establish my own credibility and identity. I didn't know if I could or if I even belonged there. I felt disenfranchised, marginalized and out of sync with everything. The disillusionment of re-entry was perplexing as I searched for some emotional hand-holds to steady myself. Clearly, having served in Vietnam was a major liability. I had to begrudgingly realize that I had been disconnected from my old environs to a much greater degree than I had imagined. Mine was to be a bumpy ride back to The World if I chose to take it.

Lifeless Integration

"Anyone who isn't confused really doesn't understand the situation."
Edward R. Murrow

My return to civilian life teemed with incompatible thoughts about how to get started. My natural instinct was to work furiously while in denial to re-assemble the pieces I thought I had left behind as if nothing had ever happened. But at the same time, I wanted someone to recognize what I had survived and to acknowledge my sacrifices. I also wanted to be somewhat invisible--probably forever---another strange sensation. I didn't want to be questioned about what had happened, and I didn't want to talk about it, but I wanted people to know I had done my job and had overcome some enormous personal hurdles doing it. It was bizarre. I wanted to stay out of the political and social sewers of the anti-war circles, but my pride at being a survivor was top of mind. It caused multiple internal conflicts. Mostly, I just wanted what I wanted. Being left alone seemed in order temporarily, while I sorted out many acute divergent thoughts and emotions.

Furtively, I craved special treatment for what I had done and given, but I had enough sense to never share my thoughts of entitlement with anyone. I felt it was too risky and would have elicited nothing but rejection and argument. By then, I had had enough forced intrusions into my psyche, and I was determined to control any incursions going forward.

The first week home was packed with details big and small because I had less than 6 days before I had to be in the classroom for graduate degree studies. Registration, books, class schedules, and more had to be attended to. The new stereo equipment I purchased on R&R in Hong Kong and the personal things I sent home from Vietnam needed to be picked up from the U.S. Customs Office. I had saved enough combat pay to buy the sports car I had lusted after for 12 months. It was a promise I had made to myself if I made it home. So in the first week I became the proud owner of a brand new racing red Italian sports car. Moreover, Mary and I had to plan our wedding while we worked around her teaching and my classes. If I was going to fall into the rhythm of school/married life with my future wife, I had a lot to do in great haste.

There was also a nagging administrative re-entry detail that needed my attention. Official separation from the Army took one full day at Oakland Army Terminal. During the process, I was told I had to immediately sign up for Guard or Reserve duty to complete my obligation. On my first day back, I couldn't bring myself to do that. I didn't. Stubbornness whispered in my ear that the Army would find me if they needed me. To my pleasant surprise, they never did. Years later I found out my separation orders read that due to my combat service, unit actions, and the awards I won, I was not to be re-assigned without prior permission from the Pentagon. When I stumbled across it, I actually felt confirmed. My faded memories of pride and accomplishment had finally been authenticated.

Disconnection.

I took the indignity of being shamed and shunned for serving in Vietnam as a personal affront. Beyond the ignominious public who dispensed the humiliation, it also came from those with whom I thought I would be able to reconnect. Friends, classmates, relatives, teachers, and co-workers made for peculiar encounters. I am sure to them I seemed a different person, but I couldn't comprehend why I was so different that I would be rejected and feel the sting of being ostracized.

Ostensibly, I thought people wanted me to be the old Paul I used to be, and to forget Vietnam had ever happened. But I couldn't revert back. My views on many things had been altered. Yet I didn't recognize they had or why. I did know I didn't want to reminisce about a previous part of my life which now seemed so insignificant and immature by comparison to my combat time. Not surprisingly, in the new life I was searching for, a purpose and direction were not at all clear. After being consumed with the fears of war and service day to day for 6 years, the need to make a meaningful life plan was foreign to my kind of thinking. That created colossal distress because of the transformation I had gone through. I did not like the new version of the civilian world I was facing, and the people and places in it made me very insecure. Nothing seemed to fit together smoothly.

Classmates in graduate school wouldn't talk to me. I was older, and obviously being fresh from the war, no one wanted to be seen consorting with a "baby killer". Some of my relatives snickered at me and thought I had been stupid for not getting into a reserve or guard unit in order to avoid Vietnam. Former friends were the most difficult to deal with for any number of reasons even though there had been early warning signs when we were classmates only a few years before.

I ran into a friend who happened to be in the company of one of my high school religion teachers, Father Al Torrelli, S.J. Both were finishing their law degrees at USF Law School. We were catching up, but when Torisi heard where I had been, he told me I should be ashamed of myself for being a murderer. At first I thought it was a politically correct sarcastic joke. But as he continued his chastisement, it was all too clear he was deadly serious. He went on about the sins I had committed by participating in an immoral and illegal war which murdered civilians. He told me I was going to Hell.

In other random encounters, I met people with whom I had been close friends during school years. One fellow didn't acknowledge I was visible or present. When I said hello, he looked past me and refused to hear me. Another didn't consider me invisible but rather the deserving target of his anti-Vietnam venom. He determinedly told me I was a shameless killer of innocent people, and I had participated in immoral and heinous crimes against the Vietnamese.

One obtuse college friend phoned me the first day I was home. I had no idea how he knew I was home because I hadn't had any contact with him for 3 years. He was in law school and wanted to know if I could help him smuggle drugs from Vietnam through my men who were rotating home. He said he made really good money selling them and would share it with me if I could help him. I was incensed. I declined and never spoke to him again.

In the compactness of San Francisco, it was almost impossible to avoid these kinds of prickly encounters. The first Sunday back I tried to go to Mass at S.I. Cathedral to give thanks and to ask for help. It was one of few sacred places from my past to which I really wanted to reconnect. Midway through Mass, an anti-war group took over the altar and unfurled the Viet Cong Flag. They proceeded to hijack the ritual with a protest speech and song against the war. I got up and left swiftly. My anger and frustration almost took complete control of me.

I just didn't want to debate or argue with anyone about the politics or morality of the war or the right or wrong of my participation in it. I was exhausted and still irresolute about so much, including my own service. But that was for me to sort out privately...not in some public forum filled with rancor and prejudice. I wanted people to understand how difficult it was for me. But it just was not possible in the highly condemnatory environment. There were fewer and fewer places where confrontation could be avoided. Alcohol continued to be my best friend. It soothed me. And it numbed my lingering bitterness and anger.

The Intruder

In my disorienting quest for reconnection, I tried going back to some old hangouts. I was hopeful I could run into a friend with whom I could talk and dream about a future, not to re-live my adolescent past. The Laurel Lodge had always been a place to ideate, contemplate and speculate as a student while imbibing a warming drink. For many of us, it was our off-campus Student Union that served alcohol. The Lodge was always loaded with USF undergrads, night school and law students who sat around the cozy fireplace debating issues like world hunger and the existential meaning of life. A group of young Sears people would occasionally drop by after the store closed. It was really convenient because it was close to both USF and the Geary Street Sears. It was owned and run by Gordy Esposto, a close high school friend of my brother Jim, so I knew I was always welcomed there. I decided one night to try going back.

A Laurel Lodge Matchbook

When I went in, nothing looked changed. I was buoyed by the fact that the place looked, felt, and smelled the same as it always had. People were sitting around the fireplace in quiet conversation and there was the familiar musty smell of stale beer on the floor mixed with freshly popped popcorn and cigarette smoke. It was just what I was hoping for.

Gordy was tending bar as usual and the seats and tables were filled. The optics seemed perfect. 'This might be the place for connection,' I thought. I looked around at each table and barstool a couple of times looking for a friendly face. And then it hit me, there was not a soul I knew. Same age group as always, same array of students from USF and the law school, but they looked a generation younger and a galaxy apart from me.

I felt I was an intruder, but took a seat at the bar anyway. Gordy had always been great to me and he always liked to get his news on Jim's whereabouts. As I sat down, Gordy shouted out, "Hey, Paulie! Hey good to see you. It's been awhile. Where you been and whaddaya been doin'?" 'Ha! A friendly familiar face.' I thought to myself. I finally felt a spark of connection.

"I did two years in the Army and just got back from Vietnam," I said calmly. Gordy looked at me for a long time as he recovered from the unintended emotional slap to his face and tried to think of what to say next. There was a long pause……

"Naaaaawwwww! That's not possible. Weren't you here just a couple a months ago?! Yeah! I remember. You were just here. I swear you were here just a couple of months ago. You didn't really go to Vietnam did you? I am *sure* I just saw you. That's crazy. How come you didn't get out of it like everyone else? Vietnam! Wow. That's bad shit. You didn't see any action did ya? Vietnam? Wow! Hey, how's Jimmy? Is he doing okay? Is he still married? … and he has a kid. Man, that's so hard to believe."

The Comforts of FSB Berchtesgaden

We made a little more small talk, but it was difficult to stand Gordy's obvious discomfort with me. So I finished my drink, said a warm goodbye and left. As I sat in my new sports car thinking about what had just happened, I was struck by a blinding flash of the obvious. I didn't know how to talk about what I felt and other people had no idea how to talk to me. It was a profound and embarrassing admission for me--another secret for me to guard and hide. The military was over for me and I was in a new civilian world. Back in this world there was a different language; different texture to life; different protocols and new models which didn't integrate or transition. Right or wrong, there was so much distance between me and the "civilians" I felt like an extraterrestrial on a brief visit to Planet Earth.

Furthermore, it was obviously intolerable for people to be confronted with someone who had personally lived through a war which most knew only as the lead story of the nightly news for 6 years. Points of reference were impossible for both parties to align. The politics of the war had infected everyone's point of view and, consequently, their emotions about it. Overwhelming numbers of people had an automatic bias against the Veterans. As if they feared us to a certain degree. I hated the bias. It was consistent and it hurt. But hurt became an integral part of re-entry for every Vietnam Veteran. We didn't realize it at the time but we needed to stay undercover so as not talk to anyone about our feelings, just as we had been trained in combat.

In the early days of being home, I would get an occasional call from my men as they rotated through California on their way home. I was honored and thrilled they thought to contact me. However, there was never an attempt by Mary or anyone in my family to make them feel welcomed. It was as though they were as dangerous and blemished as I was. So, we would have an awkward phone conversation, maybe a meal together, and then they would go on their way. Definitive and abrupt separation from such an intense time in my life became more pronounced the longer I was home. To all those around me, my military service was over, and there was absolutely no need for me to resurrect one millisecond of it. I needed to keep it buried. There was less pain and trouble for everyone. I had to stay focused on the here and now or the future.

The Silent Conversation

My family was happy to have me home, and they were happy to have me get my life back on a track to which they could contribute as quickly as possible. They wanted to share their marital knowledge and experiences with Mary and me. To be perfectly fair, the fact I got home safely and needed their help to start married life was the center of interest for all of those who loved me. They wanted to help, and I knew they felt rehashing things, no matter how significant, would slow my transition and re-launch. As was the case with others, no one in my immediate circle of support had any idea of how to have a conversation with a warrior. I had to accept that.

As Mary and I prepared for a life together, I occasionally tried to share some troubling memories of Vietnam with her. It was my attempt to clear my head and get a proper orientation to our new life. She was my partner, and I felt we should have no dark shadows or secrets between us. But Vietnam was a non-starter for her. She didn't want to know anything. She never asked me what happened, how I felt or what I did. I believe she genuinely thought nothing good could come from it. But I felt otherwise. I needed to talk about it, yet I didn't know how to or nor could I articulate why without feeling stupid. More than likely, I simply wanted someone to listen. But I didn't press it. On the few occasions when I asked her if we could talk, she declined and said she didn't need to know. Her father's deafening silence about his combat time at Attu in WWII was her behavioral model. Furthermore, her family never spoke about difficult issues, so she had no practice with the discomfort of a reflective conversation. It was a pivotal rejection early in the marriage that was a leading indicator of our future.

I had alcohol to help me box up my memories. It took the edges off of the rough emotions and helped me lock away the shame and anger. Moreover, I feared I wouldn't be able to sleep or my nightmares might get worse if I didn't drink myself to sleep every night. Even though the old drinking rationalization was no longer valid in the non-combat environment, I was too habituated by then to go tea totaling along. The habit caused me some concern, but not enough to find out why or to seek help. I didn't want to know. I needed the alcohol and couldn't imagine living without it. So nightly drinking continued privately while I focused on what had to be accomplished.

I told myself to concentrate on looking forward, not backwards. The future held hope, the past nothing. There was a wedding to plan for in just 9 weeks, April 4, 1971. Initially, it and grad school were my primary focus. Mary had done a great deal of thinking and planning about it, so for me the wedding was actually easier than I had anticipated.

The most challenging part of the marriage preparation was navigating the resentful feelings of her parents. They had an impossible time accepting and forgiving me for my breakup with her 3 years before. They actually never did. They also did not approve of my blue collar family and made certain my mother knew it. Their sullen reception and their rejection of her hospitality and food at a specially prepared rehearsal dinner the night before the wedding devastated Mom. My relationship with them was never loving, easy or cheerful. I did the best I could with their rejection of me and my family. After 24 months in the Army, I was prepared to handle anything. The detached attitude I had forged there coupled with alcohol consumption when in emotional pain worked just fine in dealing with my unreasonable in-laws.

After a fair amount of worry, the wedding came off beautifully. For such a tense and abbreviated planning period, it was near flawless. Mary was embraced by my family, made to feel welcomed and took to our family dynamics easily. In the developmental years of her life, love and warmth were non-existent from her mother and father, so she flourished in the larger warmer Italian family. In their eyes, we were a picture-perfect match and extremely happy. After a quick honeymoon we hurriedly returned to school and work. We had only just begun.

One chunk of the life I had been desperate to recover had now dropped into place. Despite the obstacles, the first phase of my new life was a success. Focus, effort and determination had paid off, and I thought they would be the keys to my life's success. After the Army, I knew nothing different anyway and in the civilian world I was too busy trying to catch up or run away. I'm not sure which.

UNEXPLODED ORDINANCE

> There is the guilt all soldiers feel for having broken the taboo against killing; it is guilt as old as war itself. Add to this the soldier's sense of shame for having fought in actions that resulted, indirectly or directly, in the deaths of civilians. Then pile on top of that an attitude of social opprobrium, an attitude that made the fighting man feel personally morally responsible for the war, and you get your proverbial walking time bomb.
>
> *Philip Caputo*

Post-Traumatic Stress Disorder was not in our vocabulary during the years following Vietnam. As is now common knowledge, most Veterans of combat are not open to naturally talking about their experiences. For Vietnam Veterans we felt the same way, but we also knew that no one wanted to hear from us even if we did want to talk. Clearly, the general public's opinion was that if we suffered, it was our own fault and our own problem. On multiple fronts, the country wanted nothing more than to forget about the embarrassment of Vietnam. The bad communal aftertaste of the war aggravated the anger and dissent on both sides. The phrase, "Oh, get over it!" describes the standoff best.

Collectively and individually, we didn't know how to deal with the disquiet because it was such a new phenomenon for us. Once the troops were finally home, the public was exhausted and it had no appetite to repair any of the damages which had occurred. People wanted to get on with life and get the failing economy back on track. There were few places to vent anger—for everyone, but especially the Veteran. A few found a little comfort in friendly hideouts which might take them into their circles like the VFW, American Legion, or Vietnam Vets. For all of us, however, time was supposed to take care of the bad feelings and the memories. For me, it didn't. I just hid everything.

My trust in civilians and the changed world had been severely damaged by my military experience. I laid much of my anger and frustrations on both. And I found myself working hard at consciously denying that I had undergone any change. Denial was a strong defense mechanism I had learned in combat. It helped. I also wanted to avoid any more shame or hurt from ugly confrontations. Even though I was married, I felt isolated and lonely. My conversational skills had been significantly retarded. I am naturally inclined to be friendly with people, but I had a difficult time getting aligned with people's new opinions and behaviors. I could not tolerate the whining about what I believed to be their relatively stress-free existence. Nothing in their vanilla lives seemed as difficult or dramatic as the time I had lived in a war zone.

Social and entertainment options were somewhat limited in newly married life because Mary and I had no desire to participate in recreational drugs or communal drunkenness (my drinking was hidden and private), each seemingly age-appropriate and expected of our generation. Furthermore, I resolutely refused to become an active participant in the new Revolutionary socio-political environment. My refusal triggered chronically aggressive self-pity in me that manifested itself in my isolation from others. That chip on my shoulder, in turn, caused emotional edginess which demanded constant "medication". The medication was alcohol. It helped me block out anger and sorrow. Nevertheless, some symptoms resisted alcohol.

Nightmares were common. They were vivid and frightening. A recurring one of reporting for a second tour in Vietnam and my groveling and pleading that I had served my time still occasionally haunts me today. I needed to keep the nightmares at bay because I thought they indicated mental weakness, and I would never admit to them or seek help. I felt I had to be self-sufficient and had to fix myself. "Help" was not in my vocabulary. I had been trained to be mentally tough.

I became compulsive about proving my substance, toughness and unassailability in order to offset feelings of depravity, vulnerability or unworthiness. Unidentified anger was always near the surface. Guilt haunted me. At times I would be overwhelmed about being alive…when I thought I didn't deserve to be. This ongoing perception led me to odd risk assessments, hyper-competitiveness, and an obsession with accomplishment to prove my worth. Keeping these internal forces in check required constant attention. I would do risky things to prove to myself I was worthy of life, or to give it up if I wasn't—sometimes they worked and other times they didn't. Subsequently, accomplishments and taking risks provided the exhilaration and synthetic doses of self-esteem I needed to keep going.

In my first year back, I was driving home from work one day when I saw a police car chase on the wrong side of a 4 lane divided road. I thought I could help so I jumped the median and joined the chase down the wrong side of the road. The adrenaline rush kicked in right away as we shot through on-coming cars. When the cop pulled the suspect over and cuffed the guy to his car, I pulled in behind him and asked if he needed any help. The cop was incredulous. He told me to get back in my car before he arrested me. I was actually a little miffed. I truly couldn't recognize that I had no sane point of reference for my behavior. I thought only of the action and cared nothing about the risk.

A few months later while working on installing a new electrical outlet in the house we had rented, I left the power on to the circuit as I worked on the rewiring. I knew full well it was a big risk. As I screwed things back together tightly, the screwdriver caught the hot lead and shorted against the grounded box. The screwdriver shaft melted in a flash of spark as I held on to the insulated handle. Luckily the handle saved me from a fatal electrocution.

In a driving rainstorm with my windshield wiper fuse blown, I drove 104 mph in order to keep the rain sheeting up the windshield so I could see the road. Once again, the adrenaline pumped furiously through my system as I was riding on the edge. I got pulled over by the CHP and almost arrested for reckless driving, but talked my way down to a speeding ticket provided I got the windshield wipers to work. I snapped in the spare fuse I always carried in the glove box while the officer waited for proof it worked. When the wipers came on, I took the ticket from him and drove off indignantly.

During a labor strike at the Sears stores in San Francisco, I worked 43 consecutive days from 7am to 7pm doing everything from driving my father's eighteen wheeler, cleaning restrooms and stocking the warehouse to working the sales floor and paying bills in accounting so I could prove my worth to Sears and to myself. It was just like Vietnam to me. Embrace the mission and accomplish it. But no one else on the management team saw it that way or worked more than their normal 40 hour week. They complained about working conditions or the dangers of crossing picket lines. I thought both were fun. They thought I was a maniac. I considered them nauseatingly weak and perfidious.

At the time, I really had no idea why I did these kinds of things so detached from reality. On the surface I *appeared* to be pretty normal, but these idiosyncrasies defined me until I was eventually able to mask and control them better.

I was unaware of other symptoms which had become a part of me. The constant hyper-vigilance; compulsive orderliness; claustrophobia in large crowds; no Asians at my back; face the door in a restaurant to see who enters; easily startled; panicked by sudden loud noises; a consistent lack of trust; flashbacks; explosive anger, and lack of patience with protracted decision making seemed natural to me, but not to the others who had to live with me.

These peculiarities were intertwined in my being, but were never identified as a package of potential trouble. I was teased about some of them by family members, friends or colleagues, and so I laughed along with others and worked hard to control or hide them. It wouldn't be until 35 years later that I could see the depth and impact this template of odd behaviors had affected others and me. Post-Traumatic Stress Disorder was identified, and mine was a classic case.

While it is not a curable disorder, in today's mental health world, an individual can learn to live with PTSD effectively. Therapy can help the sufferer. After centuries of humankind knowing about it, it is really only in the last few decades through study and examination that effective treatments have come to the fore. The following article sheds some light on what we now know about PTSD, starting with its history and its relationship with humankind.

A Short History of PTSD from Thermopylae to Hue Soldiers Have Always Had A Disturbing Reaction To War
by Steve Bentley

Post-traumatic Stress Disorder is an emotional disorder that can be found among survivors of traumatic experiences such as combat. The fact is, PTSD is an old story—war has always had a severe psychological impact on people in immediate and lasting ways. PTSD has a history that is as significant as the malady itself. It's been with us now for thousands of years, as incidents in history prove beyond a doubt.

Three thousand years ago, an Egyptian combat veteran named Hori wrote about the feelings he experienced before going into battle, "You determine to go forward. . . . Shuddering seizes you, the hair on your head stands on end, your soul lies in your hand."

History tells us that among the Egyptians, Romans, and Greeks, men broke and ran in combat circumstances—in other words, the soldiers of antiquity were no less afraid of dying.

Herodotus writes of the Spartan commander Leonidas, who, at the battle of Thermopylae Pass in 480 B.C., dismissed his men from joining the combat because he clearly recognized they were psychologically spent from previous battles. "They had no heart for the fight and were unwilling to take their share of the danger."

One thousand years later, things had changed very little at the front. The Anglo Saxon Chronicle recounts a battle in 1003 A.D. between the English and the Danes in which the English commander Alfred reportedly became so violently ill that he began to vomit and was not able to lead his men.

Many consider the Civil War the first step on the road to modern warfare. Civil War soldiers made the first frontal assaults into repeating rifles and pistols, as well as the Gatling gun and delayed-time artillery rounds that allowed air bursts. Civil War technology also included telescopic sights and rifles with spiral barrels that greatly increased their accuracy and destructiveness in battle.

The immediate result was that psychological symptoms became so common, field commanders as well as medical doctors pleaded with the War Department to provide some type of screening to eliminate recruits susceptible to psychiatric breakdown. Military physicians, at a loss to treat the problems, simply mustered the extreme cases out during the first three years of the war. They were put on trains with no supervision, the name of their home town or state pinned to their tunics, others were left to wander about the countryside until they died from exposure or starvation.

Unfortunately, the attitude that combat veterans with psychological problems are really malingerers trying to gain economically is still with us today. That attitude, combined with veterans' pride and distrust, accounts for the fact that, while 830,000 Vietnam veterans have full-blown or partial PTSD, by 1990 only 55,119 had filed claims.

By the end of World War I, the United States had hundreds of psychiatrists overseas who were beginning to realize that psychiatric casualties were not suffering from "shell shock." These psychiatrists came to comprehend it was emotions and not physiological brain damage that was most often causing soldiers to collapse under a wide range of symptoms. Unfortunately, they continued to believe this collapse came about primarily in men who were weak in character.

In World War II, it became clear it was not just the "weak" in character that were breaking down. This is reflected in the subtle change in terminology that took place near the end of World War II when "combat neurosis" began to give way to the term "combat exhaustion."

Detachment may be heartless but it makes it possible for sensitive people to survive the war relatively undamaged. While it's true that we detach ourselves from war in order to survive, it's also clear that the act of detachment is itself a kind of willed destruction. It's the price paid; it's why we never learn. The psychic numbing necessary to survive combat is not something you step into and out of easily. You can't do it halfway.

You carry it home, where you live with it. You share it with your family and your friends and your kids, and ultimately with your society. And it is poisonous, exceedingly poisonous—and it alters "the very soil in which society's roots are nourished.

It takes time and effort to overcome such detachment—some people never do. It can be overwhelming. In Vietnam, 2.8 million served. Given the nature of guerrilla warfare, it is hard to estimate the number exposed to hostile fire. However, the Research Triangle Institute's Vietnam readjustment study concludes 480,000 have full-blown PTSD and another 350,000 have partial PTSD.

The dynamics were different in Vietnam, where conditions of the war were such that moral revulsion combined with psychological conflict lead to both acute and delayed reactions. Months or even years after their return to this country, many Vietnam vets combined features of the Traumatic Stress Syndrome with preoccupation with questions of meaning—concerning life, and ultimately, all other areas of living.

Having closed off and numbed themselves in order to survive, soldiers are then faced with the task of working their way back toward humanity. The struggle is to "re-experience himself as a vital human being." However, it is not all that easy, for "one's human web has been all too readily shattered, and in rearranging one's self-image and feelings, one is on guard against false promises of protection, vitality, or even modest assistance. One fends off not only new threats of annihilation but gestures of love or help."

This goes to the heart of current concerns about PTSD—that, paradoxically, its tremendous incidence in Vietnam was ultimately a sign of the sanity of those who fought in the war. Otherwise, why be disturbed by the killing, by the stuff of war? But ever after, in peacetime, the reconstruction of "the human web" becomes more and more implausible: if societies are sane—if, in fact, they are civilized—why are there wars?

The arguments are circular. The question of PTSD is always thrust back upon us. The reason there are wars is because most societies are not civilized, but might be someday. There are "cures" offered in the best of societies for PTSD, programs that are established to reintegrate sane men and women into the established order. But always the absolute cure to the eradication of symptoms of PTSD is to eradicate their causes. We are disturbed by war, and justly so.

As we know it today, Post-traumatic Stress Disorder is marked by a re-experiencing of the trauma in thought, feeling, or dream content, which is in turn evidenced by emotional and psychological numbing. Today, PTSD is characterized by depression, loss of interest in work or activities, psychic and emotional numbing, anger, anxiety, cynicism and distrust, memory loss and alienation, and other symptoms. And why not?

Who would not be alienated from the scenes of death witnessed by soldiers? The point is that throughout history, men and women have acted to suppress the horrors that they've seen. It's time we recognize that for what it is—as not only the outward manifestation of PTSD, but the clearest evidence we have that wars are destructive in other ways than in body counts. It takes many years for even the most sane among us to arrive at what we have seen and wanted to forget.

I have been exceptionally lucky in many ways. For all of my professional life I was able to subconsciously camouflage most of the symptoms of my

PTSD. Clearly, my career goals and my insatiable appetite for achievement provided good cover for their full blown exposure. As long as career promotions continued at a rapid pace and my head was filled with issues of the job and accomplishments, the memories of war had a difficult time catching up with my conscious state of mind. It was after I left my career at its peak that the curtain was lifted on the indicators I had carried for 35 years. Then they were exposed in every day behaviors, and it became obvious there was something really wrong.

Like a typical PTSD casualty, I didn't want to ask for help or be associated with the stigma of having a mental health need. But my wife Max asked me to give the VA Hospital the opportunity to help. There was absolutely nothing to lose, and if any counseling could help me, surely the VA could direct me to the help I needed. I reluctantly agreed and set a date.

At the initial appointment, I had to fill out a screening questionnaire. It was a simple format. I answered the questions honestly and with no hesitation. The psychiatrist I met with said I had a perfect score. I said, "Great! I guess we're done." She said, "No! No! No! You have really bad PTSD. One hundred percent of your answers indicate you have PTSD." I still had my doubts. I was further evaluated in a series of sessions and was subsequently diagnosed with a typical case of PTSD for my age and background. After living most of my life in purported normalcy, I was actually relieved to drop my defenses and get the help I could admit I needed so badly.

I started counseling shortly thereafter and have continued since. It has been a tremendous help. The realization I will never be cured is not as bad as it may sound. Not everything in our world is curable and there are some memories I don't want to lose. I have learned to live with PTSD by making a rigorous effort to learn from it and to allow healing. The most important ingredient for my living with it is service to others. Volunteering at The Wall has proven to be a one of the most important acts of healing I can do for myself. It has provided rewarding and effective relief.

THE 12 STEPS OF PTSD

1. We admitted we were powerless over nothing. We could manage our lives perfectly and we could manage those of anyone else that would allow it.
2. Came to believe that there was no power greater than ourselves, and the rest of the world was insane.
3. Made a decision to have our loved ones and friends turn their wills and their lives over to our care.
4. Made a searching and fearless moral inventory of everyone we knew.
5. Admitted to the whole world at large the exact nature of their wrongs.
6. Were entirely ready to make others straighten up and do right.
7. Demanded others to either "shape up or ship out".
8. Made a list of anyone who had ever harmed us and became willing to go to any lengths to get even with them all.
9. Got direct revenge on such people whenever possible except when to do so would cost us our own lives, or at the very least, a jail sentence.
10. Continued to take inventory of others, and when they were wrong promptly and repeatedly told them about it.
11. Sought through nagging to improve our relations with others as we couldn't understand them at all, asking only that they knuckle under and do things our way.
12. Having had a complete physical, emotional and spiritual breakdown as a result of these steps, we tried to blame it on others and to get sympathy and pity in all our affairs.

Author Unknown

I enjoy helping others, and I am comfortable laughing about my ongoing recovery from the pains of PTSD.

Closing the Gap

When I think of work, it's mostly about having control over your destiny, as opposed to being at the mercy of what's out there.
Gary Sinise

Big Pimpin' with Sears in the '71 Fall Catalog

Work is the Answer

In my return to civilian life, I quickly became focused on doing, not being. The time I had spent out of a civilian career path felt like a massive disadvantage for me. My self-imposed pressure to offset that shortcoming had steadily intensified while I was gone. And it was exacerbated by surviving Vietnam. As previously mentioned, I felt marginalized, one down, misfit, and distrustful of my peers and others. I became obsessed with the thought that I was woefully behind, and felt compelled to always run at top speed. The compulsion produced a form of controlled manic behavior. Deciding and doing things with little hesitation and no regrets were key manifestations as exemplified by my getting married as soon as possible. The accumulations of enviable houses, cars, children, or materiel were forms of competitive measurements for me. I needed physical evidence of my progress. By my own design, therefore, my existence was to be defined by an endless schema of achievements in my pursuit to earn a place in The Good Life.

Eventually I accepted that I wasn't going to fit in. But I would not compromise my principles to fix the misalignment I had with others or the world. I felt I had much to prove to everyone. At the same time, I didn't want to draw much attention to myself. I just wanted to succeed. I needed to develop tools for my aspirations. I started with the thought that focused common sense and tenacious energy were minimum requirements. That worked in the military, why not in civilian life?

Grad school had been my planned accelerant for catching up and overtaking cohorts. It didn't take long for me to realize the grad school program did not offer me the acceleration or stimulation I craved. It was agonizingly slow and theoretical presented by passive-aggressive and sometimes hostile faculty for whom I had little respect. Frankly, I had outgrown their pseudo-intellectual concepts that smacked of immature idealism. My edginess and need to conquer had no patience for it. The younger students, with their different beliefs and agendas, their different sense of right and wrong, and their tedious academic pace made me restive. I needed more. And, truthfully, as a newly married couple, we needed money.

As far I was concerned, Mary's teaching income and my G.I. Bill could not get us the things I wanted in order to catch up and maintain a new pace. Initially, she was provisionally okay with the way we lived our life together. I wasn't. I needed something more exciting to stimulate me and more demonstrative to validate I was progressing towards acceptability. We talked things over, and with her agreement, we decided I would return to the workforce while I figured out how far to go in grad school or when to start on a different career path, U.S. Army included.

Sears was top of mind, as much as I didn't want it to be. It was the place I had worked before leaving and it was familiar. But I wanted to keep my distance from that period of my life if it was at all possible. There was just too much old baggage there. Sears did, however, give me the guarantee of immediately making my old salary which would sustain us while I considered other career options. That was a big incentive. Beyond that, however, I was unsure what I could expect from a return to Sears. I knew I didn't want to work in either of the San Francisco stores because they were too much a part of my past. One store was where both my parents had worked and the other where I had been a part timer and a trainee.

After gathering some intelligence on the situation, I called the Regional Office and spoke with Percy Menzies, the Human Resource Director whom I had never met. I inquired about a possible assignment to one of the five new stores outside of San Francisco which had been opened while I was gone. Menzies was empathetic and professional but explained that because I had previously worked in a union store, I had to return to one of the two San Francisco union stores.

I pleaded with him that I needed to start anew in a different environment, so I asked for a special exception to the policy. He said he couldn't grant a precedent-setting exception. I knew Sears did not want anyone from union stores migrating to the new non-union environments but I thought it was worth asking. Mom still worked at the Mission Street store and policy dictated relatives could not work in the same unit. That left the Geary Street store. With no exception to policy granted, I had no choice. I reluctantly agreed to go back to Geary...at least to start.

Menzies arranged for an interview with the new store manager so I could meet him to consider whatever limited options I might have. I was not happy. It was exactly what I didn't want to do. But I needed to start working and to make some income. My career clock was ticking.

Sears, Where America Shops

Most of the people at the Geary Store had known me from the day it opened in 1951, so it was like returning to an old school for me. The store manager, however, was different from the one who was there when I went on active duty. The new man was Howard Lasky. I didn't know him. Menzies told me Lasky was a rising star and he urged me to consider taking a long view of the possibilities that might develop from working for someone on the rise. I thought it might be good advice, but remained skeptical and somewhat petulant. I checked with other sources about Lasky's pedigree to confirm Menzies' advice. It was good counsel, so I approached the appointment marginally optimistic about getting back into the workforce with someone of Lasky's caliber, even if it was only temporary. Work and pay were better than school.

The day for the interview came, and I slipped into the store undetected. I wanted to get to Lasky's office on time and not get hung up risking uncomfortable conversations with the people that knew me. I was ushered into his office and immediately appreciated Menzies' advice. Howard Lasky commanded my respect from the moment we shook hands. A Stanford MBA, bright, high energy, and charismatic, he was easy to like and he communicated well. He had a great sense of humor and an all-business mind.

San Francisco Sears Geary Street Store

By this time, I had been home for only four months. The transition to civilian life had been difficult and disconcerting. I was nervous as was Lasky. Even though I knew Sears had to take me back as a matter of policy and law, I was completely uncertain about the specific assignment I would be offered and concerned I had done the right thing in asking to return. Lasky was equally cautious being forced to interview an unproven, un-quantifiable unknown like me.

He said I could be re-hired and credited for my military service including a small calculated raise. That was good news. He made some light talk about my background, the service, and why the increase would be small, but I was fine. After discussing the pay, his nervous demeanor peaked and he got suddenly serious.

He said there was a caveat I needed to consider before I made a decision about accepting the offer. A new government program called Affirmative Action had been instituted by Sears while I was gone. It was a system developed to accelerate the careers of under-recognized minorities. It impacted me because I couldn't have the level job I had earned before my duty until four "minorities" were placed in managerial jobs ahead of me. I would be held in reserve as an assistant manager until it was my "turn" to get my position back as a department manager.

Whatever else Lasky explained after that was obscured by my resentment. I tried to process what he said but his voice was muted in my head. I was struck with the inequitableness. I was going into a queue until the appropriate numbers of minorities were advanced ahead of me regardless of their capabilities, my past performance or service to the country? Relegation to the back of the line by law and policy was extremely difficult for me to accept as a returning Veteran. Times had really changed.

He asked me to think about "the offer". I tried to think of options or questions while my anger, frustration and bitterness bubbled inside like hot battery acid. There was nothing I could think of to say, so I thanked him, shook his hand and asked when he might want an answer. He said to sleep on it and then let him know what I wanted to do to work out details.

As impressive and professional as Lasky was, he had no connection to me. He did what his job required of him and owed me nothing. But I was dispirited by the recurring shocks of inequity and rejection civilian life continually eructed. I wanted to anesthetize my feelings and to know when I would feel wanted and comfortable back in the "World".

I needed money and work to give me a sense of esteem, accomplishment, and control, i.e. some defense against the forces that buffeted my emotions. Making a decent salary and building some standing were my impulsive remedies. Clearly, school was not going satisfy either need. Should I go back to the Army as a Captain and live in a more familiar world? Should I take Lasky's offer? Or chance drowning in the hierarchal Sears bureaucracy? I felt trapped again.

Semper Gumby: Always Be Flexible

When Mary and I discussed what to do about the Sears offer versus continuing school, there was hardly any deliberation. I never loved the academic world because I considered academia a dress rehearsal for life taught by people who had no life experience---they lived in classrooms and libraries hiding from accountability. I wanted to move on, and I rationalized that Sears might give me an opportunity at a career. She agreed. It was a risk. But because of the military experience, my mind had become more conditioned to risk. Of course, I promised myself to finish the graduate work as I processed through the managerial labyrinth of Sears or wherever else I might go. So, I finished a semester of graduate courses and reported for work at the Geary Street store in July of 1971. Trapped or not, it was the best option I had at the time.

Returning to Sears, I initially felt an obligation to re-connect with the group of people I was close to before I left, even though we had not stayed in touch. Many had progressed to larger jobs, but there was still enough in common to re-ignite old friendships. However, I had to quickly face the fact I had no interest in the daily indulgences of gossip, speculation, complaints, and wish lists the group gorged on. I didn't want to be excluded from the clique, but I also didn't want to waste energy on issues over which I had no control. I remained friendly to all, made no judgments about them, but realized I had to take a different path to accomplish what I needed—one for which my military resume had prepared me well.

For instance, I was pleasantly surprised how "hard work" was defined in the new non-life-threatening civilian environment. It was very different from combat. The challenge of a 40 hour work week was so minimal it made me chuckle. And no one was trying to kill me! My perspective was very different from my co-workers. It, along with my extreme work ethic, substituted for the exhilarating highs I had experienced flying dangerous missions. Both provided me distance from the memories I wouldn't entertain or share. Speed, action and passion for accomplishment set my cadence apart from others.

The pace was a strain for Mary early in our marriage, but it serendipitously provided her with what she desired from our relationship. It gave her a strong partner, safety, financial security, and was acceptable as long as we made steady and rapid progress. An overcrowded priorities list and my bloodstream filled with alcohol at the end of a day to help tranquillize my maniacal approach was the formula I needed to run at top speed. Busyness and the pursuit of indeterminate success helped distance me from everything from which I needed to run.

I wanted to escape from the bondage of my past. The nostalgic recall and revision of youthful memories is an important part of the social fabric and currency for my generation in San Francisco even today. But I had no appetite for re-living my past. I was resolute that I would have no connection to those times, geography or relationships, except for family. Beyond them, there was absolutely no community to which I could relate or embrace. I had been ostracized once and I didn't want it to happen again. Furthermore, I wanted to look forward. That was difficult for my family to understand--especially Mom and Dad. They couldn't imagine I would forsake all they had taught me to treasure in our Italian-American community of The City. Sears was destined to help me escape hurts and resentments and to become the community I would embrace.

As expected, it became the sole stimulator for me. I kept a high-performance edge in order to pass others ahead of me, while the company provided the recognition, ego nourishment, self-esteem, and the advancement for which I was hungry. My work ethic was the key. I worked harder, faster and smarter than my peers, and I was consistently rewarded. My leadership and coolness under pressure were attributes Sears valued highly, particularly when there was a troubled situation. The detachment I had developed in Vietnam tempered by compassion and understanding of people was a prized quality that motivated me to utilize all the military learnings in every assignment. . Throughout my career, Sears executives consistently reported that they had rarely seen such well-developed leadership qualities in one of their own "home grown".

In surprising but consistent steps, from my first management job until my last as President of the Automotive Group, I was given the toughest, most difficult jobs to turn-around and make profitable. I eventually became the unofficial "company relief pitcher". I was usually called into a situation as though it was the bottom of the 9th inning with a full count; nobody out; bases loaded; and a 1 run lead. I had to strike out the last three batters to win the game. And I did every time. I loved every second of the drama. It never failed to be an adrenaline-charged high.

Each new assignment gave me the satisfaction I had experienced as a platoon leader. I always led from the front, not from behind; attacking and progressing, never satisfied with small movement; pushing forward and building pride and a sense of accomplishment in each individual as they supported teammates. And every successful turnaround made me hungry for the next.

During my career, I was promoted through 23 assignments in 35 years. I always believed the broken situations presented me were opportunities to have fun and to prove myself when I compared them to the dreadful existence in war. To be reminded, I kept a picture of a firebase close so I didn't forget what real danger looked like. It kept the pressures of Sears' challenges in the proper perspective most of the time. I couldn't save my men then, but I would save anything Sears gave me. Every job was a very personal test beginning with my first staff assignment as the Customer Service Manager at the Geary store.

Then one year into that job, I was called at home at 6:00 am and asked to report to the Mission Street Store to become the Operations Manager (Assistant Store Manager). I was astounded because it was completely unexpected and was a quantum leap from the Customer Service job. I was 28 years old and had been back in the Sears work force for only 3 years. The promotion catapulted me 3 moves and probably 6 career years ahead of everyone in my peer group.

I was thrilled but confused. My mother worked at the Mission store and I knew we couldn't work in the same unit. In my excitement and confusion, I felt sure I had to fix the policy conflict quickly. So at the appropriate time on my first day, I called Mom at home to tell her the news, "Mom, I've got good news and bad news this morning. The good news is I have been promoted to Operating Manager of the Mission Store. The bad news is I am signing your retirement papers as we speak." Was I precipitous, awkward, and clumsy? Yes. But Mom was elated for me and relieved she could retire with panache and grace. She had been troubled by a bad back for years and our family had been trying to convince her to retire or go on disability. Her time to enjoy life had come and more family folklore had been recorded.

I got my first geographical move and promotion out of the S.F. union environment to Operations Manager in Redding, California after less than a year at the Mission Store. I was promoted there to get new store opening experience. It was exhilarating to develop a brand new store from the time of construction to its opening and running. Moreover, with the move to Redding, I immediately enjoyed a feeling of independence and separation from my past. I took to the corporate wanderer lifestyle almost naturally. New relationships, surroundings, friends, and challenges were stimulating not troubling for me. I often wondered why I enjoyed the wanderlust after being raised in a traditionally static family environment.

Redding was followed by moves to Modesto; Pocatello, Idaho; Hollywood, California; Northridge and more. And for a few years I shuttled back and forth between Chicago and California in assignments of greater prestige and responsibility. Inevitably, there were problems and moments of doubt along the way, sometimes harsh, sometimes not. But every assignment built on the previous one, so my accumulated knowledge and experience continued to increase in value. I tried to always look at every situation as a learning opportunity. Whenever I had to articulate my career aspirations or what I ultimately wanted to accomplish, I invariably said I wanted to be in an assignment in which I could learn and make a difference to the company and the people with whom I worked. That perspective never left me. I enjoyed a magical ride.

Whether it was dealing with the two longest labor strikes in the history of Sears; the three broken stores to which I was assigned as store manager; the first closure of a retail store in the history of the company; the restructure of the California stores and the Installed Home Improvement Business; the re-birth of the Service Repair Business; or the re-construction of the Automotive Business after a 50 state national crisis-of-confidence disaster; I always found the appropriate prescription to overcome the challenges of the situation and lead the business to higher ground.

The World's Tallest...in 1971

I was captivated living on the edge of one turnaround after another and by the confidence I gained from each test. That coupled with a work ethic I owe to my parents and the U.S. Army are prized gifts that propelled me to success I never imagined. As a result, I became comfortable in my own skin whether I was in front of a TV camera for a nationally televised story or walking through an Auto Center to listen to a customer complaint or technicians trading stories about their work. The customers and the employees were always my primary priorities. What I could do for either group provided meaningful value to my work.

They are the backbone of any organization. I loved working with them, I loved the company and its values, and I loved the work.

Throughout this fabulous ride, I had always dreamed of retiring a wealthy man at 55. It was the dream that kept me there for 35 years. The vision of security in retirement with the riches and freedom to do whatever struck my fancy was a great incentive to complete my career with the same company. Not completely unexpected, at 53 years old, the opportunity to retire early with full pay and benefits came when I sold off a part of my responsibilities.

After the spectacular recovery and reconstruction of the multi-faceted Automotive Group, Sears decided it had no appetite for the auto parts portion of the business once it was performing properly. It needed the capital for other growth opportunities. So I developed and completed a transaction to sell the Western Auto Supply Company to Advance Auto, another automotive parts retailer. It was a great deal for Sears and a profitable exit from the business. But by completing the deal, I had also eliminated one half of my job.

As a result, I was offered the opportunity to retire and be paid full salary to the age of 55 with full benefits. A *golden parachute for me!* My dream had come true 2 years early, and I leaped at the offer. I had proven myself beyond my expectations and accomplished more than I had the capacity to comprehend. I had gone from the stockroom to the Executive Suite; had the rare experience of being a key leader of an American icon Fortune 50 company; and, built deep lifetime relationships with the people with whom I had worked. When I walked out the door for the last time, I could honestly say there were very few days at Sears I did not cherish.

My work at Sears was done. There was nothing left for me to accomplish. It was time for younger, smarter, faster runners to take the baton from me and for me to turn to others in my life. I was surprised yet satisfied my leaving had arrived so swiftly and gently. The addiction to proving and performing that started in Vietnam was finally sated. I had been embraced by the Sears community for more than 35 years. It paid handsome dividends in money, power, prestige and position while keeping the curtains pulled over many personal ghosts and shortcomings.

Unfortunately, I was unaware of the collateral damage that had accumulated.

Sears West Side Homan Ave Headquarters until 1971
The Glory Days

> Early in my business career I learned the folly of worrying about anything. I have always worked as hard as I could, but when a thing went wrong and could not be righted, I dismissed it from my mind.
> *Julius Rosenwald*

ALCOHOL

"I have absolutely no pleasure in the stimulants in which I so madly indulge. It has not been in the pursuit of pleasure that I have periled life and reputation and reason. It has been the desperate attempt to escape from torturing memories, from a sense of insupportable loneliness and a dread of some strange impending doom.

Edgar Allan Poe

We laugh....He's serious

Cunning, Baffling, and Powerful

I didn't drink in high school...everybody else did, but I didn't. I was too afraid I would get in trouble and embarrass myself or my family. I drank in college to be one of the guys but didn't like it much because I was the one who always had to drive everyone home. Actually, being with Mary was more important to me than being with drunken friends. I was kind of an asymmetrical social drinker. Friends didn't include me in their partying most of the time because I was rarely available and didn't want to drink to oblivion. My habitual drinking started when I went in the Army.

According to the National Council on Alcohol and Drug Dependency, throughout our military history, holding one's liquor has been akin to being a "real soldier"...on a par with knowing how to handle one's weapon. Even today, heavy drinking, glamorized in the culture of those serving in uniform, is common. After active duty, many Veterans who served with honor abuse alcohol. There are many reasons, and one of the most common is because of the PTSD associated with combat deployments. Of course, I was unaware at the time I was a classic candidate in many dimensions for both eventual outcomes. And I can now see how my addiction progressed at an archetypal rate.

Embedded in the daily life of an officer, particularly a 2nd lieutenant was the Officers Club. It was practical (you could eat meals there) and you didn't feel lonely. The Club was part of an unwritten social code for officers. There, new friendships were artificially sweetened by alcohol and old ones were effectively recharged with the same ingredient. Real war stories were proudly told. It was a place to hang out, showcase manhood, de-brief, fit in socially, and solve the Army's problems, all under one roof. The ethos of the Club, the intrigue, the action (lonely wives trolling for company) and the drama was more lively with the ubiquitous presence of alcohol. It was a convenient and seemingly harmless social process. While I was assigned stateside, I easily became a regular patron.

For my particular version of loneliness, alcohol was the perfect social lubricant which helped me fit into what I initially perceived as "foreign" military life. It was also a necessary and convenient tranquilizer for my paranoia about my inevitable assignment to Vietnam. I paid no attention to the problem drinkers I ran into every night at the Club. I always reassured myself quietly I was not one of them.

However, by the time I was ready to deploy, my social drinking at the O Club had transitioned to having my own well-stocked bar in my bachelor officer quarters. I justified the hoarding by telling myself it was more convenient and cheaper than going to the Club. But I began to suspect there was something unnatural about drinking alone in my room and not wanting friends to see my supply. And, the closer I got to actually going to Vietnam, the more I needed to numb my fears. While I remained confident I would be able to easily address it if I ever needed to, my consumption went up steadily.

In Vietnam, alcohol became the way I chose to deal with my fear, the intensity of my assignment, and the level of danger to which I was subjected. Drugs were not a consideration for me although their use was common, particularly among the enlisted.

Modest off duty drinking was an accepted practice among the 101st officer corps. As long as you were not working, you could drink in your hootch. On duty, it was a court-martialed offense. I was technically on call 24/7, but because my job involved choppers and we didn't fly our missions at night, I was not considered on duty unless I was the Officer of the Day with NDP (night defensive perimeter) duty. On most days, it was a relief to have my "maintenance" alcohol at night with peers who didn't question my frequency or need. It kept me going and sane enough to get the job done.

But it wasn't long before I couldn't live without a drink every day. Three dead at Henderson and my own near death episodes were more than enough to get me indulging on a daily basis. I knew I would never jeopardize another's life because of drinking, but the dangers of my job, the deaths of the men and the unending fear of more possible failures continued to justify whatever amount of alcohol it took to keep me functional and calm each day. Since I was convinced I wouldn't survive my assignment, the risk of my getting into trouble seemed inconsequential.

I was not a sloppy or excessive drinker—just numbingly consistent. I never blacked out or got sick. I drank enough to feel a warm glow take over my tension and relieve it. What could be wrong with that? I believed that if I made it home and out of the danger of the war, I wouldn't have a compulsive need for alcohol because the world would be so much safer to navigate. Then I would stop. It would be easy I thought.

But when I got home, I found I couldn't break the habit. In the civilian world, the daily trials and tribulations were Lilliputian by comparison to combat, but the maniacal pace I had to have stimulated my need to drink every day. I was frustrated about it but not overly concerned because I didn't think it was excessive (my definition). It was always just enough to give me the calm and deadening I needed at the end of every day. To rationalize the frequency and amount of consumption, I furtively compared my drinking to others whom I considered "heavy drinkers" and was quite satisfied I was not any worse than they were. I ignored any signs of addiction because I knew I couldn't live without the calm I craved.

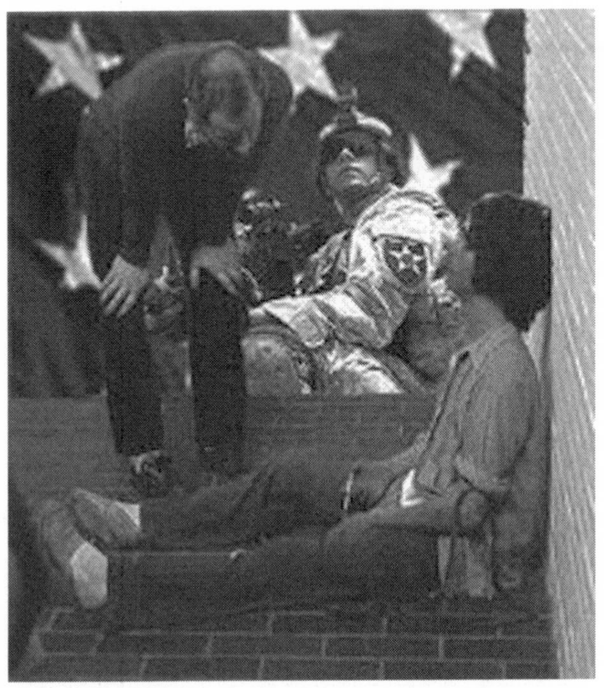

A Long and Intangible Road Back for Many

The Cycle of Addiction

As time progressed, drinking steadily increased in direct proportion to the degree of difficulty of each assignment. The greater the challenge, the more I needed alcohol to cope with problems and unidentified anxieties. This phenomenon highlighted two components of my addiction. First, the living-on-the-edge adrenaline rush I needed to duplicate a combat high was replicated each day by the myriad of difficulties with which each new assignment came fully supplied. They required alcohol to subdue their over-stimulating effects. Second, the overload of problems and the sorting of priorities that flooded my mind, protected me from facing fearful Vietnam memories or my march towards addiction. Managing these two components left no space to consider grieving, healing, sobriety or recovery.

Alcohol became my best friend and my dependable coping tool. It helped me rationalize my selfishness, block out my tensions, and run every day from my fear, shame and guilt. Furthermore, I was convinced people couldn't detect the habit because I always drank alone. I even thought I hid my problem pretty well from my family, but I didn't. In order to maintain a façade of normalcy, I thought I had to pretend at any given time to be one of three people: father, husband, or powerful executive. I managed the three personalities during agonizing cycles of drinking and dryness, but had to constantly suppress the hypocrisy that resulted. I was an addicted person who couldn't see beyond my need for alcohol, and that eventually became the number one priority. It was a destructive closed loop. Hung over every morning, I would promise myself each day was going to be a new beginning.

In truth, I really didn't like me. I knew I was an impostor living a lie waiting to be discovered at any moment. But I couldn't solve the conundrum of living a superficially successful life, accomplishing the things I accomplished, having all the symbols of success, and simultaneously be a full blown alcoholic. That didn't fit the alcoholic imagery I had in my mind. 'I couldn't be one,' I told myself, 'I'm not living in a refrigerator carton and peeing in my pants.' I was a big time executive with all the right success symbols. Unfortunately, as is typical alcoholic behavior, I was lying to myself.

I continued to rationalize, 'Yes, I have to drink every day but I can stop for any period of time,' Deceptively, I always had a target date for when the "abstinence trial" would end. I was determined my drinking was wholly tied to the challenging assignments I accepted. Yet I knew I couldn't live without the mental high or the feelings of accomplishment and superiority those jobs provided me. Alcohol was the calming counterbalance to the unbridled external forces of job, family, income, financial security, prestige, relocation, and more that pressurized me. More of one thing begat more of the other, and the glamor of achievement camouflaged any addiction problems I might have felt I had.

While providing great material satisfaction to my family, there was an additional price paid for my overachiever, alcohol-supported success. Family life was tumultuous, harried, hurried and transient. Move and uproot. Move and uproot. Move and uproot. Everyone had to put on a compulsory happy face and make the best of the disruptions. Unfortunately, there was harm done to the family living in constant uncertainty that in turn produced more tacit guilt for me.

The guilt was validated when we had to face our second move back to Chicago after being in California for only 10 months. When told we had to move, my younger son Jeff broke down and said he couldn't do it. He couldn't face finding new friends and starting another new world. Jon was frustrated changing high schools, but was resigned to reconnect to sports friends he had made in junior high school. Mary was exasperated with another move, another house, more relationship issues, and more distance from her aging parents and my family in California.

I had been officially put on notice that I would be an officer of the company in less than two years, so I felt I had to make the move. It was the brass ring, and I was finally one step from it. For me, there was no choice. Finally, Jeff said he would try one more time. Mary agreed to a last move. We made the move back to Chicago for me. I, in turn, made a solemn promise to everyone that we would never move again. I am now lucky enough to be able to say I kept the promise.

Two years later in February of 1992, I reached my life-long career goal. The Board of Directors approved me to become one of only 17 elected officers of Sears, Roebuck and Company, a 44 billion dollar enterprise of 400,000 employees. I had made it. I was the youngest officer in company history and, as expected, was given the most difficult of the officer assignments. I was charged with cleaning up a mess of staggering proportions in the service and repair business which at one time had been the most profitable unit in Sears. It was also the most complex to run. Unfortunately, it had deteriorated so badly it was losing millions and taking the entire company brand with it because of poor customer service. Predictably, my need for more alcohol intensified with the assumption of the new assignment.

As a new naïve officer, I was foolish enough to think that if I just uncovered a single major problem in the complex business and fixed it with my newly acquired power, all would be well. But I couldn't find just one. There were more than I could count and each one had an insurmountable number of tendrils. There was major trouble in the fundamentals of the business. It was drowning.

A magic bullet solution was out of the question. It was patched with so many temporary fixes and workarounds, nothing short of a complete re-build could restore it to profitability. That was an awful truth I had to reveal to the Board who had just made me an officer. They were embarrassed, and, as expected, asked me how quickly I could fix it. I gave them a conservative estimate, but it did not satisfy them. They wanted profitability to happen faster. I heard their concern as a mandate to produce a miracle.

I perseverated for weeks trying to piece together a demanding but realistic profit plan for my first full year in the assignment. Depressingly, each scenario looked more grim and disappointing than the next. The more I considered the size and number of problems, the more I became constricted by my self-imposed unrealistic goals. Resources like money, people, expertise, organization and, time were needed. All were in short supply. I was becoming overwhelmed by the possibility of failure in this high profile situation, and was embarrassed by my needing to ask for support. I couldn't grasp how much fear was affecting me and clouding my thinking. Alone and isolated, I worked desperately to keep my terror hidden. I drank more and more each day to wash away the torment and depression. But no amount of alcohol could make me feel better.

Eventually, I drank around the clock and showed up for work with bottles of mouthwash to hide the smell on my breath. My fragile world collapsed around and inside me rapidly. Hope faded as I struggled to find my way out of the personal and professional quick sand. Finally, I had a complete breakdown. I could no longer manage the job and the drinking. Alcohol had been my best friend and magic medication for years, but I couldn't control it. I was beaten and I didn't care.

Surrender

Ten months after making the Sears record book as the youngest elected officer, I was close to catatonic. I couldn't get out of bed; too hung over; too depressed; and too scared of being discovered a failure. I was unreservedly hopeless. After three days of hiding in the bedroom and claiming I had the flu, Mary called 911. The EMTs arrived and easily recognized what was wrong with me. They knew I needed to be detoxed and took me by ambulance to a hospital that had an alcohol rehab program. I didn't even question them. I just wanted some relief and perhaps a spark of hope.

After two days detoxing in the locked mental ward, an orderly helping me brush my teeth informed me I was a garden variety alcoholic. At that point, I was easily convinced it was true, and that I was just as sick as the alcoholic I envisioned in a refrigerator carton. When the orderly said out loud what I couldn't admit to myself, I felt instant relief. To have him say it gave me incredible liberation from the oppression of my secret. The confirmation of my addiction that I had denied for years marked my surrender and the start of recovery. It was a miraculous moment of personal truth long overdue.

From that chance conversation, I began to take very tiny steps forward. I learned alcoholism is a sickness not a moral weakness, and that I could be treated if I wanted to recover. I was hospitalized for 4 days and then released to begin the rehab program of my choice. No mandate. No prescription. No medications. It was up to me to take action against the illness. No one would force me. I had to want it, and I did.

Sears wanted to know something about my absence from work. So I told them I had a bad case of the flu and that exhaustion had overtaken me. Based on my work ethic and my perfect attendance for over 30 years, it was easy to believe and to understand my absence.

I began out-patient rehab a week later and then considered how to handle the lethal forces of the job which had broken me. I made a tentative goal to try to go back to work while still in treatment when I was ready. I was unsure of many things at that juncture but very sure I wouldn't tell anyone about my alcoholism or recovery demands. I wanted to be fully committed to recovery and live without alcohol going forward, as unrealistic as it may have sounded at the time. But personal pride and dignity were still large considerations for me. I didn't want to suffer the shame or risk of being pilloried in the company.

I knew I had to eventually return to work. I had no choice. My job and financial security were of paramount importance to me and my family. Early on it looked as though it would be impossible to manage everything together. The first priority was to focus all my efforts on staying sober each hour and day. If I didn't do that, the job would be lost. Slowly and painfully I started to put together one day at a time instead of getting entangled in unrealistic thoughts about months or years of sobriety. I hung on to each tenuous daily reprieve while I searched for a way to work and live an abstemious life.

Outpatient rehab was four nights a week. After two weeks of getting through it, I got permission from the counselor to work back into my job on a part-time basis. I needed to create a new work environment for myself by developing a different work load and speed. Full agenda and full throttle for every waking moment would not be possible anymore. That *modus operandi* was actually a dangerous trigger for my addiction.

Learning ways to limit, pause, and renew were the starting points. I had been scared sober by a disease about which I knew nothing and from which I thought I was immune. I needed to learn from it and heed all the signs for relapse. Humility was an early critical ingredient for recovery. It gave me perspective and re-orientation to what was important in my life. Gradually, the problems at work which had seemed so insurmountable looked a little more manageable. Taking things a day at a time was completely new for me. I started to adjust everything slowly to that cadence. I learned how to anticipate, delegate, and approach internal and external demands in a different way.

Simultaneously, the disastrous condition of the business improved ever so slightly as the staff stepped up and incrementally instituted reasonable tactical solutions and developed a viable long term strategy to re-position the business. The search for magic bullets ended. Bold honesty and responsible planning was surprisingly refreshing to the Board. They understood and endorsed the turnaround strategy we presented. It was a tremendous endorsement that personally motivated me and it gave me confidence to move forward with my recovery.

Rehab turned out to be a starter course in Alcoholics Anonymous focused on the 12 Steps, meetings, and spirituality. All three were new for me. Increasingly, I came to understand and believe that AA could help me stop drinking for more than just a few days or weeks. It didn't seem possible, but the program worked if I maintained honesty, openness and willingness. Alcoholism almost broke me, and I was certain I couldn't withstand more daily internal destruction that had rotted my being. The bottom I hit made me appreciate that alcoholism's progression is fatal.

One of the most fortuitous things that happened to me in my first days in the hospital was the visit of a sophisticated recovering alcoholic who came into my room to offer his support. He had been sober for over 30 years and looked like the furthest thing I could imagine from an alcoholic. He wore tortoise shell glasses, had white hair, well dressed, articulate, soft-spoken and unassuming. I first thought he was a psychiatrist on staff. Fortunately, he was an AA member who made a habit of checking in every week at the detox ward of the hospital to offer his support to each patient. It was his way of giving back, staying sober himself, and being of service to the community.

The quality and length of his sobriety had earned him the highest respect of the local AA community. He was a solid, reliable pioneering AA member in town. I was privileged to have him invite me into his circle of sobriety. He helped me through my difficult first 6 months as I navigated my way back to my job at Sears, and then mentored me for more than 15 years while

I finished a spectacular career. He was a guiding light during an absolutely critical part of my life. I still think of him daily and all he gave me during good and bad times. He taught me how to deal with life on life's terms rather than trying to bend it or forge it into what I wanted. He gave me the faith I needed to succeed with life's continual diversions and interruptions while not succumbing to the temptations of alcohol or my ego.

With his support and that of the AA community, I have been able to enjoy the benefits of sobriety. I was able to complete a fabulous career overflowing with excitement and success while I learned how to live without alcohol. I have been graced to have found AA. I am forever grateful.

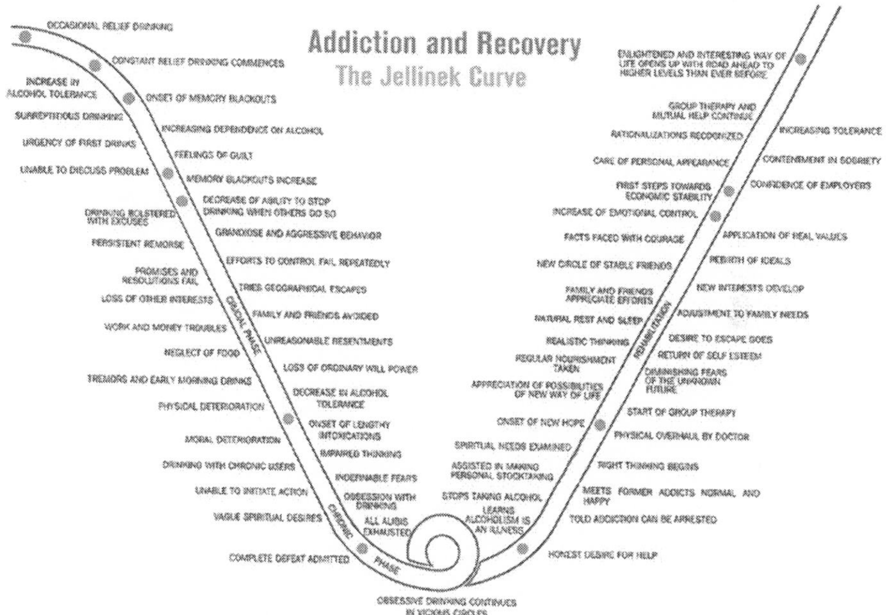

The Wall That Heals

"When you are part of the same tribe, you give blood together and you take blood together."
Tim O'Brien

Kenneth B. Luttel

During my time in the Army, one of the more dreaded extra duties for a junior officer was being a Casualty Notification Officer. Had I been sent to Ft. Hamilton, the home of the Army Chaplains as was originally planned, more than likely I would have been the designate for the Brooklyn area. Considering the possibility, I am glad I went to Ft. Hood, TX instead of Ft. Hamilton, NY.

The Notification Officer is the poor devil who rings the doorbell and delivers the news that a loved one has been killed or gone missing. The officer has a maximum of 10 minutes to be with the relative. He is not allowed to speak about anything beyond what is required to be read to the next of kin.

1. Name, rank, and serial number.
2. Date of death and limited details about it.
3. Approximate date the body is scheduled to arrive home.
4. A strong recommendation on whether the casket should be opened or kept closed.

It is a horrible job requiring implausible resiliency. Today, there are specialists trained for notification so it can be done with the utmost care and dignity. In my time, it was considered an extra duty usually relegated to a junior officer and there was little to no training to prepare you for the impact of the reaction of the loved one receiving the news.

I didn't know how the notifications for my five men were received by their families and I have always wondered about them. I was not involved in that portion of the tragic process. My responsibility was to inventory and catalog their personal belongings and send them to their Home of Record with no comforting note or information I may have wanted to convey. That was hard enough for me, and it was especially grim in the cases of Luttel and Bohrman because I knew them and I was responsible for sending them on the mission.

It haunted me that my relationship with both of them ended so heartlessly and catastrophically, especially when I thought I should have done more to prevent their deaths in the first place. To pack their simple possessions into a duffel bag for shipment home was intrusive and demoralizing. I wanted some kind of bridge back to them to say how sorry I was, and to tell them I would have traded places with them if I could have. I know it sounds irrational, but saying, "It don' mean nothin" was not how any of us really felt. Every death meant a lot yet there was no place to say it, nor anyone with whom to share the grief. Grief makes you weak, and in a hostile environment with sudden death challenging your every decision and move, weakness is not an option. Focus and strength are the only defenses for the emotional minefield you walk daily.

For years after, however, I thought about Luttel and Bohrman privately and wondered if I should try to make contact with their families to offer my condolences. In fact, when my PTSD began to consume me in my later years, the thought of making contact became a fixation. I wanted to make amends to someone for my guilt. So I went looking for their personal information and was surprised when I discovered both the families were within a short driving distance from where I live.

I checked in with different counselors I was seeing at the time to get guidance. Separately each of them said unequivocally not to try. That it was self-serving on my part and the families were probably not prepared. After all the years, more than likely they had moved on with their grief. I accepted the advice and dropped the idea, but not the desire to express my apologies for the part I had played. I had to learn to live with it. I could, and I did until…

In September of 2009 I had just landed at Washington National Airport in DC for my weekend of volunteer work at The Wall. I was in a cab on my way to my hotel and anxious to get checked in and down to The Wall when my cell phone rang. It was a strange area code I didn't recognize, so I assumed it was a marketing call. I was just about to let it go when I decided to ask the caller to take me off of their call list. I answered brusquely and a voice came on, "Is this Paul Baffico?"

Impatiently, I answered, "Yes it is, what can I do for you?" expecting a pitch for some cheesy investment scheme.

"My name is Richard Luttel. I am Ken Luttel's brother." Pause. Pause. Pause. Flashback! My memory crackled with voices and images.

"Oh my God you sound exactly like Ken," I said slowly. In an instant, 39 years of my life were compressed into a crystal clear memory of Ken Luttel sitting on his cot across from me assuring me he wanted to go out on the mission. The memory was as vibrant as if it had happened that morning. Immediately, I felt Richard's call was more than just pure happenstance. There had to be some abstruse reason for it. I had to know more.

I asked him how he found me, and he said he had read a 2006 Chicago *Tribune* article about me on the internet in which I had mentioned the death of his brother Ken. That led Richard to call the writer, Bonnie Rubin. Against all rudimentary journalism protocol and policy, Bonnie was kind enough to give him my contact information. She recalled how much I wanted to talk to the families from the time she had interviewed me for the article. She knew how much it would mean.

The cab pulled up to my hotel and I needed to recover from the amazement of Richard's call, so I suggested I call him back when I was a little settled in. I wanted to get the right orientation to talk—it had been a lot of years. I checked in quickly, and hurried to the room. I couldn't wait to talk more. I crowded up to the window to be sure I got a good cell signal and dialed his number. Somehow I had a concern it might be a cruel prank and I didn't want to be part of it. When Richard answered we got caught up on my history and more importantly the Luttel family. I lost any concern for his intentions.

Richard is the youngest of 10 children, and Ken was the older brother whom he idolized. He remembered the day the Notification Officer came to the door of their house on the family farm in Greensburg, Indiana. He said, "I'll never forget seeing my mother drop to her knees in the front room when she saw the Army car come up the road to the house. She knew he was dead."

He asked me if I would be willing to go to Greensburg to meet the family and to tell them about Ken's time with me. Before I could respond, I felt a huge pressure inside of me start to release. A deep breath later, I said I would be honored. I didn't know how serious he was, but was hopeful he could really make it happen. We exchanged phone numbers so we could work on getting a date to meet. I thanked him for tracking me down and told him how much I had wanted this kind of contact for a very long time. We agreed to talk in a week.

As I considered the implausibility of what had just happened, I flopped on the bed flabbergasted. The pain from the loss of Ken and others for whom I was responsible was suddenly re-opened and exposed. Maybe that was good. Maybe it was dangerous to my own well-being. I didn't know, but I wanted to find out. I had to find out. My conscience needed an answer. I was determined to move forward with this chance encounter.

About a month later the meeting was arranged. Richard and I set the date for Saturday October 24, 2009. Meantime, I checked in with my PTSD counselor about making the trip. I got a green light because the meeting was initiated by the family. I also talked with a Pentagon Army Chaplain and got some tips and advice. I felt I needed experienced guidance for the meeting, and he was helpful. He said to limit my time; know what I am not going to say; be mindful of the family needs more than my own.

I drove to Greensburg the night before. The plan was to have a meeting with the Luttel family at the county fire house in the small village of Letts, directly in the middle of Indiana farm country. It was the only building close the Luttel farm that could hold all of the family at one time. It was a chilly morning and we had set the time for 11 am to give everyone time to gather. Richard met me in Greensburg and led me to the firehouse in his truck, but not before hugs and introduction to his son. I was able to tell Richard again how grateful I was to him for finding me. It was then he told me there were going to be about 40-50 people for me to meet--four generations of Luttels who wanted to know about Ken.

Shortly after we arrived at the fire house, people started to trickle in. The station was set up for a family meal, and each relative brought their special luncheon dish. I was introduced to each, one by one, including Ken's mother. As only a family suffused in love and tradition can, I was deeply touched by the effort every one of the Luttel family made to make me feel comfortable. If I had designed the day, it was exactly how it would have been: family, food, and warmth on a cold October morning in America's heartland.

After the meal, I got the chance I had agonized over and anticipated for 39 years. I offered my condolences to all of the family, and said I was grateful for the opportunity to share my heart. I had carried the guilt of Ken's death with me for a long time and kept it buried so I didn't have to re-live it each day. Today was the opportunity I had looked forward to so I could tell them what they already knew about Ken. That he was a good man, he was a hero and he had paid the ultimate price for his love of his brother warriors and our country at an extremely difficult time in our country's history.

They asked me if I had any pictures of where we were, and I said I had video footage I was happy to show even though it was old, crude and shaky. They didn't care. Richard cued up the equipment and ran it as I explained what Ken's job entailed and showed them video of the base camp and some of the firebases we flew to in a typical day.

I spoke of Ken's service time with the platoon and the fact he was adamant about seeing action. A rear assignment was of no interest to him. His oldest brother asked me if I could explain the medals he won and why. They had put them into a display shadow box his mother kept on the mantel in her house. There was a Bronze Star for Valor, a Purple Heart, an Army Commendation, and the usual others.

As I started to explain the significance of each award, I saw by the expressions on many faces my explanation didn't register properly. When I got to the Bronze Star for valor, another brother asked what Ken had done to receive it. I explained he had volunteered for an extraordinarily dangerous mission and when I tried to talk him out of it, he insisted on going.

Someone said, "So was the Jeep hit by enemy fire?" Suddenly I thought I had inadvertently confused the facts, so I cautiously asked what they had been told.

"Well, we were told Kenny was killed in a Jeep accident...that he hit some kind of mine or something."

I realized I was in uncharted waters, so my response was careful and deliberate, "Oh no," I said. "Ken was not in a jeep, he was killed on an ARVN firebase when it was overrun by the NVA. Ken was a hero, and these medals reflect his heroism. He volunteered for the mission and absolutely would not take no for an answer. He was doing what he said he had come to Vietnam to do."

Someone else interjected, "You mean he was killed in combat, not in some accident?"

"Believe me, I sent him. It was no accident. He volunteered to go out and fight in a very daring operation. He was killed in a fierce battle."

"And he'd do it again!" his mother shouted out through her tears. "That's the kind of man Ken was!"

"You are absolutely right, Mom," I replied. "Your son was a hero and he was doing what he wanted to do. I'm just so sorry he didn't get a chance at the life he so richly deserved."

I turned back to the rest of the family and picked up the thread, "I believe you were told he was killed in an accident because our battle activities were classified at the time. There was fear of more anti-war press propaganda, so the media was kept away from us. The White House needed to show the world that our involvement in the war was winding down. Those of us there had no idea of the change in policy. Like Ken, we all did our jobs day to day. And Ken did a great job. All of you should be very proud of him. It was no accident. Ken Luttel was the real deal."

The smiles and the tears of joy for the family were powerful. The true story had finally been told. There was calm and a sweet silence in the firehouse as the family quietly absorbed the news of their hero.

I thanked them again for allowing me to come to tell Ken's story. I thanked Richard and hugged him as I said hushed goodbyes to each of the family and slipped out the door. Their time had finally come.

There it was, the Final Chapter for Ken, his family…and for me.

> "There were times in my life when I couldn't feel much, not sadness or pity or passion, and somehow I blamed this place (Vietnam) for what I had become, and I blamed it for taking away the person I had once been."
>
> *Tim O'Brien*

A Safe Place for Healing

"The wound is the place where the Light enters you."
Rumi

The Wall was designed to be a public space for healing, and now I understand that. It has given me the place I have desperately needed for years to hear my own voice; to remember; to share; to talk openly; to honor my men and all the other warriors whose names are there. For me, The Wall has closed an enormous breach in my identity. It is no longer necessary for me to be ashamed about my service. I don't have to hide a part of myself or wander around in my own mental darkness. Now I can accept who I am and feel proud to be a part of The Wall's national importance.

It has allowed me to de-code the underpinnings of my character as a leader, successful executive, Veteran, father, husband and as a reluctant patriot. It helps me face my problems with survivor's guilt, PTSD, lingering anger, resentment, and alcoholism. They are the unintended consequences of my service. They are not the after effects of personal failures, lack of strength or moral fiber. The Wall helps me accept that I am human and flawed like every other human, and the acceptance motivates me to be a better person. Finally, it helps me appreciate that regardless of my flaws and afflictions, I have had a remarkable life.

The heart wrenching encounters at The Wall with Billy, Jack, Major Landry, the Luttel family, or the taking of Jon, Jeff, and Tiffani to share my secrets have easily convinced me that I have been granted a massive amount grace and forgiveness for a good reason. It is to serve others of the Veteran community fully and faithfully.

The personal insights I have discovered there are astonishing. I feel compelled to pass them on because they have given me a new purposeful life. A life dedicated to sharing them with other Vietnam Veterans who come to touch a part of their history before they pass on. It's also about devotedly serving *all* Wall visitors: Veterans of all wars, school children, families, foreign tourists, and more. I am honored to teach those who want information about the Memorial or the difficult history that it represents. It is powerful for most to hear it from those of us who lived it. Finally, my purpose is about listening to contemporaries who need to tell their stories or to make amends.

Not surprisingly, Vietnam remains enveloped in a seductive mystique because of its imprecise currency in many of today's conversations. But for more and more people, both young and old, Vietnam has become more than just a piece of vague history from which they have been detached. Now people want to know much more about it than is readily available. Those who are disconnected from the emotions and the divisiveness of five decades ago want to know specifically what happened and why, and they want to understand its relevancy to today's conflicts and how the lessons learned from then apply today. One of the most common questions we are asked at The Wall is, "Did we learn anything from Vietnam?"

There are potent and persuasive lessons learned from Vietnam, but they are not always obvious. First, we have learned not to blame the soldiers. They are doing their job. That is what they are supposed to do. They follow orders. For that, we treat them with honor and respect, regardless of the politics in doing their job. Today there is substantially better treatment before, during, and after active duty for those who serve. The all-volunteer concept; recognition; honor; retribution for injuries; recovery services and more are to name but a few. Second, we have learned to hold our armchair warriors accountable for their decisions and the orders those decisions create. Third, we have learned that war is an *instrument of politics.* Politicians can and should be openly challenged about using force as a means to accomplish an end. Fourth, it is not immoral or unpatriotic to protest their decisions. It is every citizen's responsibility.

Finally, and possibly the most powerful lesson of Vietnam is that the moral burden of war should be shared by *all* of us, voters and politicians alike, regardless of what side they may take. War is not simply a function of black and white decision making. The moral burden of killing people demands that all of us weigh and examine the mission and goals of a potential conflict. They, in turn, mandate a scrupulously realistic assessment of risk before there is a commitment to combative actions. Otherwise, it is too easy to indiscriminately squander young lives and resources. We are just beginning to comprehend this obligation.

To some, The Wall can be a physical reminder of the lingering guilt on our collective conscience that Vietnam denotes in U.S. history. As has been stated, the burden of the guilt and embarrassment the war produced continues to prowl in the background of each successive Administration. Its fingerprints are unmistakable on many of the military, political, and diplomatic actions of the last four decades. And yet that burden of guilt is equipoised by the mysterious reflections on The Wall's polished surface. They are the reflections of the living and are the reminder of the hope and life meant to be enjoyed in appreciation of the sacrifices made...and to pass on the baton of honoring human sacrifice that can be so easily forgotten.

Most visitors who talk with me are surprised when they learn I volunteer from Chicago every month on my own time and at my own expense. This inevitably leads them to asking a little more about me and why I do it, sometimes with awkward questions, but mostly with great respect and curiosity about how it came to be for me.

It has taken me some time to package uncountable thoughts and feelings into something I can explain in a few sentences. I try to be sensitive to the visitor's time constraints and needs, so I let them lead the conversation with their questioning. I answer about why I do what I do by saying volunteering is cheaper than therapy and works a lot better for me. That is my prosaic answer. Sometimes it works well, but many times it can lead to a longer conversation.

The real answer is more complicated and deep inside me. I had to retrieve it with hard work. That happened when it became okay for me to think and talk about my memories. Before then, it was impossible for me to have a relationship with that time of my life. All of it was packed up with the emotions and feelings I worked hard to avoid every day.

Now I feel The Wall calling me to share and to help; to volunteer and guide other Veterans to connect with an important part of their life. That is often difficult. For most, it is emotionally shocking to physically touch their dreadful memories after so much time has passed. The recall is traumatic and many times debilitating. The tidal wave of feelings the act elicits requires support by another combat Veteran who can provide empathy and understanding to the sufferer. We represent the solidarity he once shared in battle, and that is immediately comforting. Invariably, Vietnam Veterans of any age, color, or economic status feel like close brothers again at The Wall. It is reassuring for them to recall one more time the intimacy, safety and intense bond that was forged in combat and never duplicated again. I am honored to be a part of it and to participate with them.

My calling also includes a passion to teach and carry forward a piece of history that needs rehabilitation. If nothing else, a greater understanding of Vietnam in the proper context is required to counteract the fragmented rhetoric to which most are wedded. The Wall is the venue to make a difference. With the help of VVMF, the situation is improving.

There is also the satisfaction of being a positive part of the legacy of Vietnam Veterans. It feels good to be included because it is a gift for me to pass on my knowledge to visitors. I try to not overwhelm them with war stories or sensational tales, but rather to clearly articulate the carefully studied history of U.S. involvement in the war, the tactics, the country, the global context and the symbolism The Wall represents. All of us are committed to accuracy. We aspire to be living authorities, and we do not take the aspiration lightly.

Besides volunteering in D.C., as a part of my healing process, I have become actively involved in serving younger Veterans who are affected by the trauma of their combat deployment(s). Today, Iraq and Afghanistan Veterans are most interested in talking with Vietnam Veterans because we blazed a path in dealing with the difficult problems of PTSD and more. Subsequently, I became a certified Peer Support Specialist to counsel and guide Veterans of all eras in their life transitions. It has been a great tool. I am also involved in a federal grant pilot program for Veterans and their families suffering from the problems related to the trauma of deployment.

These programs along with my work at The Wall are therapeutic and meaningful for me. I feel it is the least I can do to honor them and to give back some of the grace given to me. My service to their needs is an integral part of my healing and my life. It is my therapy, my desire, my purpose and my mission.

Because I have involved myself in serving this community, I've been fortunate enough to have had more than my share of recognition. I was honored to be the 2012 Red Cross Military Hero of the Year for Greater Chicago. I was chosen to be the front page feature story in the Chicago *Tribune* on Veterans Day. I have been the Grand Marshal of the American Legion Parade honoring Vietnam Veterans in our town. And was the feature story of the local magazine. I even had my story appear in a special Vietnam Veterans edition of USA Today. After years of hiding, the attention feels a little embarrassing, but it has also fostered an unanticipated pride about my service.

One of the most meaningful recognitions for me came in 2009 when the 101st Airborne invited all its Vietnam Veterans and their families to Ft. Campbell, Kentucky, the home of the 101st, to be personally thanked and welcomed home by the Division Commanding General, his staff and the entire division. A total of 982 Screaming Eagles from Vietnam lined up in formation and marched into a hanger for the standing ovation welcome home ceremony which brought tears to my eyes and those of every warrior marching with me. Even though it was almost 40 years later, the warm welcome home and congratulations was a lifetime highlight for every one of us.

Ft. Campbell 101st Welcome Home in 2009.
No Slack. No Dry Eyes.

Finally, as the Boomer Generation nears the completion of its life cycle, the legacy it will leave behind has become increasingly clear. Like it or not, Vietnam (like WWII for the generation before) is taking its place as the signature event in the lives of this highly touted segment of population. We may have wanted it to be Sex, Drugs, Rock N' Roll, and Revolution, but the passing of time confirmed the cyclic nature of these synthetic fads long ago and, thus, their unsustainability. History has provided a clearer lens for each of us to assess our contribution to our legacy and to the Greater Good. It's a lens which provides a larger and broader context than the narrow hedonistic one of our self-centered youth.

For all of my generation, the word "Vietnam" evokes a profound range of emotions. But for every male, it triggers a meticulous recall of a chilling, virginal experience. It denotes a single, powerful, unnerving, and crucial decision-making time in our youth that is recalled by each of us in the greatest of detail.

By comparison, no other decision came close to impacting our lives as much as the moment when the war forced us to separately stand up and decide what to do about service and obligation to the country. None of the choices seemed satisfactory. For most, there was no clear answer. Everything looked out of focus. Whether it was to volunteer, be drafted, get married, have children, manipulate the system, bribe, hide out in school, get a job deferment, or simply run away. Each option was a risk for which we had no context. Vietnam demanded of us an incredibly lonely and isolating decision that we suspected would alter our lives. And it did, whether we were aware of it at the time or not.

Now as years of war in Iraq and Afghanistan come to an end and we assess the cost of those actions versus the value of the outcomes, current events situate our old Vietnam decision into an intense spotlight. Men of the Vietnam Generation now feel compelled to make an accounting for their choice of many years ago, either privately or publicly. Perhaps it is a part of the natural aging process or because our life stages seem more potent as the sands run out of our hour glass. Remember Patton's prescient comment about answering a grandchild's question about what you did in the war? He was right. There comes a time to be personally accountable. That accounting is autonomic when you walk past the 58,300 names on The Wall.

Those who didn't go or serve at all often say they should have when they see the names. For them, their conscience is their stubborn companion. They are burdened with a prickly reminder which cannot be explained away in time. And then there are those who falsely claim they are Vietnam Veterans. The figure is as high as 67% by some counts. Oddly, we don't have nearly as many claiming they went to Woodstock. While their behavior is infuriating and insulting to the Vietnam Veteran, I suspect those who make the claim want forgiveness for not participating as much as those of us who fought once wanted forgiveness for our participation. The demons inside all of us will probably never be calmed.

Fortunately, today our culture is crafting a different story about Veterans of Vietnam. The story now grants us honor, pride and recognition for our service, and that helps fortify us against the deep sorrow and grief we continue to feel for the losses we witnessed. Most of us who went are now openly proud of our service. The victory in the Cold War, the building of an economy second to none, and the success in rebuilding the best military organization in the world from the rubble of the war are all directly attributable to Vietnam. The Gulf War, Iraq, Afghanistan and the all-volunteer armed forces have proven to be powerful lessons about duty, honor and country for the Vietnam Generation...and about, "...what you can do for your country".

The passage of time continues to clarify the Vietnam narrative and to purify the minds and souls of those of us who served, whether alive or dead. It says we answered the call; we did our jobs; and we fought like tigers in a war people are still trying to understand. It has taken a couple of generations to get away from the highly charged emotional schism Vietnam produced, but now there is genuine acknowledgement for service. And, as was intended, The Wall has played a major role in the healing process for all. For me, The Wall is an enduring representation of my last mission.

I am humbled by the sacrifices made by the young men and women whose names are on The Wall. In service to their country and for each of us who fought alongside of them, they paid the ultimate price. Now I understand why. So that in my whispered prayers for each of them every day, I can finally say I am at peace with myself, my country, and my men.

Doing a Name Rubbing at The Wall

> *What is a Nation?*
> *The nation, like the individual, is the culmination of long past efforts, sacrifices and acts of devotion. The cult of ancestors is the most legitimate of all: the ancestors made us what we are. An heroic past, great men, glory---I mean real glory---this is the social capital on which the national idea is based.*
> *Ernest Renan*

Acknowledgements

The name of the author on the cover of this book is mine, but I would be foolish to singularly take credit for its development and substance. There are many upon whose shoulders I stood to make this a collective effort: historians, novelists, writers, researchers, volunteers, friends, family and more. My writer friend Julie Morse was the first to embolden me and to publish a part of the story years ago. Visitors at The Wall motivated me to write down my thoughts along with counselors who gently and sometimes not so gently pushed and pulled me along. They were enormously important for sustainability over the years of writing. My children, Jon and Jeff and their wives, Tiffani and Brigid each either inspired me to tell the story or quietly reinforced the venture with their abiding care and interest. I could not possibly have done the work without their support and inspiration.

I am also immensely indebted to those who took the time to walk with me through the process by reading all or parts of the manuscript and carefully modifying the organization, style, words or anything else which needed attention. Author Jon Entine looked at the first layout and told me it was worth developing. Writer/producer Rachael Milton read the entire rough manuscript and told me I had something worth publishing. My brother James worked closely with me through two complete re-writes, even though it was painful for him to hear of my experiences for the first time after 40 years of my secrecy. My son Jeffrey read some of the early lead chapters and gave me his valuable unvarnished professional input. Journalist Bonnie Rubin of the Chicago *Tribune* gave the work her blessing. My two wonderful friends from D.C., Ari and Sharon, reviewed early versions and helped me shape the concept. And they continued to nurture it with me when I would be in town for my volunteer weekends over the course of three years. And finally, my writer step-son Austin Smith whose tireless review, critique and final approval was the confirmation and validation I wanted so very much so as to move ahead with completing the job.

I am forever grateful to all of these people for their unrelenting support and encouragement; especially at the times I was ready to end the mission.

About Ann McNamara

The preceding was shaped largely by conversations over many years with my wife, Ann (Max) McNamara. 'Max' holds degrees in Philosophy from Trinity College Dublin, and Religion from Yale Divinity School. Her wide reading, teaching, and public lectures have provided many of the prisms, and concepts used in this book. Her own scholarly research brought generously and routinely to our breakfast and dinner table sharpened and honed my perspective on my experience as a Reluctant Patriot. In fact she conceived the title of this opus.

My struggle to find meaning and purpose in the seemingly incomprehensible events described herein, has been far more clearly elucidated by Max. The clarity of the mission I now have and the coherence I now sense in my life are the result of the depth and breadth of her work in theological and philosophical ethics, as well as her deep faith in me.

Max is the founder and director of Ethical Cartography ™, which offers counsel and programs in Ethics, Forgiveness, Reconciliation, and Moral Psychology. She is the author of *What's Good? For Dinner: recipes for ethical conversations at family meals*, she is the creator of Maximize The Moment ™, questions for lively conversations, and has her own blog site on maxthemoment.wordpress.com

References

1. Ahamed, Liaquat, *Lords of Finance, the Bankers Who Broke the World,* New York, The Penguin Group, 2009
2. Alexander, Larry J., *Biggest Brother: The Life of Major Dick Winters, the Man Who Led the Band of Brothers,* New York, New American Library, 2005
3. Ambrose, Stephen E., *Band of Brothers: E Company, 506th Regiment, 101st Airborne from Normandy to Hitler's Eagle's Nest*, New York, Simon and Schuster, Inc., 1992
4. Ambrose, Stephen and Brinkley, Douglas, *The Rise to Globalism, American Foreign Policy Since 1938*, New York, Penguin Books, 1971, 1976, 1980, 1983, 1985, 1988, 1991, 1993, 1997
5. Atkinson, O'Brien, D'Este, Millett, McPherson, Hastings, Weinberg, *On War, the Best Military Histories,* Chicago, Pritzker Military Library and Museum, 2013
6. Atkinson, Rick, *The Guns at Last Light*, New York, Henry Holt and Company, LLC, 2013
7. Atkinson, Rick, *The Long Gray Line, The Journey of West Point's Class of 1966*, New York, Henry Holt and Company, LLC, 1989
8. Buruma, Ian, *Year Zero, a History of 1945,* New York, Penguin Press 2013
9. Caputo, Phillip, *A Rumor of War,* New York, Henry Holt and Company, 1977, 1996
10. Caro, Robert, *The Passage of Power,* New York, Vintage Books a Division of Random House, 2012

11. Childers, Thomas, *Soldier from the War Returning: the Greatest Generation's Troubled Homecoming from World War II,* New York, Houghton Mifflin Harcourt, 2009
12. Compton, Lynn, *Call of Duty: My Life Before, During and After the Band of Brothers*, New York, The Berkeley Publishing Group, 2008
13. Dallek, Robert, *Nixon and Kissinger: Partners in Power,* New York, HarperCollins, 2007
14. Dower, John, *Cultures of War,* New York, W. W. Norton & Company, Inc., 2010
15. Edelman, Bernard, *Dear America, Letters Home from Vietnam*, New York, W.W. Norton & Company, 1983
16. Eisenhower, David, *Going Home to Glory,* New York, Simon & Schuster, 2010
17. Evans, Richard J, *The Coming of the Third Reich*, New York, The Penguin Press, 2003
18. Guarnere, William and Heffron, Edward, *Brothers in Battle, Best of Friends*, New York, The Berkeley Publishing Group, 2007
19. Ghaemi, Nassir, *A First Rate Madness,* New York, The Penguin Press, 2011
20. Hackworth, David H., *Steel My Soldiers' Hearts: The Hopeless to Hardcore Transformation of U.S. Army 4th Battalion, 39th Infantry, Vietnam*, New York, Touchstone, 2002
21. Halberstam, David, *The Best and the Brightest,* New York, Ballantine Books, 1969, 1971, 1972, 1991
22. Hastings, Max, *Armageddon, The Battle for Germany, 1944-1945,* New York, First Vintage Books, 2004
23. Hastings, Max, *Retribution: The Battle for Japan, 1944—45*, New York, Alfred A. Knopf, A Division of Random House, Inc., 2007
24. Kagan, Robert, *Of Paradise and Power: America and Europe in the New World Order,* New York, Random House, 2003
25. Kalb, Marvin and Kalb, Deborah, *Haunting Legacy, Vietnam and the American Presidency from Ford to Obama,* Washington, DC, The Brookings Institute Press, 2011

26. Karnow, Stanley, *Vietnam: A History*, New York, The Viking Press, 1983, The Penguin Group, 1984, 1991, 1997
27. Kempe, Frederick, *Berlin, 1961, Kennedy, Khrushchev and the Most Dangerous Place on Earth,* New York, G. P. Putnam's Sons, The Penguin Group, 2011
28. Kennedy, Robert F., *Thirteen Days: A Memoir of the Cuban Missile Crisis*, New York, W.W. Norton and Company, 1969
29. Ketwig, John, *And a Hard Rain Fell: A GI's True Story of the War in Vietnam*, Naperville, Illinois, Sourcebooks, Inc., 2002
30. Logevall, Fredrik, *Embers of War: The Fall of an Empire and the Making of America's Vietnam,* New York, Random House Publishing, 2013
31. McCabe, Allen and Arant, Daniel, *Wall Facts: 2014 Edition*
32. Macmillan, Margaret, *Paris 1919, Six Months That Changed the World,* New York, Random House Trade Paperback, 2003
33. Maraniss, David, *They Marched Into Sunlight: War and Peace Vietnam and America October 1967*, New York, Simon and Schuster, 2004
34. McMaster, H. R., *Dereliction of Duty: Johnson, McNamara, the Joint Chiefs of Staff, and the Lies That Led to Vietnam*, New York, HarperCollins Publishers, 1997
35. McNamara, Robert S., *In Retrospect: The Tragedy and Lessons of Vietnam*, New York, Random House, 1995, 1996
36. Moore, Lt. General Harold G., and Galloway, Joseph L., *We Were Soldiers Once...and Young: Ia Drang - The Battle That Changed the War in Vietnam*, New York, The Random House Publishing Group, 1992
37. Mullaney, Craig M., *The Unforgiving Minute: A Soldier's Education,* New York, Penguin Press, 2009
38. Nasaw, David, *The Patriarch, The Remarkable Life and Turbulent Times of Joseph P. Kennedy*, New York, The Penguin Press, 2012
39. National Commission on Terrorist Attacks, *The 9/11 Commission Report: Final Report of the National Commission of Terrorist Attacks on the United States,* Washington, DC, United States Government, 2004
40. Nolan, Keith, *Ripcord: Screaming Eagles Under Siege, Vietnam 1970*, New York, Ballentine Books, Random House Publishing, 2000

41. O'Brien, Tim, *If I Die in a Combat Zone, Box me Up and Ship Me Home,* New York, Broadway Books, 1999
42. O'Brien, Tim, *The Things They Carried,* New York, Houghton Mifflin, 1990
43. Perry, Mark, *Partners in Command: George Marshall and Dwight Eisenhower in War and Peace*, New York, The Penguin Press, 2007
44. Prochnau, William, *Once Upon a Distant War: David Halberstam, Neil Sheehan, Peter Arnett----Young War Correspondents and Their Early Vietnam Battles,* New York, Vintage Books, 1995
45. Ricks, Thomas E., *The Generals: American Military Command from World War II to Today* New York, Penguin Group, 2012
46. Scruggs, Jan C., *Why Vietnam Still Matters: The War and the Wall,* Washington, DC, Vietnam Veterans Memorial Fund, 1996
47. Sheehan, Neil, *A Bight and Shining Lie: John Paul Van and America in Vietnam,* New York, First Vintage Books, 1988
48. Sontag, Sherry and Drew, Christopher, *Blind Man's Bluff, The Untold Story of American Submarine Espionage,* New York, HarperCollins Publishers, 1998
49. Sorley, Lewis, *A Better War: The Unexamined Victories and Final Tragedies of America's Last Years in Vietnam*, Orlando, Florida, Harcourt, Inc., 1999
50. Thomas, Evan, *Ike's Bluff, President Eisenhower's Secret Battle to Save the World,* New York, Little, Brown and Company, 2012
51. Timberg, Robert, *The Nightingales Song,* New York, Touchstone, 1995
52. Young, Marilyn B., *The Vietnam Wars, 1945-1990,* New York, HarperCollins Publishers, 1991

Made in the USA
Middletown, DE
20 September 2019